52
110
152

Critical Views
of Isaac Bashevis Singer

Critical Views
of Isaac Bashevis Singer

edited by Irving Malin

New York • New York University Press
London • University of London Press Limited
1969

© 1969 by New York University Press
Library of Congress Catalog Card Number 69–19262
Manufactured in the United States of America

Acknowledgments

Illustrative passages from the following books by Isaac Bashevis Singer — *The Spinoza of Market Street,* copyright © 1958, 1960, 1961 by Isaac Bashevis Singer ("The Spinoza of Market Street" and "The Destruction of Kreshev," copyright © 1961 by Isaac Bashevis Singer and "A Tale of Two Liars," copyright © 1958 and 1961 by Isaac Bashevis Singer); *Short Friday,* copyright © 1961, 1962, 1963, 1964 by Isaac Bashevis Singer ("The Last Demon," copyright © 1962 by Isaac Bashevis Singer and "Blood," copyright © 1964 by Issac Bashevis Singer); *In My Father's Court,* copyright © 1962, 1963, 1964, 1965, 1966 by Isaac Bashevis Singer ("Bilgoray," "The Miracle," "The Suicide," "Winter in Bilgoray," and "The New Winds," copyright © 1966 by Isaac Bashevis Singer; "The Purim Gift," copyright © 1963 by Isaac Bashevis Singer); *The Slave,* copyright © 1962 by Isaac Bashevis Singer; *The Magician of Lublin,* copyright © 1960 by Isaac Bashevis Singer; *The Manor,* copyright © 1967 by Isaac Bashevis Singer; *The Family Moskat,* copyright 1950 by Isaac Bashevis Singer; *Gimpel the Fool,* copyright © 1957 by Isaac Bashevis Singer ("Gimpel the Fool," copyright 1953 by Isaac Bashevis Singer; "The Old Man," "The Unseen," and "Joy," copyright © 1957 by Isaac Bashevis Singer and *Satin in Goray,* copyright 1955 by Isaac Bashevis Singer — are reprinted by permission of Farrar, Straus and Giroux, Inc. and Martin Secker and Warburg Ltd.

266409

Critical Views
of Isaac Bashevis Singer

Contents

x   *Contents*

Introduction

I first read Isaac Bashevis Singer in 1958. *Satan in Goray,* which was published in 1955, had not been reviewed much, and it was soon remaindered. I found a copy, studied it carefully, and became hypnotized. I wondered about the writer. How could he dare to write an account of demonic possession as a terrifying religious experience? Why was he so "attracted" to the false Messiah? Was he an orthodox Jew? These questions captured me ten years ago (and they still do). I resolved to read more of his novels and to write about them.

I next encountered "Gimpel the Fool" in the Howe and Greenberg collection of Yiddish stories. The story, so apparently different from *Satan in Goray,* also fascinated me. I kept quoting the now-famous line: "No doubt the world is entirely an imaginary world — but it is only once removed from the real world." It seemed to capture elusive tensions between reality and unreality, life and art, sanity and madness. I was struck by the fact that Saul Bellow had translated the story; it was interesting that one writer I was studying had been moved to translate "Gimpel the Fool" for the *Partisan Review* audience (before the subsequent appearance in the Howe and Greenberg collection). I did not then make more of the coincidence.

While I was planning *New American Gothic* (1962) and *Jews and Americans* (1965), I managed to read other Singer novels. I was tempted to include discussions of him in the critical studies because he seemed to touch both groups of writers.

There is a remarkable resemblance between *Satan in*

Goray and *Wise Blood* (or, for that matter, *The Heart is a Lonely Hunter* and "Master Misery"). These fictions deal with the false Messiah; he is worshiped by misfits who, eagerly seeking signs, mistake their narcissism for divinity. They walk the line between madness and revelation. I am unsure whether or not Gothic always draws this line, but I know that Singer's characters are as possessed (and possessive!) as those of Flannery O'Connor or Carson McCullers. (I am pleased that Melvin J. Friedman notes the resemblance in his essay.)

I was, of course, tempted to include Singer in my *Jews and Americans.* I did not finally make room for him because I felt that he is more of a "special case" than Malamud, Roth, Bellow, and Karl Shapiro. Although he deals as they do with the dualities of Jewishness (as I shall note), he writes in Yiddish; he pictures small towns in East Europe; he "accepts" imps and demons; and he delights in references to the Cabala. On one level, he is "out of their world"; on another, he is not. Thus as the contemporary reader has become more aware of the American-Jewish writers I have mentioned, he has been discovering Singer; and today Singer is discussed by the audience of *Playboy, Harper's,* and *The New Yorker.* (He has come a long way in ten years. But this is not correct. *We have caught up to him.*) I am pleased that I now have the chance to introduce a collection of essays entirely devoted to his work.

There are several ways of performing this task, but I think that it is best to call Singer a "tightrope" writer. This "tightrope" stance not only relates him to classical Jewish thought, it also brings him to the heart of contemporary literature. I hope that by exploring three works, the autobiographical *In My Father's Court,* "The Slaughterer," and *Short Friday,* I can convey his characteristic themes, images and attitudes.

In My Father's Court is a valuable starting point. Although it is possible to dismiss these memoirs as exotic or old-fashioned — they describe "simple" people who long to ride on trains, to see cellars inhabited by demons, or to study Talmud day and night — we cannot easily do so. They capture our interest because of those uncertainties and insanities which plague *us*. They are remarkably "modern."

"The Will," for example, gives us a man who lives for his last testament. He delights in changing it, specifying different floral arrangements and body purifications. It becomes his identity. Singer does not explore the causes of this obsession — is this the right word? — but he does suggest that it is the search for a definite, perfect world. The man with the will wants so desperately to rise above the petty fluctuations of daily life that he neglects the "tight-rope." He falls because he tries to fly.

Other people in these memoirs resemble him. They compulsively study omens and portents, not even realizing that they do. Although some find comfort and meaning in orthodox belief, as does Singer's bookish, other-worldly father, many embrace low religion. They place their faith in idols. Because the salesman in one story believes that he shares in eternal life, he attempts to sell his share to others, who eagerly clutch at the "holy" merchandise. The line between real and unreal faith, between revelation and madness, is thin here; it puzzles and disturbs us. When Singer forgets these ironies and gives us elsewhere ideal Reb Asher the dairyman, we remain unconvinced and bored.

It is strange that *In My Father's Court* ends with the word "love," for it follows the course (and victory?) of hatred. Perhaps Singer himself knows this: although he celebrates the court of his father — and, by implication, justice, family closeness, and good will — he realizes that it is "out of this world." The tension between the law-abiding court and the criminal world — that tension never openly admitted by Singer in his "author's note" but which occurs in much of his fiction — rescues these memoirs and makes them live for us.

Singer's memoirs are dualistic. They fight our cozy feelings of nostalgia and romance because they assert that the Jew has always lived on the edge of being. They reflect traditional beliefs. Abraham J. Heschel has written: "Jewish thinking and living can only be adequately understood in terms of a dialectical pattern, containing opposite or contrasted properties." (He cites, among others, dualities of Zion and exile, head and heart.) Because the Jew has been a "tightrope" walker, he has learned to value the ironies of life in a "radically sophisticated" way (to use Max Schulz's phrase). He has not yielded to the idols of the crowd. I think that this stance is especially attractive to the contemporary reader who recognizes his own need for skepticism and irony, especially when he is told by statesmen and "admen" to believe self-satisfying lies and to call these truths.

Singer's awareness of dualities is even more powerful in "The Slaughterer," a story which appeared in the November 25, 1967, issue of the *New Yorker*. Although it deals with orthodox rituals and settings, it presents a bleak, ironic view of our fate, a view expressed (but surely not as well) in such other *New Yorker* contributions as *In Cold Blood* and *The Fire Next Time*. By experiencing the tensions of "The Slaughterer," we can more easily understand the nature of Singer's attractiveness and pertinence.

"Yoineh Meir should have become the Kolomir rabbi," we are told in the very first sentence, but he is frustrated by the "stubborn opposition" of the Kuzmir wise men. He "dangles," to use Bellow's word, especially after he learns that he must become the town's ritual slaughterer. Although he tries to comfort himself with the thought that his new role is holy, he is full of fear and trembling. We do not know why Yoineh is so upset; we want psychological motivation, but we are compelled to accept this fear as a *given*. The significant point is that by isolating blood as a totemic image, Singer can arouse our deepest feelings and bridge the gap between "exotic" Kolomir and violent America.

Silently rebelling against the law — slaughter is, after all, sanctified in the Torah — Yoineh gradually exiles himself from the past, the community, the family. This displacement weakens him. He tries to create his own tradition as he imposes new laws upon himself. He will become his own "father" — his own lawgiver. But he cannot find consolation because he is "cut off." There is more irony. Although Yoineh learns to perform his duty (where does duty end and punishment begin?) he believes that bodies resist his unwilling knife. All the shrieking animals — the hens, the roosters, the geese, the oxen, the goats — refuse to die. They rebel against him as he rebels against himself. Thus he identifies with his victims. (The master and the slave unite in Singer's fiction.)

Where can Yoineh go? He wants the "higher spheres" where there is no pain, no blood, no death. Perhaps nature is the answer. He looks up into the "radiant" sky — the stars flash with "heavenly secrets" — but he cannot forget the earth. (Note the "tightrope" again!) He continues to see blood before his eyes. (The emphasis upon the elements, especially earth and fire, accounts for the intense "objectivity" of Singer's fiction.) He feels trapped; he cannot move.

Elul is "the month of repentence." It can bring "exalted serenity" (light and air), but it is full of blood. "A great many beasts" are killed because the New Year begins during this month. Yoineh's feelings reach their climax. The linking of personal feelings and the public occasion is beautifully rendered. Nightmares take over as they do in much of Singer's fiction, revealing dark truths: "Cows assumed human shape, with beards and side locks, and skullcaps over their horns." The cows are elders because they embody the Laws. Yoineh wants to destroy the Laws, but he cannot kill. This nightmare ironically demonstrates his ambivalent longings. So does the next one.

"Yoineh Meir would be slaughtering a calf, but it would turn into a girl. Her neck throbbed, and she pleaded to be saved." The animal becomes sexual; slaughter and rape are related. He is unmanned because he cannot perform *the act.* Finally he wakes up and runs out of the house, but the outside world is strangely dreamlike. Nightmare and reality, violence and love, animalism and humanity – these typical Singer contraries have been joined in less than three paragraphs.

Because Yoineh has been sacrificed to his role (or has sacrificed himself?) he no longer recognizes his identity. He becomes others; he sees himself in "all that crawls and flies, breeds and swarms." He loses his mind. By accepting the validity of his obsession — it is not "right" to kill even for religious reasons — he can no longer act rationally. He even wonders whether the Lord Himself is a slaughterer. He is above (or below?) reason when he runs to the river and destroys himself. How ironic that he slaughters himself for a noble, mad purpose!

The story, however, does not end here. We are reminded that it is the holiday (holy day) season and that the ritual slaughtering must continue. Tradition reasserts itself in the last line when the community dispatches two messengers to bring "a new slaughterer." A hopeful conclusion?

"The Slaughterer" deals with universal themes — Justice, Truth, and Love — but it does not sermonize at length. It vitalizes abstractions until they *bleed.* How does Singer achieve this effect? There are several possible answers. First, he concentrates upon one specific, controlling image. Second, he uses as his hero an intense, obsessive human being. Third, he stylizes his plot. Fourth, he unites theme, consciousness, image, and plot, cutting out unnecessary details. "The Slaughterer" creates and destroys Yoineh.

I have spent so much time upon this story because it exemplifies the dualistic thinking of Singer. The tension generated here depends greatly upon rhythms of contractions and expansion; it is when these rhythms are lost, as in "Short Friday," *The Slave,* or parts of *In My Father's Court,* that we notice mere exoticism or hopefulness, not the "tightrope" stance.

In the collection *Short Friday,* which, like "The Slaughterer," is not discussed at length in the following essays, we can again see the strengths and weaknesses of Singer's narrative strategy.

The narrator of "Alone," one of the sixteen tales in the collection, tells us, ". . . many times in the past I have wished the impossible to happen — and then it happened. But though my wish came true it was in such a topsy-turvy way that it appeared the Hidden Powers were trying to show me I didn't understand my own needs." His remarks reveal characteristic concerns of his creator: Singer explores, for the sake of "goodness," the "topsy-turvy" world in which "Hidden Powers" baffle human understanding. He dialectically opposes — or marries? — the impossible and the possible, reality and dream, and in doing so, he demonstrates that the patterns we usually adopt are less truthful and secure than they seem.

Singer is too involved with high mystery to care about modern psychology. He omits Freudian speculations, glib analysis; he never really explains the motivations of his characters. He sees that passion is more inexplicable than the sophisticated terms (or idols?) we worship; he refuses to rationalize and debase it.

"The passion for blood and the passion for flesh" rule his stories. These passions are frequently so extraordinary that we are tempted to label them "obsessive" and "unnatural." Simmele, for example, cannot rest until she obeys the voice of Esther Kreindel and becomes this woman. Risha must take pleasure in killing and loving. Their passions upset their apparently stable world.

Although Singer does not delve into the reasons for "madness," he is able to capture it in striking images:

"The chicken, its throat slit, fell to the ground where it fluttered about flapping its wings in its attempt to fly and spattering Reuben's boots with blood. Finally the little rooster gave a last start and then lay still, one glassy eye and its slit neck facing up to God's heaven." Not only does this image suggest the writhing of Reuben and Risha, the two lovers, it also forces us to see the world as miraculous and earthy, painful and beautiful. Indeed, the dialectical oppositions of up and down ("lay still" and "facing up") , tremor and stasis, spirituality and beastliness (the thoughtful, "glassy eye" and the "slit neck") represent the effect governing much of Singer's fiction.

Two images recur: (1) The world is a wasteland or hospital. The narrator of "Alone" enters his hotel room: "inside mosquitos, moths, fireflies, and gnats fluttered and buzzed about. . . ." Jechidah views Earth in this way: "It was spring, and Earth's corruption grew leprous with blossoms. From the graves with their memorial trees and cleansing waters arose a dreadful stench. Millions of creatures forced to descend into the domains of death, were becoming flies, butterflies, worms, toads, frogs." Gunegund, the witch, cultivates "poisonous berries" and thorns "that seem to bite one's clothing." (2) Human life is nonsubstantial, thin, or ambiguous. Reb Falik's "strength began to leave him; his hands trembled; and when he spoke his head shook sidewise." We are told in "Jachid and Jechidah" that "the body is composed of such weak material that a mere blow can make it disintegrate." Anshel disappears in "Yentl the Yeshiva Boy." Shmul-Leibele, in the title story, is "shorn of all his strength."

Because these visions constantly beset us, we "sympathize" with them and forget that they are partial. We lose sight of transcendent possibilities, ideals, promises. Singer may praise the Lord, in other words, but he apparently worships His adversary. The narrator of "The Last Demon" explains: "I, a demon, bear witness that there are no demons left. Why demons, when man himself is a demon? Why to persuade to evil someone who is already convinced? I am the last of the 'persuaders.' " I think that Singer himself is convinced that men are demons; that somehow life itself is "cursed." And he holds this belief so passionately, if unconsciously, that the power of witches, evil spirits, and imps attracts him. He makes their daily business come alive as they defeat weak humanity. Thus he is less powerful in the title story — "a quiet singing" of Paradise — than in his other ones.

Or is Singer fooling us? He does refer to tricks, deceptions, and masquerades, using these symbols in many stories. He may want us to yield to the demonic (as he does) so that we can see our own irresponsibility and wickedness. He tempts us to forget about the real meanings of life. If we grant the possible heresies that govern Singer's world, we must still admire his best stories and novels for their tension between body and spirit, hell and heaven. This tension or, rather, perilous balance arises because he refuses to offer easy evaluations or to take simple sides. He does more: he gives us religious humor.

And it is this humor that accounts for the Jewish flavor. Singer considers existence a painful joke; he smiles at our attempts to struggle with demonic passions (given to us by the Lord?). *But at the same time he admires the whole secret design; life is, after all, such a beautifully odd comedy:* "the world is full of puzzles. It is possible that not even Elijah will be able to answer all our questions when the Messiah comes. Even God in seventh heaven may not have solved all the mysteries of His Creation. This may be the reason He conceals His face." By concealing his true religion (does he smile or sneer?) Singer captures the ambiguous tightrope of existence.

He is, therefore, a frightening, essential writer. He asks the right questions (even in translation!) and makes us unsure of our usual answers. He forces us to walk unsteadily on the tightrope.

For My Spiritual Guides

Joel Blocker and Richard Elman

1.

An Interview
with Isaac Bashevis Singer

INTERVIEWERS: *Perhaps we could begin by asking you some questions about what has happened to Yiddish literature. Yiddish literature was, in its prime, a body of work which was very close to the masses by whom it was read — in language, in point of view, and in drawing from a common basis of experience. The annihilation of six million Jews during World War II changed all that drastically. The Yiddish-reading audience was decimated and continues now to dwindle from attrition. How, then, do you feel about writing in Yiddish today?*

SINGER: You don't feel very happy about writing in a language when you know it dies from day to day. Although I don't feel that Yiddish will die completely, it's a fact that the number of readers is becoming smaller and smaller, and we — I mean Yiddish writers — are all conscious of it. The only thing is, I don't have this feeling while I write; I don't choose to remember it. I think that's a lucky thing because if I did remember while I was writing that some of my readers were dying and others were not being born to replace them, it might have some influence on me. Writers, as a rule, don't think about their readers while

*Reprinted from *Commentary* by permission; Copyright © 1963 by the American Jewish committee.

they write. As a matter of fact, thinking about the reader is a terrible pitfall for a writer. A writer should not think about who is going to read him because the moment he thinks about this, some other power interferes. In my case, writing Yiddish and thinking about the readers would really destroy the writer completely. But happily I never think about such things. When I sit down to write I have a feeling that I'm talking maybe to millions or maybe to nobody.

INTERVIEWERS: *Nevertheless, are you and other Yiddish writers disturbed by this tragedy — not at the moment of writing, but in general?*

SINGER: We are all conscious of it when we are not writing. There is a lot of discussion about it in the Yiddish papers and in meetings of the PEN Club. We all feel the same thing and we express it in Yiddish by saying: "We talk to the wall." We sometimes have the feeling that we are talking to nobody. On the other hand, I can tell you that those people who still read Yiddish are a peculiarly sensitive group. No writer gets the response a Yiddish writer does, if the readers really like him. The Yiddish reader, as a rule, is either very bad or very good. There is no such thing as a neutral reader. Either he loves the writer or he hates him. I have had good luck writing in the Yiddish paper, the *Jewish Daily Forward.* This paper still has eighty or ninety thousand readers and many of them — as a matter of fact, most of them — are readers of fiction. I still have a lot of readers and have the feeling sometimes that I am talking to thousands of people. I know, for example, that my novel, *The Slave,* which the *Forward* ran in its week-end literary supplement, had an audience of twenty thousand readers. Not many writers have such an immediate audience.

INTERVIEWERS: *Then writing in Yiddish today has its advantages as well? You're not completely "talking to the wall"? In fact, you're probably better off than most serious American writers today who have no immediate mass audience of that size. If a writer in this country does enjoy such readership, it is not of the same kind as your Yiddish-reading audience.*

SINGER: I must say that the *Jewish Daily Forward* has a tradition of publishing good fiction. Its editors have always considered it a very important part of the newspaper. Our readers ask for fiction. It isn't like American newspapers. The New York *Daily News,* for example, also publishes fiction, but I don't think the *News* would lose many readers if it stopped publishing stories. The Yiddish reader is accustomed to reading novels and stories in the newspapers. For him, it's a must. In this respect, we are lucky.

INTERVIEWERS: *Do you see any future for Yiddish literature?*

SINGER: The future looks very black. They say that if a Yiddish reader dies, there is no one to replace him. This is true. How it happens that the *Forward* still has eighty to a hundred thousand readers today, and the *Jewish Day Journal,* another Yiddish newspaper, has close to fifty thousand is a riddle to me because twenty-five or even thirty-five years ago they said the Yiddish press would only last another five years. One of the great pessimists then was Abraham Cahan who helped build the *Forward.* He said that the first generation of Jews in this country would speak Yiddish, but the second generation would not. It was so, but somehow the Yiddish press goes on living. It's like the Jews generally. They die all the time and they keep on living all the time.

INTERVIEWERS: *If that's the case, who then are you writing for — this still considerable Yiddish audience, a different audience in English and other languages, or both?*

SINGER: As I said before, I'm not very conscious of the audience. The only audience I'm conscious of — you may laugh at me — is myself. I have to please myself. After I have written something I am the first reader. I'm most interested in pleasing myself. It's not modest to say so, but I think this is so with every writer. In my case it is especially important because Yiddish readers are not a homogeneous audience. They are of different kinds, some very educated, some not educated at all. For example, we have readers who will read good fiction, but their intelligence is so small and their taste so dubious that you just don't know how they will judge and what they will accept. We get letters at the *Forward* from readers who say, "I read the wonderful novel of Sholem Asch. I also read the wonderful novel of ———," referring to some mediocre detective story we might publish at the same time. To him they are both alike. Yet we also have many very perceptive readers who know world literature and are very sensitive to literary values. That's why when a Yiddish writer worries about his audience he gets all mixed up.

INTERVIEWERS: *You don't at all – somewhere in the back of your mind — have an image of someone reading you in a foreign language — English, for example?*

SINGER: That's a very important question. They accused Sholem Asch of writing for the translator. I don't say the accusation was true, but there were those who pointed to specific passages in Asch's work and said: "You see these lines. They were written for the English, not for the Yiddish reader." I take great care not to think about the reader in English or French or any other language. Nothing can spoil a writer more than writing for the translator. He must feel that he writes for people who know everything he knows — not for the stranger. It's only when you write for your own people and when you don't think about anybody else that the other people reading in a foreign language will appreciate your work and like it. Can you imagine Gogol writing for the French or the American reader? He was a Russian and wrote like a Russian and assumed that the reader knew everything he knew. You know, many of my Yiddish readers complain that I am too Jewish. They say: "We have already forgotten about all these things." "You remind us of things we would like to forget." But this doesn't bother me. I assume that the reader knows as much about Jewishness and Jewish life as I do.

INTERVIEWERS: *Would it be fair to say that you are actually writing in a somewhat artificial or illusionary context, as if none of the terrible things that happened to the Jewish people during the last two decades really did occur?*

SINGER: Yes, very fair. There was a famous philosopher, Vaihinger, who wrote a book called *The Philosophy of "As If,"* in which he showed that we all behave "as if." The "as if" is so much a part of our life that it really isn't artificial. After all, what could be more artificial than marriage? When a man marries a woman he assumes that she's going to be devoted to him and he acts as if his wife will treat him in this fashion. And so on and so on. . . . Every man assumes he will go on living. He behaves *as if* he will never die. So I wouldn't call my attitude artificial. It's very natural and healthy. We have to go on living and writing.

INTERVIEWERS: *But you do agree that at the heart of your attitude there is an illusion which is consciously sustained?*

SINGER: Yes. But take the case of a mathematician who writes a book and knows that there are only ten or twenty other mathematicians who will understand him. Still he doesn't write for twenty people. He knows there will be mathematicians in later generations. Every man who creates something does not and should not worry about being understood. I would say I write for the best possible reader no matter how many readers there really are.

INTERVIEWERS: *Then you're not really a popular writer in Yiddish, just as in English those critics who originally acclaimed your work were part of an avant-garde rather than a mass audience?*

SINGER: No. I'm not a popular writer among Yiddish readers. As a matter of fact I had many quarrels with Abe Cahan who told me: "You write well, but it's not for our readers." Even my present editor at the *Forward* sometimes complains that my language is too difficult, my subjects too obscure. And when I write about devils and ghosts, for instance, he asks: "Who among our readers remembers such things?" No, I'm not a popular writer. But the truth is, in spite of this, I have become, to a degree, "popular." Still, my work is only published in the week-end supplements which are devoted to literary works, rather than the regular week-day pages in which appears conventionally popular fiction.

Occasionally, however, I write more popular work under a different name — the name of Warshofsky. Generally I sign my name in the *Forward* Isaac Bashevis, but once in a while I publish under the name of Isaac Warshofsky. When I write under the name of Warshofsky I take less care, but I never publish such things in book form. I use a different name to distinguish between two different kinds of writing. Since I must write a great deal and I cannot work on every piece of writing the way I work on the stories which I take very seriously, I publish some pieces which I consider belle-lettristic journalism. It sometimes happens that some of them come out well. In fact, one of my books, *Mein Taten's Bes-din Shtub* ("My Father's Courtroom")[1] is a compilation of this kind of work, published under the name of Warshofsky. Only later I adopted it, as it were, and signed the name Bashevis . . . after I cleaned it up and worked on it.

INTERVIEWERS: *Is it a common practice among Yiddish writers to use pseudonyms?*

SINGER: It's not uncommon. I. L. Peretz wrote under many different names. Some say as many as fifty pseudonyms.

INTERVIEWERS: *And you make a definite distinction between your literary and your journalistic work?*

SINGER: Yes I do. I must say I don't work very hard on my journalism. I just write it and let it go. I write memoirs of my boyhood, reviews, *feuilletons,* and all kinds of things. As a matter of fact many of my readers like my journalism better than my stories, and some of my best stories were never published in the *Forward.* For example, "Gimpel the

Fool" was first published in a Yiddish literary magazine.

INTERVIEWERS: *About this business of names again. What is your real name?*

SINGER: My real name is Isaac Singer. My brother's name was Israel Joshua Singer. In Yiddish I sign my fiction Isaac Bashevis. For some reason this name is sacred to me, and I won't sign my journalism with it. Perhaps it's because Bashevis is derived from my mother's name. Her name was Bathsheba.

INTERVIEWERS: *To come back to Yiddish literature for a few moments. Do you regard yourself as writing within that specific tradition, or do you feel that you have been more influenced by non-Jewish European authors?*

SINGER: I'll tell you, I feel myself naturally a part of the Jewish tradition. Very strongly so! But I wouldn't say I feel myself a part of the Yiddish tradition. Somehow I always wanted to write in my own way, and I never felt that I was somebody's disciple. For instance, Sholem Aleichem, who was a great writer, always used to say that he was a disciple of Mendele Mocher Seforim. That was very modest. But I don't have these feelings. The only person I have a lot to thank for — from whom I learned a great deal — was my brother, I. J. Singer, who was ten years older than I. But even here I wouldn't say that I was my brother's disciple. I would almost say that I tried to create my own tradition, if one can use such words.

INTERVIEWERS: *Then what do you think you* did *learn from your brother?*

SINGER: My brother wrote a number of novels — *The Brothers Ashkenazi,* which was translated into English; also *Yoshe Kalb,* which was translated under the name of *The Sinner,* and many others. I learned a lot from my brother, particularly in regard to construction. I consider him a great master of construction, and his writing was always quite close to me. Much more so than Sholem Asch's, for example. So whatever there was to learn from my brother I learned, and I think it was a lot. My brother al-

ways used to say to me that a writer should not mix the
essay with fiction. Many writers are half essayists and half
fiction writers. Thomas Mann, for example. He writes a
story, and in the middle of the story he inserts an essay or
an article. He is himself both the writer and the critic.
Even a writer like Dostoevski used to do this. In *The
Brothers Karamazov,* while he is describing Father Zosima,
he suddenly inserts a whole essay on what a saint is and
what a saint should be. It is the old-fashioned way of writing. My brother always used to call this a literary mannerism. It's true that the great novelists used this in a successful
way. But for a young writer, modern writer, it's not the
best model. I avoid these things. When I tell a story, I tell
a story. I don't try to discuss, criticize, or analyze my characters.

INTERVIEWERS: *Apparently, your brother was very much
aware of Flaubert's dicta on the purity of the novel?*

SINGER: Yes, you're right. I think in this case I also agree
one hundred per cent with Flaubert — when you tell a
story, tell a story. Use the words that give information
about your characters, but don't talk about them. When I
write about a character I will say that he looked so and so
and behaved so and so, but I won't say he was a good man.
Sometimes I read writers who say their characters are
"noble" men. To me this is ridiculous. If the man was
truly noble this should come across from what you tell
about him. It's up to the reader to judge.

INTERVIEWERS: *Along these lines, then, do you consider
yourself to be a "modern" or a "modernistic" writer? The
American critic, Irving Howe, has tried to define this
modernistic element in your work.[2] Do you feel this was
just?*

SINGER: When I read Mr. Howe's piece I was greatly surprised to find myself described as modernistic. First of all,
it never occurred to me that I was a "modernist." Secondly,
I don't know what a modernist is. This word . . . you cannot define it. What is modern today will be traditional

twenty years from now. When Mr. Howe called me modernistic, I assume he meant that I write in a way similar to other contemporary writers. Maybe you could tell me. What does it mean to be a "modernist"?

INTERVIEWERS: *Well, perhaps it means your work is different from traditional Yiddish writing. For instance, there are certain conventions that Sholem Aleichem uses that don't appear in your writing. One example would be the "dear reader" device, the writer addressing the reader directly.*

SINGER: Yes. I try not to use the "dear reader." It's curious, however, when I write under the name of Warshofsky in an article or memoir, then it pops up when I need to make a connection of some sort. But in real fiction the "dear reader" device is always a trick, a substitute for telling the story. It's only when the writer can't think of anything else or has some spiritual interruption that he resorts to "dear reader" — as if to say, "Dear reader, forgive me for not telling the story the right way."

INTERVIEWERS: *Do you mind if we ask a few biographical questions at this point? You were born in 1904 in Poland and grew up in Warsaw. Warsaw at that time, during the first two decades of the century, was a center of Yiddish writing. Did you go to the University in Warsaw?*

SINGER: No. But I studied in a rabbinical seminary which was a kind of college.

INTERVIEWERS: *How old were you?*

SINGER: I must have been about eighteen.

INTERVIEWERS: *What did the studies encompass?*

SINGER: We studied secular as well as religious subjects and the Hebrew language. I never finished the seminary because a lot of things they taught there I knew already. My knowledge of secular subjects was backward, but in religious matters I knew a great deal. My family was very religious. My father was a rabbi. So were both of my grandfathers.

INTERVIEWERS: *Were they Hasidic rabbis?*

SINGER: My father was and his father as well. But my maternal grandfather was an anti-Hasid, a *misnaged.* There was always a conflict between my father and my mother about Hasidism because my mother was a little bit of a skeptic where that was concerned — especially about the *zaddikim,* "the wonder-rabbis." My father always used to say that if you don't believe in the *zaddikim* today, tomorrow you won't believe in God. My mother would say, it's one thing to believe in God and another to believe in a man. My mother's point of view is also my point of view.

INTERVIEWERS: *But did your family want you to be a rabbi?*

SINGER: Very much so. But I made up my mind very early not to be one because I began to doubt, not the power of God, but all the traditions and dogmas. I saw how one sentence in the Bible was made into volumes and volumes in the Talmud and later books. From earliest childhood I had a feeling that one thing was God and the Higher Powers, which are above us and with us, and another thing is what human beings make of the divine. I think that many of the misunderstandings of religion stem from this . . . the failure to distinguish between God and man.

INTERVIEWERS: *What kind of boyhood did you have? Many of your books portray urban lower-class Jewry in Poland. Were you, a rabbi's son, exposed to this as a boy?*

SINGER: Yes. We lived on a very poor street in Warsaw, Krochmalna Street. Naturally I was in contact with poor people. Many of them used to come to my father for advice. Many of their questions were religious and moral, but they had a direct bearing on everyday life. Many of the women used to come and tell stories of woe to my mother. I always listened, and I had plenty of chances to listen, to poor people and rich people. My father was a *dayan,* a kind of a judge. So people used to come with all kinds of business problems and conflicts, and I remember trying to decide for myself which of them was honest and which of them was dishonest.

INTERVIEWERS: *Well, is the clan you describe in* The Family Moskat *a family you knew in the Warsaw of that day, or is it purely invention?*

SINGER: No. It was invented. It is true that there was such a rich family in Warsaw in those days, and many people have thought that I was describing this family, but it isn't so. *The Family Moskat* is a composite of many families I knew.

INTERVIEWERS: *What do you think first impelled you to write?*

SINGER: There was one important circumstance: My brother was a writer. My father was also a writer. He published religious books. So writing and publishing were always familiar. However, the real reason for wanting to write was that I very often met situations which baffled me, and from the moment I knew that there was such a thing as literature, I thought how wonderful it would be to be able to describe such things. Incidentally, some of these situations now seem not as unusual as they seemed at the time. When I was about twelve years old I began to read worldly books. Before that I had read only Hebrew books. Well, the first worldly book that I read was a Sherlock Holmes collection by Conan Doyle in a Yiddish translation, and I cannot tell you how delighted I was with this book. I'm afraid even today to try and read it again because I know I would be disappointed. Every story of Sherlock Holmes sounded to me then like heavenly music. Something only an angel could write. As a matter of fact, I tried to imitate Sherlock Holmes. I considered myself a detective. I remember once walking in Warsaw and seeing a man who I immediately thought was suspicious. I said to myself, this man is suspicious. There was no reason whatsoever for me to believe this, but I followed him over half of Warsaw. After a while the man began to look back. At that moment I was Sherlock Holmes and I hoped that he would commit a murder and that I would catch him, and so on and so on.

INTERVIEWERS: *This familiarity with criminals and their behavior comes across very strongly in* The Magician of Lublin....

SINGER: Now that you say so, I think you are right, but it would never have occurred to me. This is the reason that critics sometimes know more than writers.

INTERVIEWERS: *When did you begin to write seriously?*

SINGER: Let me continue with what I was saying before. One day my brother brought home a copy of Dostoevski's *Crime and Punishment* in Yiddish....

INTERVIEWERS: *Also a detective story....*

SINGER: Yes. But I understood very little of it. I was just too young. I knew that the hero had committed a murder, but that's all. There is one moment in the book where the District Attorney speaks to Raskolnikov and Raskolnikov suddenly gets up and is ready to leave and then he sits down again. When I read these few lines I thought how wonderful this was. I don't know why this made such an impression on me. . . . Now you ask, when did I begin to write: When I was about sixteen I began to write in Hebrew, not in Yiddish. I wrote terrible poems, although they were admired because the Hebrew was good. Then, after a while, I began to write stories, again in Hebrew. I even published a few in a Hebrew newspaper. But later I saw that writing Hebrew was an artificial thing because there was a lot of dialogue in my writing, and as my characters spoke Yiddish, I had to translate what they said into Hebrew — which was not a living language at that time. So, after a while, I said to myself: What am I, a writer or a translator? And I came to the conclusion that I must write in Yiddish because it was my mother language and the language of the people I wanted to write about. Since then I have written mostly in Yiddish. Wait — here's something more I remember, a very interesting thing. Even before I learned to read and write, as a child, I liked to imitate my father and my brother. I used to take a pen and scribble on paper. All week long I would scribble and when Saturday came I had to stop. This for me was an ordeal — to have to wait until the Sabbath ended so that I could continue my smearing. Why? I don't know even today.

INTERVIEWERS: *You once told us that during your adolescence you spent three or four years in your grandfather's village, and that this was a strong influence in determining your future as a writer.*

SINGER: Yes. Because this town was very old-fashioned. Not much had changed there in many generations. In this town the traditions of hundreds of years ago still lived. There was no railroad nearby. It was stuck in the forest and it was pretty much the same as it must have been during the time of Chmielnicki. I learned a lot about Jewishness in this town. The town was called Bilgoray. I could have written *The Family Moskat* (which takes place in Warsaw) without having lived in Bilgoray, but I could never have written *Satan in Goray* or some of my other stories without having been there.

INTERVIEWERS: *Why? What did you do there?*

SINGER: I studied the Talmud. I studied the Bible. I studied Cabbala, although it was forbidden. According to the Law, a man should not study Cabbala before he is thirty, but I used to remove the books from the study house. In fact, I almost stole them. I took them to my house and read them often. I was fascinated by the Cabbala.

INTERVIEWERS: *Considering all this, how did your parents react to your wanting to be a writer?*

SINGER: It was a great shock to them. They considered all the secular writers to be heretics, all unbelievers — they really were too, most of them. To become a *literat* was to them almost as bad as becoming a *meshumed,* one who forsakes the faith. My father used to say that secular writers like Peretz were leading the Jews to heresy. He said everything they wrote was against God. Even though Peretz wrote in a religious vein, my father called his writing "sweetened poison," but poison nevertheless. And from his point of view, he was right. Everybody who read such books sooner or later became a worldly man and forsook the traditions. In my family, of course, my brother had gone first, and I went after him. For my parents, this was a tragedy.

INTERVIEWERS: *You and your brother left Poland about 1935, your brother first. Why did you leave, and were you able to pick up right away and continue writing?*

SINGER: Yes. We were both pessimists. We both believed that it was inevitable after Hitler came to power that the Germans would invade Poland.

When I came to this country I lived through a terrible disappointment. I felt then — more than I believe now — that Yiddish had no future in this country. In Poland, Yiddish was still very much alive when I left. When I came here it seemed to me that Yiddish was finished: it was very depressing. The result was that for five or six or maybe seven years I couldn't write a word. Not only didn't I publish anything in those years, but writing became so difficult a chore that my grammar was affected. I couldn't write a single worthwhile sentence. I became like a man who was a great lover and is suddenly impotent, knowing at the same time that ultimately he will regain his power. I shouldn't have even tried to write anything, but I did try, again and again, without success. The novel I tried to write then I eventually threw away. In later years when I looked at it I was startled to find that it was the work of an illiterate man — and this was after I had written *Satan in Goray* and knew Yiddish fairly well. It was a real case of amnesia. One has to get a very great blow to act in such a way. But after a while I got over it, just like that lover whom I spoke of. I've seen this phenomenon at work in other writers. For example, those Yiddish writers who went to Russia, hoping that Communism would help them in some way, became so disappointed that some of them could not even write a single worthwhile sentence. Bergelson, who was a good writer, published a book in Russia called *Birobijan*. When I read this book I had the same feeling that I had in reading the stuff I wrote upon first coming to

America. The man couldn't write a word. It wasn't merely a question of style.

INTERVIEWERS: *At that time, did it ever occur to you to write in English?*

SINGER: I used to play with the idea, but never seriously. Never. I always knew that a writer has to write in his own language or not at all.

INTERVIEWERS: *Did you ever think of going to Palestine in 1935?*

SINGER: Yes. I did think about it. But since I wanted to write in Yiddish and I knew that in Palestine Hebrew was the spoken and written language of the Jews, I decided not to. I could never really think seriously about going to Palestine even though I knew that Yiddish had no real future here. Perhaps I was selfish. I chose Yiddish not because I was a *Yiddishist,* but because I felt that this was the best way for me to express myself.

INTERVIEWERS: *About the time that you were growing up in Warsaw, Jewish radical movements of one sort or another had a very strong influence. Jewish socialism in the form of Bundism was a powerful movement, and of course the Zionist movement was burgeoning. Did you ever feel yourself attracted to any of these groups?*

SINGER: For some strange reason, just as I was skeptical about religious dogma, so was I skeptical about political dogmas. Certainly I was very close to these people, and maybe that was the trouble: you know, sometimes when you see the cook, the food doesn't seem very appetizing. While the ideologies sounded very attractive, I was close enough to see who was preaching them and how these people fought for power among themselves. The truth is, if you ask me, that the aches and troubles of this world cannot be cured by any system. Nevertheless, there are better and worse systems. Democracy seems to me to be one of the better systems, and there is no system which gives more power to the devil than Communism.

As for Zionism, I always believed in it. I think that

Israel is a great hope for the Jewish people. But it is true that just as I knew the socialist cooks, I knew some of the Zionist cooks in Poland. . . . Yet, in the case of Zionism, I felt that whoever the cook was, the food was wholesome. It is true that when I was in Israel five years ago, I found there things which I didn't like. But you find these things in your home or in your own heart. Am I so delighted with myself and with my writing?

I always felt about the Soviet Union that it would never come to any good. From its very beginning it was a butcher shop, and it has remained so even today . . . even if there has been some "improvement." When people have extreme power over other people, it's a terrible thing. I always pray to God (and I do pray because I am in my way a religious man), don't give me any power over any other human beings. I have always avoided this kind of power like the plague. As a book reviewer, I sometimes have some power and it is my hope that someday I will be able to stop reviewing books, because even this little bit of power I inevitably abuse. You know, I review the easier books first or I leave the more difficult ones for last. I do what is easier for me, and in this way I abuse my power.

INTERVIEWERS: *Can we talk a little about translations now, the translations for your books? Do you feel that much of what you have written comes across in English translation?*

SINGER: I am very happy about my books being translated into English. In English my audience is a very real one. I don't have to assume or imagine it. It's not *as if*. And of course many of my English readers are intelligent Jews who know no other language, and I am very happy to reach them. I always take this business of being translated seriously. I am very scrupulous about English translations. Even though my knowledge of English is small, I always felt from the moment I found an American publisher that I wanted to work hard on the translations, because when I read some of the Yiddish writers in English, particularly some of Sholem Aleichem, I knew how bad translation could be. It was so bad you couldn't read it. So I made up my mind that I would contribute as much as I could to the effort. For years I worked together with the translators on *The Family Moskat*. Incidentally, by working on that translation, I learned the little English I know. Since that time I have taken part in the translation of every one of my books. I think only in this way can a translation come out bearable. I say "bearable," because you know just as much as I do that writers inevitably lose a great deal in translation. A friend of mine, also a Yiddish writer, once came to me for some advice. He thought that because I had been translated into English I could advise him on a translation of his own book. I told him that he must be prepared to lose at least 40 per cent in translation, and to make sure that the other 60 per cent had some worth. Or better still, to write something 140 per cent. . . .

Translation is an endless process, really. Every translation, like every book, is a problem in itself. The same translator can do a good job on one book and a bad job on another. Nevertheless, good translation is possible, but it involves hard work for the writer, the translator, and the editor. I don't think that a translation is ever really finished. To me the translation becomes as dear as the original.

INTERVIEWERS: *Well, you've been a translator yourself, haven't you? Did you take as much care with other men's work?*

SINGER: I must confess, no. I did most of my translation as a young man, and frankly I don't think they are very good. I translated *The Magic Mountain*, Stefan Zweig, Remarque, all these from the German. I also translated from Polish and Hebrew. Although my translations were generally praised, I really didn't work as hard on them as I should have. I think *now* I would do a much better job because I have learned what it can mean.

INTERVIEWERS: *What did you do with that chapter in French in* The Magic Mountain? *Did you leave it in French, as was done in the English translation?*

SINGER: No. I didn't because French can't be translated easily into Yiddish, which uses Hebrew characters. But since it was bad French I had to translate it into bad Yiddish. You don't have to make a great effort to write bad Yiddish.

INTERVIEWERS: *While we're on the subject of translations, it seems that the six books of yours which have been translated into English fall into two categories. One of these is the kind of writing best exemplified by* The Family Moskat, *that is, rather straightforward, realistic narrative; in this case, a family chronicle.* The Magician of Lublin *is also somewhat like this. But* Satan in Goray *and most of your stories seem to have a different quality altogether. They are much more stylized; they emphasize folk elements, particularly the demonic and the supernatural. Now our question is this: is this division of your translated work, as we've outlined it, representative of your total output?*

SINGER: In asking the question that way, you also answer it. . . . It is true that my work does fall into two such categories. The reason is simple: sometimes I feel like writing about the supernatural, in a symbolic way, and I also feel that there is a place for the realistic method. These two categories are not mutually exclusive; they are only two sides of the same coin. The world can be looked at one way or another, and the theme of a story determines its style. What I have had translated thus far is a good part of my work, but there are still many things which have not been translated and published. For instance, I have written a novel called *Der Hoyf* in Yiddish. In English I originally wanted to call it "The Beginning," because it deals with what we spoke about earlier: the beginning of socialism and Zionism in Poland. But it will probably be called "The Manor." The translation is now being completed. It is a large book written more or less in the style of *The Family Moskat.* There is another book which I have written about Jewish life in America. It's called "Shadows by the Hudson" and it's again written in a different style, a kind of combination of the two styles.

INTERVIEWERS: *Why don't you tell us something about* "Shadows by the Hudson." *Isn't this one of the very few things you've written about America?*

SINGER: Yes. "Shadows by the Hudson" is a story of a group of people who came to this country at the end of the Second World War or immediately thereafter and settled on the Upper West Side of New York — on Riverside Drive, West End Avenue, Broadway and so forth. While they live here, their minds and spirits are still in the old country, although, at the same time, they take roots here in New York. The times are mixed up and they are mixed up, and their story is full of confusion, unusual love stories. In fact, I think it's an unusual kind of novel.

INTERVIEWERS: *What are you working on now?*

SINGER: A book called "A Ship to America." This is the first time I've ever written a novel in the first person. It has autobiographical elements, but it isn't autobiography. It begins in Poland in 1935, but most of the book takes place in New York. It's the story of a writer who comes to this country, loses his passport, and becomes, against his own will and intentions, an illegal visitor. In 1939, he gets his first papers and a permit to go abroad. On the eve of the Second World War, he goes back to Poland to marry his lover and bring her, and his son by another woman, back to America. I won't tell you the end, because the book is now being serialized in the *Forward* on Fridays and Saturdays.

As for the style, I would say it's different from anything I've done before. Writing in the first person is a new experience for me, and creates new problems in description and construction. The idea that writing in the first person is easier than in the third person is far from true. It is a style with many possible pitfalls and demands more caution from a writer. One of the chief dangers of such a novel is that it always threatens to become a mere memoir.

INTERVIEWERS: *Now what about this folk element in your work? What use do you feel you are making of it, and how do you regard the so-called demonic trait?*

SINGER: There are two reasons for this: one is literary and the other is more than literary. The more than literary reason is that I really believe there are spirits in this world, and that man has a soul, and that the soul is not the only spiritual entity in this world. I really believe that. Of course, many people, Jews and Christians alike, have believed in demons and spirits. But that's not why I believe in them. I truly believe that there are forces and spirits in this world, about which we know very little, which influence our lives. A hundred years from now, when people know more about other things, they will also know more about these spiritual powers. I believe that psychical research is a science of the future, not the past. I find it very easy to believe in reincarnation, possession by devils, and other such things. We have many proofs that these things exist.

INTERVIEWERS: *Then why is it that you are so cynical about Hertz Yanovar and his group of spiritists in* The Family Moskat?

SINGER: *I* am not. It is my characters who are skeptical about this group. All the skepticism belongs to Asa Heshel and his wife. Still, I myself am a little skeptical about spiritism. Why? Because this is already a planned business. You sit down at a table and call forth a spirit. I don't believe that a spirit can just be called forth to order. In the same way, I don't believe that a man can just sit down and write a great poem. It won't work; it's not so easy. Spiritism has become a money-making thing, a kind of church, a dogma. So I don't believe in it; but I do believe that it is possible for a human being to see a spirit in a spontaneous way. This perhaps explains why I write critically about spiritism in *The Family Moskat.*

INTERVIEWER [*sic*]: *Just for the record, have you yourself ever had what you would call a spiritual or supernatural experience?*

SINGER: Never, really. But other people, whom I trust, have. And I have read a lot about such things. If there is any field of knowledge in which I am some kind of scholar, it is psychic research. I have read a great deal on this subject, in English and other languages.

INTERVIEWERS: *Are you familiar with Yeats's mysticism, with theosophy and Rosicrucianism?*

SINGER: No, I don't know Yeats. But I've read Madame Blavatsky. But let me come back to the literary reason for my use of the demonic and supernatural. First, it helps me to express myself. For example, by using Satan or a demon as a symbol, one can compress a great many things. It's a kind of spiritual stenography. It gives me more freedom. For another thing, the demons and Satan represent to me, in a sense, the ways of the world. Instead of saying this is the way things happen, I will say, this is the way demons behave. Demons symbolize the world for me, and by that I mean human beings and human behavior; and since I really believe in their existence — that is, not only symbolically but substantively — it is easy to see how this kind of literary style was born. I really love this style and I am always finding new symbols and new stories. In *The Slave*, for example, I was unable to write about Jewish demons because this was primarily a story about Polish gentiles. Consequently, I found out all about Polish demonology. It fascinated me. Writers, as a matter of fact, fall in love with things like that, just as men fall in love with women. And certain things repeat themselves in every serious writer. I would say that every serious writer is possessed by certain ideas or symbols, and I am possessed by my demons and they add a lot to my vision and my expression.

INTERVIEWERS: *You say that these demons and Satan symbolize the world for you. Now in many of your stories — like* Satan in Goray, "The Mirror," *and* "The Diary of One Not Yet Born" — *these imps, demons, devils, and what have you triumph either partially or completely. This would seem to make you a kind of "devil's advocate." Perhaps you mean to imply that evil is triumphing over good in man.*

SINGER: In many cases, it does; and in many cases, it doesn't. From experience we know that it happens often in this world — I'm not speaking now of the next world — that evil is victorious. Wouldn't you say that Hitler's success was the triumph of evil? Certainly, he almost reached his goal. And those Germans who went along with him, in his evil ways, have not been punished. On the other hand, the good sometimes prevails. In my story, "Gimpel the Fool," Satan tells Gimpel to do a nasty thing. Gimpel does so, and then reneges on the devil. So you see, I make no rules; evil doesn't always triumph and it isn't always defeated. Once you establish a rule, it's against literature and against life.

INTERVIEWERS: *What you're saying is that you are writing morality stories, more realistic examples, perhaps, than some of the old-fashioned morality tales, but in essence, stories of good and evil.*

SINGER: I would not characterize my stories as morality tales, but rather as being constructed around a moral point of view. Perhaps only *The Magician of Lublin* could be called a true morality tale. In this book, I had more of an "axe to grind." It's true that when I write I don't look at the world as if it is beyond judgment. I do judge, not always explicitly, but more often implicitly. I even would go so far as to say that any writer who does not think in terms of good and evil cannot go very far in his writing. This is a tragedy in much of modern writing; authors have ceased to look upon life from the eternal point of view of good and evil. They look upon life in a purely scientific way; they say that such circumstances create such people and such people behave so. The moment a writer begins to regard life from a behavioristic point of view, the writing falls flat and the writing descends to the level of his own characters. As the Talmud expresses it: *les din, les dayan,* there is no judgment and no judge. My judgment is that good does not always triumph, that this is very far from being the best of all possible worlds. That's why all my Jews are not good Jews. Why should they be any different from anybody else? The Cabbalists say this world is the worst of all possible worlds. They believe there are millions of worlds, but the worst is this one. Here is the very darkness itself. How can you expect that in the blackest darkness, in the deepest abyss of all, everything should turn out nice and proper? From a Cabbalistic point of view, I'm a very realistic writer. . . .

INTERVIEWER [sic]: *This is the second time you've mentioned the Cabbala. Have you read other mystical or occult works?*

SINGER: Well, I've read all the classic works of spiritism and occultism — not only the old ones, but the modern scientific books. *The Phantasms of the Living* by Gurney and Myers, which is a classic; there's another one, too, about life after death. These were both written in the 1880's in England, when the Society for Psychical Research was created. These were people of great integrity, and they did a great deal of research. You would be surprised at some of the things they discovered. Nowadays psychic research is undergoing a kind of crisis; but at the end of the last century it flourished. Yet even today there are many serious people engaged in it. You know that William James believed in occultism. Once you begin to study these things you are faced with the fact that here is an uncharted ocean of knowledge.

INTERVIEWERS: *Do you know personally many of the people engaged in psychic research?*

SINGER: No, I do not. And I will tell you why: there is no field in which so many liars and charlatans abound as in this one. Let's not fool ourselves: there are so many that it is incredible. But they have somehow managed not to utterly destroy legitimate psychic research, just as literature has not been destroyed by its numerous bad practitioners, by, say, the two hundred or so bad writers scribbling away

in Brooklyn or the Bronx, in Paris and San Francisco.
Both of these fields are good ones for liars and charlatans;
they can really go to town. In the case of psychic research
people, there is much obvious nonsense. They publish
magazines about people who visit other planets and come
down to tell who they met there. I am not so foolish as to
believe all these fakers. Still, I do read their magazines. I
find their lies interesting. If nothing else, they are revealing
fantasies. I do believe, however, in phenomena like clair-
voyant dreams, extrasensory perception, and the like. And
I think these things are all reflections of Higher Powers,
whether divine or otherwise, of powers which surround us
and are at work all the time.

INTERVIEWERS: *Of course, then, you believe in God.*

SINGER: Yes, I do. I'm not, however, an observant Jew. I
believe in God but not in man insofar as he claims God has
revealed himself to him. If a man came to me and tells me
he has been to the planet Mars, I would call him a liar, but
I would not stop believing in the existence of the planet. I
believe that the Higher Powers do not reveal themselves
so easily; you have to search for them. Consequently, I have
no faith in dogmas of any kind; they are only the work of
men. Man is born to free choice, to believe, to doubt, or to
deny. I choose to believe. I also believe in the power of
personal prayer. While I shun organized prayer and religion, I would call myself a religious man. The Higher
Powers, I am convinced, are always with us, at every moment, everywhere, except, perhaps, at the meetings of
Marxists and other left-wingers. There is no God there;
they have passed a motion to that effect.

Notes

[1] See the four selections published in the January 1962 and April 1962
issues of *Commentary*.

[2] "Demonic Fiction of a Yiddish 'Modernist,' " *Commentary*, October
1960.

Marshall Breger and Bob Barnhart

2.

A Conversation with Isaac Bashevis Singer

Isaac Singer is a Yiddish modern. His idiom is that of the Polish ghetto, but the problems he develops are distinctly of our time. Faith and alienation, the existence of evil, man's place in the universe, these problems are all faced obliquely, in a world haunted by imps, demons, and angels. His universe is a mysteriously moral one, and the society he creates, that of the medieval Polish Jew, seems to hang timeless in a higher reality.

Since 1949 when Saul Bellow translated *Gimpel the Fool* for the *Partisan Review,* Isaac Singer has had a growing audience in English. The critics, at first impressed by his transmutation of folk material into literature, recognized the scope of his moral imagination after the publication of *The Spinoza of Market Street* in 1961. He is generally considered to be the leading Yiddish writer alive today and in the view of Kenneth Rexroth, "If only he were left writing Yiddish it would still be an important literary language."

Mr. Singer was born in Poland in 1904. His older brother, I. J. Singer, was a celebrated Yiddish novelist, best known for a family chronicle entitled *The Brothers Ashkenazi.* A journalist in Warsaw, Isaac B. Singer immigrated to the United States in 1935. Since that time he has written steadily for the *Jewish Daily Forward,* a Yiddish newspaper in New York City. His translated works include *The Family Moskat, Satan in Goray, The Magician of Lublin, The Slave,* and two collections of stories, *Gimpel the Fool* and *The Spinoza of Market Street.* A third collection of stories, *Short Friday,* was published this past November by Farrar Strauss.

This interview took place in Mr. Singer's Manhattan apartment on August 9, 1964.

I remember glancing through an interview with you in Commentary. *In it you stated that you had a great many problems of adjustment when you came to America in 1935. I wonder if you could give me some idea of the adjustments you faced as a writer?*
Every immigrant has a problem of adjustment. Even before you come here from Europe, you feel that America is almost a different planet. I don't know who made Europeans believe this, but this is what they believe. For a writer it is especially difficult because for him tradition is especially important. I will give you an example: in my country, where I lived, all the spoons are not round, but are longish — elongated. When I saw for the first time in this country a round spoon, I said to myself — "Oh, what is this?" For my business, for literature, it is good if things are steady, if they don't change. For example, in our country, a drugstore was a store where they sold drugs. When I saw a drugstore and people were eating sandwiches it was to me a kind of catastrophe. Not a spiritual one, but a kind of literary catastrophe, because then the word drugstore has another meaning. When you write in Europe, "drugstore," the reader gets a feeling what it is, he knows already with what it is connected. But when you see a different drugstore and they serve food, it means that the word has changed. I have a feeling that this is what people would say if they ever reached the planets or the moon.

The whole dictionary would have to be changed. So naturally, since I wrote in Yiddish, it was even more difficult. There I was accustomed to one language, and here it was a new language, and things were also new. It was the small variations that were new, but even small variations make a person nervous if he is accustomed to a word meaning exactly what it says. For example, we are accustomed that a table has four legs. If we would ever see a table hanging down from a ceiling, the word table wouldn't mean "table" any more. In this country, where things are always in a process of change, it makes an immigrant, especially a writer who is a slave of words, it makes him kind of nervous and it makes him feel that he has to adjust. After a while, you see that even though it has changed so much, it is very much the same.

You said you had undergone a "literary amnesia."

Yes, I would say this happens to many writers, but very few admit it. What happens to a writer is that for some reason he loses his inspiration and his power to write. In my case it was so clear that I couldn't deny it, neither to others nor to myself. For the first few years I just felt that I could not write. This was my amnesia.

What kind of thing brought you out of it? Or can you trace it to a particular event?

After a few years, when I had settled down, I convinced myself that America is the same world as there, and the change is not as huge as I thought. The people are the same and the language, even though it is a different language, has the same notions, and after a while I returned to my old ways. In every kind of amnesia this occurs. A man may forget under a shock, but a shock never lasts forever.

Do you think that part of the shock might have come from a feeling that in America you did not have an audience which you could communicate with or to?

Yes, in Poland I lived among a few million people who spoke Yiddish and I knew that I had an audience. Here, everybody spoke English and my editor, Abe Cahan, even

told me that the Yiddish newspaper which he was editing, might last only five or ten years. He was very pessimistic.
Was your education secular or religious?
It was almost completely religious. I went to a Heder and then I went to a Bet Medresh which is a school where you study religion. Then I studied in a Rabbinical Seminary. There they gave me also some worldly knowledge, but it was all connected with religion.
I have a question about your upbringing. Did you read much as a child? What type of books?
As a child I read a lot of religious books, like the Bible and the Talmud. The moment I had a chance, I began to read world literature in Yiddish, and in Polish, and also in German — I learned these languages by myself. I would say, one of the writers who made the greatest impression on me as a child was Knut Hamsun. I also naturally read Tolstoy and Dostoevski. I remember reading *Crime and Punishment* at the age of eleven, and I understood nothing. The only thing I understood was that it was a great book. I just couldn't put it away. I felt that there was something in it that just attracted me.
Today, do you keep current with American and world writing?
I still read a little fiction, but not as much. I am no longer so curious about fiction — I would rather read things that have to do with fact. I was terribly excited about the photographs of the moon. In my childhood I always dreamt about the moon, and here I hoped that in these photographs I would see unusual things. I have seen nothing more than what was published in the newspaper, and I hope that some more of these photographs will be printed. Naturally a photograph of the moon will not reveal to us the purpose of the world. I have this kind of curiosity about writing. If I would know that someone has written a very good book, a wonderful book, I would be very eager to read it. I have read in my later years so much bad fiction, that I have cooled off.

Do you think that the state of literature is deteriorating, or is it just that you have finished all the good books in your youth?

Here I am in doubt for two reasons. One is that in all generations old men say the same things. When they were young the fiction was good and everything was good, and when they became older, everything became bad. So I am suspicious that it may have to do with my age. The second reason is that so many books are published that you just cannot keep up. Forty years ago you could more or less say that you knew a little about world literature. Today, we cannot know. Twenty thousand books a year are published in this country, and in others, millions of them. The only thing I can say is that I have not seen for the last twenty years any book about which I could say here is another Tolstoy or Dostoevski or Gogol. I have written just now a review about Gogol for the *Herald Tribune* that will come out in two weeks.

Is this a new collection?

Yes. Not a new translation but a new editing of an old translation. It is a book which contains all of Gogol's fiction, and I read again everything Gogol has written. You cannot find today a writer like Gogol.

As you have come to terms with American life, do you think your writing is becoming more influenced by American writers in general, or —

No! I have read so few American writers and so late that there cannot be any talk of an influence. You are influenced when you are fifteen or eighteen or twenty and don't get influenced when you are fifty-five or nearer to sixty. In this age a man is already what he has to be. In addition, I did not read such American works which could influence me. I did read a little of Hemingway and Faulkner and the others. I admire very much a writer who is called Conrad Richter. I even got from him a very nice letter. I wanted always to write a letter to him and to tell him how much I like him. One day I got a letter from him.

Didn't he write A Simple Honorable Man?

Yes. I did not read this, but I read *The Trees,* which is a very good book. There are good writers in this country but I don't think they are of such caliber that I should be influenced by them.

I would like to throw something in right here. I know your next book being published is a collection of your stories, but what are you working on right now?

There is another book which I am not working on but is being translated at present. I have written a large novel like *The Family Moskat* which is called *The Manor.* The rough translation has already been completed, and Cecil Hemley, my editor, is working on it. He has done about a half. I guess that my next book is going to be *The Manor. The Manor* is kind of a chronicle, like *The Family Moskat.* The story begins in 1863 and ends at the end of the nineteenth century. It actually ends where *The Family Moskat* begins.

I wanted to ask something about The Family Moskat *in comparison with your other translated works, because there seems to be such a gulf in style.*

I would say that I have two kinds of style. When I write a large novel, and I have written some of these, I use a different kind of style. Not that I wrote in one epoch one way and in another epoch so. No, in the same epoch I wrote in both styles. *The Family Moskat* is more or less a realistic novel. I felt that to write this book in the style that I write my stories would not be right — I would fail with the story. So I wrote in this style and I am still able today to use both of these styles. I don't think they are a contradiction because many writers have many styles and you even adjust the style to the story.

I also understand that you write for a deadline under a different name — Warshavsky. I wonder if you could tell me something about this and also something about some of your books which have not been translated.

Warshavsky is actually my journalistic pen name. When I

write under Warshavsky I don't worry too much about style. I just write because I have to write, because I am connected with a newspaper. Under this name I wrote a number of autobiographical stories where I tell about my father's house. Some of these stories appeared in *Commentary*, some in *The Saturday Evening Post* and in other magazines. So I wrote them under Warshavsky and I considered them literary journalism. Later I published them in Yiddish, but the publisher insisted that I should give my own name under them. I may translate them into English, also under my own name, although I will say in the introduction that they were written under the name Warshavsky for newspaper publication. In a way they were more successful than my stories. People nowadays like journalism better than fiction. We are living in an epoch of journalism.

Do you find a conscious shift in your methods or technique when you decide to write under one name or another?

Yes, yes. Immediately the point of view is different. The way of description is different, everything becomes lighter, I worry less about details and I would say that I am a bit more sentimental than in my real fiction. A pen name is very important for a writer. It is kind of a different ego. It is kind of a second personality.

I want to ask you a question about translation. You, I believe, have translated Thomas Mann and Stephen Zweig into Yiddish and worked closely with those who translated your own books into English. Are there any problems of translation that are unique to Yiddish?

I wouldn't say they are unique to Yiddish but that there are problems of translation characteristic of all languages. Some people say that certain Yiddish idioms cannot be translated. This is not true. No idiom of any language can be 100% translated. It can only be a kind of an approximation. The problem with Yiddish is that there are less and less people who know the language. This is unique because, for example, there are so many people who know French that there is no problem about translating from

French. If one person doesn't do the job well another person will. In Yiddish you have to search for them. In the later years I began to translate myself together with a collaborator. *The Slave* and many of my stories I translated with the help of my collaborator. I have learned enough English to be able to translate word by word, and, then, when it comes to the construction of the sentences the collaborator helps me.

Regarding your own translations do you find that your style is faithfully maintained in the English translation?
That is a good question. It is true that in every translation the author loses — you do not gain in translation. Once in awhile you may gain in one sentence, but as a rule you keep on losing, this is true in all translations, because translation is a kind of compromise. I would say that some writers lose a lot and some lose less. This Gogol of whom I spoke before, he was one of the heaviest losers. He had a wonderful style — his language was very idiomatic and so, naturally he lost a lot, while Tolstoi, or Dostoevski or Turgenev lost less. Poetry loses almost everything; you just can't translate it. The same thing is true about humor, especially when it is connected with folklore. In my case I lose a lot, but since I myself take care of the translation I know that I am not losing everything.

When translating yourself did you stress the literal or the interpretive?
Both these are important. The ideal translation is one that would be literal and at the same time would convey the spirit of the work. Since this cannot be, translation must be a compromise.

Do you feel that a good translator must be a creative writer in his own right?
I wouldn't say that he has to be a creative writer but rather that a good translator is creative.

There are many creative writers who insist that translation is a good exercise to keep you in form when you are not actually writing.

Even in schools students have to translate to learn a language. If you never translate you have a feeling that your language can express everything — yet once you work with another language, you recognize that your own language is not as rich as you thought.

Lionel Trilling, especially in Manners, Morals and the Novel, *but in almost all of his works, stresses the importance of class in a novel, not so much class as a social fact, but class in the sense of a system of manners. He feels that class division is essential to the novelist, because it allows him the depth and range implicit in an involved and structured environment, and that he can utilize a set of manners which may suggest by nuance rather than forcing him back to the less aesthetic device of exposition by statement. Certainly, your work is rich in its utilization of class and manners. I get the impression that a society as well ordered as yours in Poland would offer much opportunity for a novelist, yet in many ways the modern reader would not be conversant with the social hierarchy of the Poland of which you write. Do you feel that this is a problem, and how do you get around it if you do feel so?*

No, it is not a problem. The good reader knows that there are many groups, and that each group has its own peculiarities, so he is not baffled when he sees that things are not just as in his own group. Rather I think that it is good for a writer, no matter how or about what he writes, to be connected with a group. In writing there is no such thing as being an internationalist or a cosmopolitan. You can be cosmopolitan in your ideas if you wish, but the moment you sit down to write you are connected with a certain group.

I would say that literature must have an address, that it just cannot be in a vacuum. This is very important. Many modern writers would like to get rid of this and write about humanity — general humanity, just abstract human beings. This cannot be done. In *Crime and Punishment,* Dostoevski does not write only about a murderer.

but about a certain man, Raskolnikov, who lived in St. Petersburg, in a certain time. I once said that if Dostoevski wanted to write a story, the same story, happening in Moscow, it would have been already a different story. There would have been a different student, a different murder, different police, the whole action would have been different. In other words, literature cannot operate in a void above humanity. It is strongly connected with a group, with a clan . . . I always write about the Jewish people in Poland proper. In other words I do not write about the so-called Lithuanians. Although from Warsaw to Lithuania is not much further than from here to Philadelphia, I feel that I don't know them enough. When a writer has visited Spain and then writes a novel about Spain, it looks to me ridiculous. I have been in this country almost thirty years, and only lately do I dare to write about American people, and only about American Jews.

You have just anticipated a question I was planning to ask. I was going to ask whether you write as an outsider looking back into another time and place, or if you more or less adopt a society as yours and write as a participant. You mean to say how I write about American people.

I was going to ask it concerning Poland, now I ask it in connection with America.

Well, about Poland, the truth is that I am still living there. I lived there my first thirty years; and, you know that your experiences in childhood are the most important for a writer. So for me the Poland of my youth still exists. About this country; slowly, I begin to feel I am also here a citizen. I mean in a literary sense. In the first fifteen or twenty years I just couldn't understand American people. Naturally, I understood from a logical point of view, but not from an emotional point of view. I didn't know what made their minds work. Today I have a feeling that, when I sit with two young people like you, I know more or less what you think and how you feel, just like the human beings in Poland.

You feel so strongly that a writer must be connected with a continuity, with a tradition. Would you reject the concept, popular at least among youth, that the writer must in some way be alienated?
You have to be both. One has to be deeply rooted and, also, in a way alienated. He has to know the object of his writing so he has to be deeply rooted, but, at the same time, he cannot be too much one of the people. If he is one of them completely, then there is no difference, and some difference is necessary. In other words, he has to be, according to my ideas, very much of a relative and very much of a stranger. You will see that this is true about many writers. Take a writer like Dostoevski. Nobody knows Russia better than he, but, at the same time, the Russians feel that he is not one of their own. He is a strange kind of fellow. This is true about all real writers.
In Gimpel the Fool, *you state, "No doubt the world is entirely an imaginary world — but it is only once removed from the real world." We sort of touched on that earlier; I was hoping that you could expand on that statement because I find this attitude toward the world is felt in almost all of your translated works.*
Many writers and many philosophers have felt the same thing. From the time of Bishop Berkeley, to whom the world was nothing but an aggregation of ideas, many have felt that what we see and what we experience cannot be more than an artificial something which has nothing to do with Being. We see the world through our categories. I don't have to expand this because it has to do more with philosophy than with literature. But a real writer also has this feeling. When I say "a table," I know it is nothing but a name; behind this word there is a thing in itself of which I have no idea. This feeling is in every writer, and because of this feeling there is a kind of skepticism in writing. In other words, even though you say things, you say them with your tongue in cheek. There is a kind of almost playing around with ideas.

And everyone who reads your works will again have to go through this same process of playing with ideas in trying to come back to what you had in mind in the first place. Thank you for saying so. If you read a writer and you like his work, you are in a way hypnotized by that writer — you begin to get his feelings — his point of view. I always feel that I really don't know exactly the things about which I talk. So naturally, since this is my point of view, the reader will get the same feeling. You know that modern mathematicians maintain that mathematics is a science which speaks about things without KNOWING what. . . . What was the name of the famous writer who worked together with Whitehead on the *Principia Mathematica? Oh, you mean Russell.*

He said that mathematics is a science where you say things, and you don't know what you are saying. When you say two and two is four, actually you don't know what this means. What does it mean this two and two is four? Two horses and two tables are not four; they have to be alike. You have to say two horses and two horses are four horses. Actually no four horses are alike, and so on.

One thing I find very interesting is that even while you consider the real the metaphysical, you make an extensive use of nature and animal images in your work. For example, The Slave *begins with a nature catalogue of daybreak and the first chapter ends with a similar catalogue of twilight. Is this a critic's generalization or do you agree with it?*

I agree. Just because a writer feels that the things outside of him are somewhat unreal, he will clutch more to description than the writer who imagines that words are objects. So I would say that description is a result of a kind of skepticism. The more you doubt the outside world, the more you will be inclined to describe it — if you have the talent to do so. Because by this you try to create, for a moment, at least the illusion that there is something beyond us.

What dangers are there in nature catalogues? Do you usually keep your original images in your final draft?
I would say that the danger is always not to become a bore. No matter what you do, if you begin to bore the reader, you yourself feel that it is boring because bad writing bores even the author. Don't overdo anything — when you feel that you can go on, you can go on. Let us say there is a situation where you can write for two or three pages about nature. It will not bore the reader because there are such circumstances where the reader will take it. But there are cases where one word is enough. There cannot be any rules about it. In literature, like in life, you FEEL how far you can go.

Irving Howe once stated that Yiddish literature is concerned with mood and controlled by an overriding theme, that of community survival and that the importance of community sublimates the study of character into the presentation of community archetypes such as Bontsha the Silent, Tevye the dairyman, or the town of Chelm. I wonder if you would want to comment on this.
Well, it is true about old Yiddish literature, but I would not say it is true about me because when I began to write many of the Yiddish writers and critics complained that I didn't behave like a Yiddish writer — that my way of writing is different. In a way I didn't then understand them. But I finally began to see what they meant. I am not writing in this way. I don't worry so much about the community as I worry about the character whom I describe.

Do you think your brother was in this category also?
He, also, was not completely in that tradition. Sholom Alechim is such a writer. To him the Shtatel and the community is everything.

From your collection Spinoza of Market Street, *I get the impression that there are two broad philosophical areas into which the stories can be divided. I was just thinking about it this afternoon, so I am not exactly sure how best to express myself. I got the feeling that either supernatural*

*forces such as imps or devils are enticing man into wrong
doing and then he is punished, or he stoically accepts the
natural order, suffers, and does nothing to improve his
condition. In either case, it seems that your characters are
not so much conscious agents as expressions. They seem to
become somewhat static.*

No, it is not completely so, because I believe, at least
consciously, in free will. Everyone of us has free will. The
only thing is that free will is a rare gift and we get very
little of it. In the stories where I describe human misery,
I describe cases where a man did not make use of his free
will and because of this you have a feeling that the imp
and satan and the devil are victorious. I always believe that
there is no power which can curb a man from using this
rare gift if he really wants to. Even though you will see in
my works many stories where I make man seem like a
victim of other powers, I don't believe in that.

*Your characters have the will to repulse the forces if they
make that choice?*

Yes. They have the will and in some of my stories you
will see that they actually do so. This war between God
and Satan means actually the war between free will and
compulsion. From the moment man is born, he is compelled, yet at the same time he is given the free will to
fight compulsion.

*You would say that when a man uses free will, he will use
it to rise above into the ethical, that his compulsion may
be toward evil but he uses his will to fight evil?*

Yes, to my mind this is actually the essence of religion.
There is not such a thing as a fatalist religion. Be it
Judaism or Christianity or Buddhism, they all teach you
that we are always given a choice. Even when it seems to
a human being that he has no choice, he still has some
choice. When a man is in prison, naturally he has no
choice — he cannot leave the prison. He cannot break the
walls, but he can always be at one wall or another wall —

he can be quiet or he can be hysterical. He can be a good prisoner or a bad prisoner.

He can reconcile himself to his position?

Yes. It is very interesting that in Europe there does not exist the fact that one gets time off for good behavior, which means that those who made the laws in this country knew that even a man in prison can behave well or badly, and he is rewarded and punished accordingly. This is a very good idea because it means that man has not lost his will completely even though he is in prison.

There are some general questions, and they are divorced from the things we have been talking about. I would be interested in having you describe your concept of demonology and briefly your concept of God.

My belief in God is not the kind of belief that God has revealed Himself to man — and He told them this is the way to behave — this type of revelation I don't believe. Nevertheless I believe there is a God. Naturally, I don't know Who He is or What He is — nobody knows exactly. God for me means the plan of the world — in other words, whatever happens in the world seems to me like a part of a huge universal plan. This authority of planning I call God. It is the Power behind all the happenings not only on this earth but everywhere. I cannot imagine one God who rules the earth and one God who rules some other planet or star. The total power which rules this world is to me God. As far as demonology is concerned, although I cannot be convinced I have this feeling, there are more entities in the world than we know of. I can play with the idea that there may be devils or angels — there is no reason why not. Microbes were living for millions of years, and we did not know them. Now man has discovered them and we may yet discover that together with us live millions of other creatures which we cannot see, not because of their smallness but because of their bigness or for other reasons. In a literary way it helps me a lot because these creatures are very much connected to folklore, and when it comes to literature they are very useful to a writer. You can say through them many things which you cannot say otherwise. When you say "Satan has tempted me," even if you don't believe in Satan, the words "Satan has tempted me" themselves have already a meaning and express a part of our thinking.

A question out of ignorance.

In these cases we are all ignorant.

I was just wondering — when you describe a demon, does this come out of a source book, folklore, or . . .

Both. It is connected with folklore, but also I will use my own imagination. But something else I discovered is that even when I use my own imagination, even this is connected with folklore.

What sources are there for Polish folklore?

The sources are very few. There is a book called *Jewish Magic* by Dr. Trachenberg, but I read this book after I had written all of these stories. The main thing is that I heard stories told in my father's house. People always came with these kind of stories. I would say there is a lot of folklore but little of it was collected and written about.

I guess that's about it.

Let me add to you that I am a sincere vegetarian. You may be interested to know that even though I don't have any dogma, this has become my dogma. I have convinced myself that as long as we are going to be cruel to animals, as long as we are going to apply towards animals the principle that might makes right, I think that the Higher Powers will apply the same principle to us. They are mightier than we are, and to whom, perhaps, we are as little intelligent as the animals are in proportion to us. This is lately my kind of religion, and I really hope that one day humanity will make an end to this eating of meat and hunting of animals for pleasure.

You see that I have two birds in the next room, and you will see that they are not in a cage. Go in and you will see that they fly around. When I went to California, I left special people who took care of them. I have a great love of animals, and I feel that in them and from them we can learn a lot about the mysteries of the world because they are nearer to them than we are.

Ruth Whitman

3.

Translating with
Isaac Bashevis Singer

Translating with Isaac Bashevis Singer means entering into a world that he has created and of which he is
an inhabitant.

One day we were translating his story, "Three Tales,"
and we came to a passage which said:

> The rabbi looked at the wall to make sure that Zein-
> vele was casting a shadow. Demons don't, you know.

We were sitting in my sunny livingroom in Cambridge,
I at the typewriter, Bashevis at my side with scraps of
Yiddish in his hand. Just as we arrived at the English
equivalent quoted above, we both looked up at the window in time to see the sun slide behind a cloud. Then both
of us glanced down at the floor beside his chair where there
was — no shadow. We laughed, but only half humorously.
He had cast the thought into my mind like a spell and he
knew it.

If it sounds sensational to describe a working asso-
ciation between a translator and an author as a kind of
enchantment, then this is merely because sophisticated

twentieth-century literary experience has become too narrow and literal to imagine such an event. Singer's world, charged with sex and the supernatural as it is, has an authenticity about it. It is the authenticity of poetry. And when a translator is in rapport with him, he cannot help but see Singer as a character in one of his own stories, characters every one of whom is driven with an obsessive passion.

Singer's passion is to know everything there is to know about human beings. He often quotes Spinoza's remark, "Anything can be a passion." For him the most consuming necessity in his life is to find out what goes on in the mind of everyone he meets. He is insatiable in his lust for information. A luncheon conversation with him leaves one stripped of one's history.

A necessary corollary of his passion for information about men and women is Singer's passion to write it all down as fast as possible. When he first arrived in New York, in 1935, his Yiddish pen became silent. He supported himself as a Yiddish journalist, writing for the *Jewish Daily Forward*, but his creative life suffered a complete drought. He felt unhappy with the new language, uncertain with the old. But the uncertainty was superficial and temporary. When the lusis occurred and he began to write, the stories came pouring out. Now he writes constantly. All the years of accumulated knowledge have turned instantly into parables of human nature and human experience, and he can hardly keep up with the flow.

But there is an obstacle between the creative flow from Singer's mind to the ear of his English reader: Yiddish. Beautiful, lovable, singable Yiddish, of which the reader seldom hears one word. This is a great frustration to a Yiddish writer, but in Singer's case the drive to communicate overrides his frustration. To comfort himself, he says:

It seems that translation, although it does damage, cannot kill an author. If he's really good, he will come through even in translation. I have seen it in my own case. Also translation helps me in a way. I go through my writings again and again while I edit the translation and work with the translator, and I see the defects of my writing while I am doing this. So I would say that in many cases, translation has helped me to avoid many pitfalls. (Interview in the *National Jewish Monthly,* March 1968)

Most of Singer's translators don't know Yiddish. Relatively few of his stories have been published in Yiddish. (An exception to this, of course, are his two long family novels, *The Family Moskat* and *The Manor,* both of which were serialized in Yiddish in the *Jewish Daily Forward.*) It is therefore seldom necessary or possible to have a Yiddish text available for his translator.

Singer's method of working is to translate with his translator, phrase by phrase, sentence by sentence. That is, he gives the literal meaning of the Yiddish in his hand or head, and then discusses the best way to put the words into literary English.

Although I was only a student of Yiddish and far from a master of the language during the time I worked with Singer, I found this method of translation very frustrating. I wanted to see the Yiddish text and see for myself how it sounded, how close or far away our English approximation could come. In only one instance, in the story "Cock-a-Doodle-Doo" (published in *Hadassah Magazine*), was I allowed to take the Yiddish text home and work over it until the translation was polished to my satisfaction. Many readers have told me that this is my best translation of Singer, that it has the real *nigun* — melody, tune, lilt — of the original Yiddish.

Singer himself laments that a tremendous percentage of meaning and aroma is usually lost in the English. He has put the loss as high as 70%. His Yiddish, the medium between his thoughts and his translators, of necessity becomes more and more abbreviated. For this reason it is entirely just that Singer has occasionally listed himself as the translator, together with his assistant. This puts the responsibility in his hands, and gives him greater leeway to change and remold the English phrase if it is not able to fit the Yiddish.

When he received the National Arts Council grant of ten thousand dollars in 1967, Singer said he wanted to use the money to publish his works in Yiddish. Perhaps this was only a brave gesture, but I hope he does this. Although millions of the readers and writers of Yiddish were killed in our generation and the coming generation shows little sign of replenishing the lost ranks, or, as Singer puts it, "Yiddish is sick, but not dead," Yiddish will become an increasingly important language for students and lovers of literature. While its importance as a daily family language weakens, its importance as the language of a great body of poetry and prose becomes stronger and stronger.

Singer has had many translators who know no Yiddish but who are talented writers — among them, Cecil Hemley and Elaine Gottlieb — writers who are able to give a shine and rhythm to his prose in English; a few, like Mirra Ginsburg, who know Yiddish; and a few who have been incompetent in both languages. But his translators are his lifeblood. He has a desperate dependence on them, as he himself declares. His only recourse is to cast a spell and catch his translator up with him into his world, his view, his insight.

He casts no shadow.

J. A. Eisenberg

4.

Isaac Bashevis Singer:
Passionate Primitive
or Pious Puritan?

I

Isaac Bashevis Singer is the only contemporary Yiddish writer to have achieved international recognition. Somehow he has succeeded in breaking out of the closed circle of Yiddish literature and in attracting widespread interest to his wild and imaginative novels and stories. This is especially remarkable because Singer writes in a language frequently condemned to imminent extinction, about a bizarre group which has all but disappeared from the face of the earth and which evokes sympathy and understanding from few of the living.

A great part of the gap between the reader and the subject-matter is, however, bridged by a consistent underlying scheme of thought which is crucial to the type of story Singer writes. By now enough of Singer has been translated into English to enable the non-Yiddish reading audience to discern his central themes and views. In effect, it is as an outsider to the language, if not to the culture, that I wish to discuss this very framework of ideas, and the crucial part it plays for his art in general. But first it is necessary to discover what precisely Singer is attempting to do in his work.

With few exceptions, Singer writes about Eastern European Jewry as it existed between the mid-seventeenth century and the beginning of the Second World War. More specifically, he tends to concentrate on the Polish Hasidic element, the fanatically Orthodox mystics, as we think of them today: Against this seemingly staid background Singer has created incredible tales of fantastic and lusty happenings. Out of situations in which modesty and control dominate there develop situations in which intemperance and insanity run wild. A strange world is made stranger by the incongruous and the unexpected. Nevertheless, the reader, for his part, is fascinated. The action and its developments are intriguing. The characters come to life with amazing vigor. And in spite of its strangeness and oddities, the world of Singer's creation comes through vividly, making itself felt in all its fullness. But what is felt with clarity is not always clearly understood.

From the very beginning the reader is beset by very perplexing problems of interpretation. Singer does not appear to be at all consistent. He seems to hop from view to view, from position to position; he never asserts a view firmly or directly. Rather, he infuses a tension of mystery into his stories by means of this apparent ambivalence. Singer himself sums up this aspect concisely in the enigmatic conclusion of "The Unseen" (*Gimpel the Fool and Other Stories*). Reb Nathan Jozefover who has had a revealing dream, just before his death, exclaims, "The truth is twofold. . . . This is the mystery of all mysteries."

Unfortunately, a number of Singer's reviewers and critics take the foregoing literally as Singer's creed of double truth, perhaps even of a double reality, each valid in its own way. But this type of interpretation does violence to his essential meaning, to the very subtle philosophic theme which runs through all of his writing.

It is, of course, understandable why the labels of ambiguity and obscure mystery are frequently used to characterize Singer's works. To begin with, he generally avoids the direct descriptive method of realism. A great deal has to be inferred from obscurely drawn events. Moral prejudices of every sort and degree underly the narration, and the reader is at a loss to discover which view is the intended one. Events are frequently interspersed with incredible elements, and often lead to a preposterous extreme. It quickly becomes apparent that the literal level of action is overshadowed by something more important. The only real exception to non-realism is *The Family Moskat,* for which the critic ought to be thankful inasmuch as this early novel gives direct insight into many of Singer's views. "Caricature" (*The Spinoza of Market Street and Other Stories*) and "The Spinoza of Market Street" (*ibid.*) are also works of realism, but for the perverse purpose of satirizing scholarly realists. For this type of intellectual satire, Singer has clearly chosen a most effective method.

Further difficulties are due to the fusing of two worlds, or at least two different realms. On the one hand, there are the believable *shtetl* types — rabbis, rich businessmen, students, water-carriers, whores, draymen, bakers, chimney-sweeps, etc. But there is also a wide assortment of the supernatural which enters into the lives of these very human people. Rich and poor, pious and profane, learned and illiterate are all afflicted by black demons, spirits, elves, imps and devils with such — to the uninitiated — exotic names as Samael, Asmodeus, Ketev Mriri, Lillith and Machlath. Holy visions and devilish apparitions become important parts of the action. The truth is revealed, mysteries are uncovered, and Satan spreads his evil gospel through these visions. The line dividing the human from the supernatural is very thin indeed.

Probably the oddest aspects of Singer's works are his themes. An inordinate stress, certainly for a Yiddish writer, is placed on sex — on evocative scenes of passionate sensualism. Astonishingly, the participants are often old-fashioned pious Jews with earlocks and beards, or devout, bewigged matrons. No combination seems incredible to Singer. Not even the aged and malformed are excluded from his lusty erotic imagination. Adultery is prevalent, orgies crown sequences of intemperate behavior, and shutters are insidiously closed in the middle of the day. The reader, conditioned to expect a more conventional version of the pre-modern world of the Hasidim, may well wonder, what ever happened to the Torah!

Then there are the vague and obscure references which abound in Singer's tales. Mysteries are played up and never satisfactorily solved. We are told that the truth is twofold, but not what the two elements are and why. The magician of Lublin repents for the sins of his adulterous and dissipated life by returning to Judaism; yet he behaves in a manner which is very unusual for a Jewish penitent. And the underground spirit Shiddah makes startling pronouncements about the fate of man and the universe: Man and the light of the universe would come to an end: "God and Satan would be one."

Closely related to this is the apparent contradiction of ideas. At times Singer's writing shows the strong influence of Spinoza. The unreality or lower reality of this life is expressed in "Joy" (*Gimpel*) and in "Gimpel the Fool" (*ibid.*). The perfect harmony of Nature is awesome to Asa Heshel Bannet, Yasha Mazur and Dr. Nahum Fischelson, but the jarring disharmony of the human passions destroys these men and others. Intellectual love of God is revered and the physical love of man is distrusted.

However, there are many elements in his writings which seem incompatible with Spinozism. Notably, there is a profound concern for death which Spinoza would not consider fitting for a truly ethical (blessed) man. For example, *The Family Moskat* ends on a very despairing note, the logical conclusion of the preceding action:

"Death is the Messiah. That's the real truth." Furthermore, Yasha Mazur repents in self-inflicted suffering for
his sins, scholars are mocked and caricatured, and traditional Judaism appears in a better light than scholasticism.
And if there are heroes, they are not the disciples of
Spinoza, the Asa Heshel Bannets or the Dr. Fischelsons,
but the pious rabbis of Komarov, Cracow and Natchalnik.

At other times completely different ideas dominate
Singer's writings. A Schopenhauerian despair permeates
the atmosphere in "The Shadow of a Crib" (*Spinoza*).
In it, the main action revolves about the intellectual Dr.
Yaretzky, whose life in the world of ideas appears to be
guided by a blind will. In "A Piece of Advice" (*ibid.*)
the moral of the story is very close to the view held by
many modern philosophies, that "we are what we do."
Placed in a religious context, the advice given stresses that
we ought to do good deeds, even if we lack sincerity and
faith in what we are doing. Even the Hegelian dialectic
is given credence. In "Joy" the rabbi moves from a simple
faith, to a total negation of religion, to a higher enriched
faith. Frequently, Singer leaves the reader with an over-
powering feeling of despair. Man's lot seems hopeless as
the anguish, humiliation and suffering increase progressively in most of his major works — *The Family Moskat,
Satan in Goray*, "The Destruction of Kreshev" (*ibid.*),
"Gimpel the Fool," etc. But balanced against this, perhaps
less powerfully and convincingly stated, is a positive hope,
as in "Joy," "The Shadow of a Crib," "The Old Man"
(*Gimpel*), "The Little Shoemakers" (*ibid.*), and "The
Beggar Said So" (*Spinoza*).

Thus the reader is left with perplexities and ambiguities of mythical elements, mystical oddities, obscurities,
indirectness, and seeming inconsistencies of thought.

II

In the writings of Singer a number of revealing
themes and attitudes constantly recur. Prominent are the

greed, lustfulness and sensuality of man. Man repeatedly descends lower and lower, to deeper states of corruption, till he is reduced to complete bestiality. Frequently, the totally innocent are forced into compromising situations by external forces and act as humans would be expected to act. Each small weakness is soon magnified into a major flaw, and the innocent gradually become hopelessly diseased. Ultimately, all suffer horribly for a state of affairs which does not seem of their making, and in which they are the slaves of their senses, not their own masters. A frightening injustice seems to dominate man's existence. On the one hand he is irresistibly attracted by the pleasures of the senses; on the other, he is cruelly punished for submitting to the temptation.

Because of this, Singer often displays both horror and contempt of the physical world. The world he recoils from is the world of the market place, of human passions, of vain ambitions, of misguided aspirations, and of all the human relationships which result from them. This is the world of Gimpel the fool, where the simple and the sensitive are gulled, deprived, humiliated and despised. It is the world in which the poverty of Frampol distorts the perspective of its people, so that the devil Ketev Mriri can play on their hungering senses till they are destroyed by their own passions. It is the chaotic world in which the penitent magician of Lublin sees lurking "unrest, lust, the fear of coming day." And it is also the world of Rabbi Bainish of Komarov, where even the most pious and devout break before the plagues which scourge mankind and are forced to sin by crying out against God — even denying Him.

In conjunction with injustice, Singer stresses the closely related theme of the moral and spiritual breakdown of man by sensual intemperance. Asa Heshel Bannet, in *The Family Moskat*, enters as an idealistic, sensitive young intellectual, but develops into an irresponsible, callous sensualist after close to thirty years in the diseased atmosphere of greed and ambition. The sturdy, upright inhabitants of Frampol are enticed by the wealth and physical excitement offered by the gentleman from Cracow, to indulge in a degenerate sexual orgy. Only after their intoxication with pleasure had worn off did they realize that they were the victims of evil forces; and now they had to continue living amid spiritual ruins, in addition to their former material poverty.

In *Satan in Goray* the townspeople are continually subjected to the pressures and assaults of the evil sensual forces of the physical world. To begin with, they are the innocent victims of the wicked Chmelnicki in 1648. Weakened after years of murder and terror, they are lured away from the disciplined traditional piety imposed by the stern Rabbi Bainish Ashkenazi and become the followers of the false Messiah, Sabbatai Zevi. In place of their strict rabbi, they accept the more relaxed and exciting spiritual rule of a sadist, Reb Mordecai Joseph, and of a masochist, Reb Itche Mates. With the relaxation of morality, Satan enters in the guise of a generous, understanding ritual slaughterer and exploits the situation to his own evil ends. Traditional values are no longer held, false prophets are trusted, customs are broken and behavior becomes wanton. Unclean meat is eaten, learning is abandoned, men and women mix freely, and adultery is accepted as the norm in the New Jerusalem. Ultimately, the falseness of Sabbatai Zevi is exposed, the corruption realized, Satan dislodged, and a modicum of sanity restored. But now the townspeople of Goray have a new legacy of guilt to bear, though the previous physical insecurities have not been reduced in the slightest.

Even within the bounds of a legal marriage, physical excesses lead to destruction. Reb Nathan Jozefover, in "The Unseen," is so preoccupied with the tinglings of sensual gratification that he is destroyed by the logical extreme of his enjoyment. Similarly, Reb Shloimele's obsession with the mystical sensualism of the Kabbalah leads to his downfall, the death of his wife and the destruction of Kreshev. In all cases, the products of sensual pursuits are chaos, anguish, futility and emptiness.

At first, Singer reacts to the horrors and injustice with an expected bitterness. He simply *damns* life and proclaims death as the Messiah. However, the direct denunciation which concludes *The Family Moskat* is soon very subtly revised. In its place Singer takes a position which many philosophers from Plato onward have taken: he simply *denies* the *ultimate reality* of the world of physical corruption. This denial, however, is not uttered with the undertone of rancor found in Singer's huge first novel. Oddly enough, it is stated in one of Singer's more positive stories, "Joy." Just prior to his death, Rabbi Bainish of Komarov utters his profound summary of the realm of corruption: "I want you to know that the material world has no substance." Singer's view is most beautifully stated at the conclusion of "Gimpel the Fool":

> No doubt the world is entirely an imaginary world, but it is only once removed from the true world. At the door of the hovel where I lie, there stands the plank on which the dead are taken away. The grave-digger Jew has his spade ready. The grave waits and the worms are hungry; the shrouds are prepared — I carry them in my beggar's sack. Another *shnorrer* is waiting to inherit my bed of straw. When the time comes I will go joyfully. Whatever may be there, it will be real, without complication, without ridicule, without deception. God be praised: there even Gimpel cannot be deceived.

Now, the problem is to decide whether Singer advocates withdrawal from life as a solution to the ills of material reality. On the surface, it would appear that the epilogue of *The Magician of Lublin* suggests just this. For Yasha Mazur set free was a destructive lecher, but Yasha Mazur immured is a revered saint. This simple interpretation, however, is misleading and does not take into consideration the special circumstances involved and Yasha's reasons for his ascetic life. He did not isolate himself specifically to become a saint, but rather to resist the carnal temptations which led to his previous disaster. As his arguments and thoughts indicate, his main concern was self-discipline. He could only convince the rabbi that he ought to immure himself in a doorless brick hut after "[he] produced for the Rabbi a variety of prototypes — saints who had had themselves put under restraint for fear they would be unable to resist temptation." The prison was to act as a fence between Yasha and the world. It was to serve the same purpose as harsh laws. For, "Harsh laws were merely fences to restrain man from sin."

Even as a saint, physically isolated in his hut, Yasha realized his proneness to the dangers of the external world:

> No, the temptations never ceased. Yasha had withdrawn from the world, but through the tiny window which he had left to admit air and light, evil talk, slander, wrath and false flattery came. . . . No hour passed without Yasha's being besieged by every sort of passion . . . empty fancies, daydreams, repulsive desires.

With his own passionate desires as his greatest enemy, Yasha was striving desperately to achieve a disciplined faith. It would then seem far more likely that his self-imposed seclusion is a particular personal remedy rather than a universal imperative.

Singer is far clearer in his views on the value of intellectual withdrawal. Little compassion is shown for the aspirations of philosophers and pseudo-philosophers. Rather, their personal failings and limitations are stressed. In effect, the philosophical thinkers emerge as weak, tormented, ineffectual, corruptible and often ludicrous.

Asa Heshel Bannet arrives with Spinoza in his pocket, but ironically is carried by his passions to destroy two women. Moreover, he is rendered intellectually impotent by his own personal restlessness and confusion. Dr. Fischelson, the Spinoza of Market St., perched between the harmony of the heavens and the chaotic passions of the rabble, gives in to his passions against the sage advice of his "Divine Spinoza." Similarly, Dr. Margolis ("Caricature") sees himself as a ludicrous, ugly figure, striving vainly and absurdly to erect a monument of thought. Neither Dr. Fischelson nor Dr. Margolis can overcome his ineffectuality, and neither is capable of producing any work of consequence. Finally, the Dr. Yaretzky of "The Shadow of a Crib" is incapable of any positive thought and action, either within or outside of his fortress of cynicism and non-involvement. The weight of human responsibility and the prospect of perpetuating mankind are too much for him, and he ultimately destroys his fiancée and himself. At no time does Singer treat a secular scholar with any real sympathy — which is unexpected in view of Singer's broad philosophical background and his brilliance in applying Spinozism to human life in his stories.

Thus far Singer appears to utter nothing but denials. Physical pleasure leads to ruin, philosophy is vain and useless, poverty and wealth both expose us to cancerous evils of the senses, and legal marriage founded on sensual gratification leads necessarily to self-destruction. Even the fanatically religious Kabbalists, seeking the inner mysteries of life, are sensualists who mislead their fellow-men to irreparable harm.

Yet Singer does make a number of significant affirmations. Implicit in his denials of the goals and behavior of men is the affirmation of one type of life. In this world, which is only once removed from reality, as Gimpel tells us, man can be involved with the problems of men, man can carry on with dignity, and man can live an upright moral existence. This becomes evident in the important short story "Joy," which treats all of Singer's major thoughts.

Rabbi Bainish of Komarov had at one time been the vigorous spiritual leader of a thriving Hasidic group. When a plague kills several of his children, including his youngest, Rebecca, he withdraws from active life. He stops eating, he stops mixing with his followers, and also stops studying. In the throes of personal grief, he adopted a totally materialistic position. The existence of God is doubted, and only the reality of the senses is accepted. One time he muses: "The sun? Close your eyes and there is no sun. The birds? Stuff your ears and there are no birds. Pain? Swallow a wild berry, and the pain is gone. What is left, then? Nothing at all."

But from these cynical depths, the rabbi has his faith restored after having a vision of his beloved Rebecca. She first asks him, "half-imploring, half-commanding," to return to his followers and to participate in life once again. Then she informs him that he is to join her after the holidays. After his mystical experience, Rabbi Bainish reached ecstatic heights . . . "nothing remained but a sense of wonder, a supernatural tang, a touch of heavenly joy." *This* is his verification for the existence of God and morality. Physical criteria of knowledge seem so puny in comparison.

With his faith restored, he abandons his philosophy of despair and strives once more to comprehend the mysteries of God:

> He [God] hides his face and the children seek him while they have faith that He exists. But what if, God forbid, one loses faith? The wicked live on denials; denials in themselves are also a faith, faith in evildoing. . . . But if the pious man loses his faith, the truth is shown to him, and he is recalled . . . a light shines from above, and all doubts cease.

Now that he is about to die and has had a great insight into truth, Rabbi Bainish asserts that the material world has no substance and that all plagues and human torments are not ultimately real. We are told to be joyous at all times. However, this cannot refer to hedonistic pleasure but rather to a spiritual joy — the joy of comprehending the divine workings of nature, the joy of *Simchat Torah*, of completing the reading of the Torah, the joy of understanding the wisdom of the Torah. In his final set of gestures, the rabbi rejoins his congregation, becomes sympathetically involved in their lives and once more guides them to the traditional paths of righteousness.

Righteous involvement in human affairs is affirmed in other places as well, though perhaps less fully or directly. In "The Gentleman from Cracow" (*Gimpel*) only Rabbi Ozer remains sane amid the lusty madness brought on by the enticements of the devil. He alone sees the sinful dangers, and he alone avoids temptation. And after the orgy, it is he who leads his followers to create order out of the chaos. Once again Singer's hero is a pious, devout rabbi, primarily concerned with the study of the Torah and the welfare of his followers.

Yasha Mazur, the magician of Lublin, reacts to his downfall by returning to piety and traditional law. Even in isolation he shows concern for the troubles of the people and tries to help them with sane, temperate advice. The chimney-sweep Moshe, in "The Beggar Said So," lives a full, rewarding life. Although he is illiterate and does not always realize the limits of traditional propriety, he is genuinely concerned with mankind, performs good deeds and lives an upright existence. And Abba Shuster, of "The Little Shoemakers," is able to live a joyous worthwhile existence by carrying on the traditional trade of his ancestors and by maintaining traditional values. He does this in the strange new world of America, against the mainstream of assimilation, after the tradition seemed to collapse with the degeneration of Europe.

Finally, there is a most astonishing affirmation of values in "The Shadow of a Crib." The Gentile Dr. Yaretzky finds one single, hopeful glimmer in a corrupt, despicable world. Although the doctor holds the assimilated Jew in contempt, he is fascinated by the strength, devotion and love of the Rabbi of Natchalnik. Late one night he peers into the rabbi's study and sees the rabbi peacefully absorbed in "a theological volume." He intuits the fullness and warmth of the rabbi's existence and the strength of his faith by the way the rabbi performs his labor of love. But the rabbi's love is not only an academic involvement with the Torah and commentaries. At midnight his wife rises to serve him tea. He doesn't look up, but an expression of tenderness illuminates his face, indicating his deep feeling for his wife. To the doctor this is the moment of truth, revealing the peace and fullness of the rabbi, living in this same world which is so torturous to him. Even after the deaths of the rabbi and doctor, the face of Dr. Yaretzky stares longingly through the same window. Despite the lesser stature of the new rabbi, the ghost is irresistibly drawn to the tradition of piety, learning and tender love.

Thus, Singer's positive affirmation of values is discernible, though in unstartling contrast to the evils that men do. Quite simply, Singer seems to assert the moral elevation of *Hasidut* (piety) in one of its more basic meanings. This is not to be confused with the Hasidism associated with the Kabbalah. For Singer has identified the Kabbalists as the worst sensualists, the worst corrupters of people. Nothing attractive results from the sadism of Mordecai Joseph or the masochism of Itche Mates or the eroticism of Shloimele. Singer's *Hasidut* is a puritanical piety, which shuns the corruptible elements of the world and is devoted to the spiritual heritage and puritanical traditions of Judaism. Only within this framework is man at peace with himself and do values survive corruption. If the foregoing interpretation of Singer is accepted, many of the difficulties disappear. For example, the epilogue of *The Magician of Lublin* is understandable. Yasha's return to piety and his striving for disciplined faith are the only ways of beginning to solve the problems resulting from his behavior in the story. And Nathan Jozefover's remarks on the sameness of his wife, who lived only to gratify her husband sensually, and a whore who destroyed him, are not obscure. Nor is the twofold nature of truth obscure if we consider Singer's moralistic metaphysics of a twofold reality of the temporal, corruptible, physical world and the timeless spiritual world.

Similarly, there is no real conflict of ideas. On some matters Singer agrees with Spinoza. For example, Singer accepts Spinoza's views on levels of reality, the destructiveness of the passions, and the positive striving for joy. But Singer disagrees with Spinoza's abstract intellectualism and his wholesale rejection of traditional Judaism. According to Singer, one need not only be concerned with the perfect harmony of God, the necessary in Nature; Talmudic pronouncements on faith, interpersonal relationships and life in general penetrate the truth as deeply. Furthermore, Singer will go along with the contemporary idea that we are what we do, or the Hegelian dialectic, only insofar as they are in conformity with his basic thesis. And when they are used, as in "A Piece of Advice" and "Joy" respectively, they appear unaffectedly and in perfect harmony with Singer's philosophical outlook.

III

One of the most striking aspects of Singer's writing, as already noted, is his deep involvement with the sensual and passionate. On these subjects his writing reaches a pitch and force not equalled in other sections. In doing so Singer causes the reader to feel a certain sympathy with the corrupt and fallen. The reader is drawn into the physical allurements. He can sympathetically understand the seeking of comfort, prestige and wealth by the early inhabitants of Frampol. He can also identify himself, to some extent, with Yasha Mazur in his aspiration for intellectual respectability, social advancement and patrician eroticism.

Such evocative writing, which often arouses our sympathies for the physical goals of man, does not necessarily mean that Singer himself is advocating lust, ambition or greed. One may passionately believe in certain ideals, yet not write passionately about them. Or one may produce involved writing about activities and deeds for which one has no sympathy. Singer's emphasis on sensual excitement is simply meant to draw attention to certain aspects. It is not an attempt to convert the reader to some form of ethical hedonism. Rather, its purpose is to produce a specific effect which is absolutely necessary if Singer's works are to be successful.

The moral element in all of Singer's works is crucial. Evil, corruption, deception, truth and uprightness are the central themes. As Singer uses them, they must be stated dramatically and vividly, or else their powerful emotional charge is not felt. Without this, the stories would lose an essential tension and probably fall flat.

To achieve this necessary effect, Singer uses a technique of Biblical writing found most frequently in the prophetic books. Quite simply, it rests on the premise that the greater the fall, the more effectively the dramatic force of the ethical concepts comes through. In the Bible the enormity of the gulf between ethical ideals and sinful behavior is strongly emphasized to achieve a similar effect. On the one hand, the iniquities of the sons of Belial are described in the most extreme terms possible; and, on the other, a vivid, awesome code of absolute morality, imposed by an omnipotent ruling force, serves as a contrast.

Then, when the downfall or retribution of the sinful takes place, it emerges with powerful, dramatic impact. For Singer is still a writer first and foremost and must avoid the direct preaching or railing of a political partisan. Instead, he brings the action and excitement to a high pitch on their own terms, by their own propulsion. He then uses the apparent design of the consequences — the inevitable fall of the sensuous — as a cosmic absolute. By so doing, the vastness of the moral gap and the magnitude of the fall come through.

For this end, the settings of the action are exceptionally well-suited. The piety and rigidity, in effect the whole moral fiber, of Eastern European Jewry is directly traceable to the morality of the Talmud and the Bible. Indeed, far more than the Westernized, emancipated modern Jew, their inheritance of the heavy mantle of "the chosen people" is conceded and discernible. They are the most recent counterparts, in terms of absolute values, of ancient Israel. With this background to the stories, the deviation from the paths of righteousness of the ancient Israelites, the deviations of Frampol and Goray are reinforced and magnified. As the heavens thundered angrily when the chosen people sinned, so they seem to do when Moses' spiritual descendants stray. In both cases, the gap between ideal and practice is great, and in both cases the falls are resounding.

In this type of moralistic writing, directness and power are needed. Jamesian subtleties would fall flat in these contexts. Allusions to sexual sublimations and discreet, indirect behavior are lost. The power and explosiveness inherent in primitivism is best brought out by the build-up to the climaxes of orgies or sexual over-indulgence. And it is precisely in this area where Singer's artistic skill is at its greatest. For the gradual transition from the pious to the sinful is done flawlessly. The reader is caught up in the involvement and goes from the normal to a seemingly impossible climax of excesses — yet never rebels at the absurdity. On the contrary, there is a true ring to the sequence of events, a validity which goes deeper than the external trappings of the events or the parochial conventions of European Hasidism.

The reason that these absurd events are credible is that there is a deeper allegorical level in Singer's writing which is perfectly coherent. It is not my intention here to analyze this extremely complex and important element to any extent. But because of its over-all significance, mention must be made of its pertinence.

In his writings, Singer has created an allegorical world composed of the absurd, the improbable, the mythological, the mystical, the traditional and the pious. Basically, these elements are used to symbolize two moral-metaphysical realms. On the lower level of reality, there is the material world of lust, greed, misery and ambition, which is characterized by absurdities, excesses, chaos and demonic forces. There is also a higher spiritual realm of genuine love, discipline and learning, which is characterized by true revelations, piety and traditional puritanical values.

To convey his vision, Singer has ingeniously adapted the built-in superstitions of the people he writes about. He takes the elves, and imps, the devils and demons familiar to Eastern European Jewry from the Bible, the Apocrypha and medieval folklore and makes them forces symbolic of evil in his broad allegory.

The way in which he does this is very effective. To begin with, he uses a Kabbalistic mode of explanation, including mysterious, mystical and mythological elements to damn pseudo-pious Kabbalistic sensualism as being very prone to corruption by evil forces. Furthermore, by employing a mythological framework which is an integral part of his characters' lives, Singer has been able to overcome the artificiality characteristic of most allegorical writing. There is nothing odd or affected about a *shtetl* type talking about Satan, *Shedim,* or evil forces. Rather, these forces played a vivid part in the *shtetl* consciousness, and because of this Singer is able to integrate smoothly the real and the mythical. As a result, Singer avoids a deadly abstractness, which is a serious danger to writing so intellectually complex. He also overcomes the boring dryness which seems to be not only part of puritanical behavior but also of the writings of its adherents. Instead, he creates a spirited allegory with lively people and vigorous spirits, capable of bringing out the bitter and humorous irony of life. Each serves his philosophic purpose admirably.[1]

IV

Because of the complexity of ideas, the ironic twists, the levels of meaning and allegory in Singer's writing, it is necessary to distinguish between the creed and art of Singer. Where conflicting views are present, the reader should not infer an ambivalence on the part of the author. In such cases, either a necessary effect is being produced, or the conflicting ideas must be considered in relationship to a larger, more basic framework. On many occasions, the symbolism undergoes a change as the stories develop. What begins as a human goal understandable from man's position becomes a temptation of non-human spirits and ends as an agent of evil and chaos. If the full dimensions of Singer's allegory are to be grasped, all views must be understood in their own right, and then correlated to the larger scale of reality. Any attempt to assign each symbol to one objective correlative would, of course, detract from the full scope of the allegory.

However, this large scale of reality overshadows all possible perspectives as the realm of absolute good and truth. In effect, Singer has painted a large canvas in which the roles of partial perspectives are portrayed. Taken in their own context, these relative views stress the values of a lower realm and lead to indignities and ruin. Only a life based on the values symbolized in the larger canvas lead to tranquility and fruitfulness. Relative perspectives conflict with one another and vary with respect to individuals, space and time. Only the proven piety of tradition is abiding and rises above all others. Thus, within the large perspective alone there are no inconsistencies and conflicts. In fact, there is a ruthless logic which seems to dominate, in which every minor sin becomes magnified in a process of corruption till it leads to total ruin.

On the positive side, a picture of the good life appears. As a moralist, Singer follows a Judaic puritanical tradition. He advocates piety, restraint, wisdom and a spiritual involvement with humans. But these are values which are widely accepted and are not the monopoly of Judaism. In his writings, Singer rises above the values which are peculiarly Jewish. The sensuous Kabbalists, a particular kind of (ghettoish) gluttony, and the foolish seeking a Messiah on their own terms as the chosen people — these have no role in Singer's vision of good.

Thus, Singer is able to exploit the universal values of Judaism without becoming affected by its parochialisms which limit the writings of other Yiddish writers. This is one of the main reasons why he has been able to break out of the confines of a narrow literary tradition to universal recognition. The other reason, of course, is the artistry he displays in executing his work. Rarely in modern literature do we find an artistic vision conveyed with such brilliance, vigor, imagination, liveliness, subtlety and effectiveness. But this is another story in itself.

Note

[1] Singer's philosophic purpose becomes even more apparent in his latest novel, *The Slave,* which appeared after this essay had been completed. In some ways it is the most extraordinary of Singer's works, and a number of very significant themes and ideas, which had been somewhat obscure in the previous writings, are clearly revealed. As in *The Magician of Lublin,* Singer is here concerned with

the deeply personal problems of an individual and the destructive forces enticing him to ruin. And, as in *Satan in Goray*, he is concerned with more general problems — the morality of the Jews under unbearable conditions; Divine Providence, Free will and Divine Justice in a horrible world. There are some poignant passages in which there is a Job-like indictment of God's plan for the world; but in spite of near-denials, there is a trust in the ultimate outcome. Once again Singer's Judaic Spinozism is evident: he believes in an overriding wisdom and perfection *sub specie aeternitatis*. But the crucial point which Singer makes in *The Slave*, more clearly than elsewhere, is in the realm of human life. Man, he says, has a dual obligation — to God and man. It is relatively easy to fulfill the former, by observing the laws of *kashrut*, putting on *tefillin*, and praying. But it is more difficult (and rarer) to perform one's obligation to man, by exhibiting humaneness, comfort, concern, and understanding. Yet the formal trappings of Judaism are insufficient by themselves. For mechanical piety without genuine sympathy *(hesed)* is empty, even immoral. The converse is not necessarily so, because the Gentile Jan Bzik and the not properly converted Sarah-Wanda have places in Heaven, alongside Zipporah, Ruth, *et al*. Thus, Singer, in *The Slave*, becomes far more explicit in his enunciation of the moral virtues stated in this essay.

Michael Fixler

5.

The Redeemers: Themes in the Fiction of Isaac Bashevis Singer

Yiddish fiction seemed about to expire essentially as it emerged — provincial, often sentimental, and appreciated almost exclusively by those for whom it was written. The talents of its writers were, to be sure, varied, and in translation some of them, like Sholem Asch, made their way successfully into the book clubs. But invariably Yiddish writers borrowed their techniques and even many of their themes from the general traditions of the Western novel. In one way or another, however, all were keyed by the experience of the Enlightenment which presented the novelist and storyteller with his basic conflict, the pull toward freedom and Westernization on the one hand, and on the other the loyalty or sentimental attachment to the old values that kept the Jews together as a people. Now, in its twilight, Yiddish has produced a novelist whose approach is so radically different from his predecessors that the metamorphosis of this theme in his works suddenly seems to render it more universal and profound.

Within Judaism the Enlightenment appeared primarily as a rationalistic reaction to traditional orthodoxy and to the continuation of what was conceived to be a self-imposed isolation of Jews from the intellectual life of Western Europe. Among enlightened Jews rationalism and the mystique of progress that went with it assumed something of the old messianic faith. Now the signs are, and Singer is one of them, that the messianic dream of rationalism is at an end. Everywhere in the vanguard there is talk about Jewish myth and Jewish symbol. For Norman Mailer, among others, the Hasidic *tsaddikim* (or saints) have the status of Zen masters as prophetic exponents of the irrational; and in modern American rabbinical literature of a pastoral nature Judaism's insights are even vindicated as a racial wisdom that, anticipating psychiatry, came to grips with the irrational and unconscious tendencies of the mind. Still, the process of reversal has been vague. After all, few modern Jews would frankly acknowledge that they believed anything that wasn't in some way reasonable. With the license of fiction Singer has done precisely that, and in so doing has dramatically identified Judaism with the irrational.

The extent to which his fiction assumes this identification has never been appreciated, certainly not by those who read him in translation and probably not by most of his Yiddish readers. Obsessed by essentially religious themes, Singer is most at home in archaic, pre-rational traditions, those surviving in the Kabbala, in late Hasidism, and in native Yiddish folklore, all of which he absorbed as a youth in Poland, and little of which is meaningful to English readers. Already enigmatic in their original setting, these traditions are more so outside of it. In his work they appear not as abstract ideas that can be "explained" but as a totality at times all the more powerful for being inexplicable. As the source of a unified and energetic vision these traditions and ideas cannot really be discussed as if they were detachable from his work. From this point of view his ideas, like those of Blake and Yeats, stand or fall with his success as an artist.

But if the irrational is a source of visionary artistic power it is also a source of eccentricity. Thus Singer believes in ghosts, imps, and the Devil; and perhaps what is more serious, he takes parapsychology to be an exact science. There is no problem about most of these things in his fiction, for there the supernatural is not simply another world, another reality, but primarily an extension of the problematic morality of this world. Trying to be "scientific" about psychic phenomena — that is to say, by definition leaving out the moral and emotional dimensions — he undercuts in some of his non-fictional writings the very area in which he is most effective. Someone who tries to find scientific explanations for psychic phenomena is evidently uneasy about parading his faith in them before skeptical eyes. Perhaps this is why he sometimes tends to treat his whole supernatural apparatus as if he didn't really believe in it but was using it as a kind of allegorical vehicle for the human predicament. In a little story, "Shidda and Kuzibah," for example, a couple of poor devils respond like unmistakable *shtetl Jews* to the trauma of dislocation in a hostile world. Such allegory discounts as fabulous the actual characters and their literal situation, which is having it both ways, for Singer just as clearly means to tease his readers with the possibility that maybe, after all, as one old crone says, "Anything can happen." Some of his characters are even more blunt. "I want you to know that the material world has no substance," says the dying rabbi of "Joy." And Gimpel, in one of Singer's finest stories, says, "The world is entirely an imaginary world, but it is only once removed from the true world." If multivalent ambiguity is an essential condition of Singer's work, by far the most troublesome is this tendency to metaphysical coyness. On occasions he seems to work on the assumption that since experience can be mystifying, the first step toward moral insight is that we should be properly mystified.

For example, some of his excursions into pure fantasy, with demons, imps, and such gear, seem motivated not only by questionable allegorical ends but by a brazen intention to force a quizzical effect. I am particularly thinking of instances where demonic narrators are used gratuitously to bracket stories compelling in themselves. The demons simply offer a coy point of view where Singer could have done as well or better with some old peasant or beggar. "The Unseen" and "The Destruction of Kreshev" are good examples of first-rate works with trival [sic] narrators. What Singer may be up to is a way of trying to expose the bare bones of metaphysical uncertainty which in the novels and novellas are covered with flesh and blood. Ironic suspension of judgment here becomes a direct admission of cognitive limitation. "Is there a God?" says an imp at the end of "The Mirror." "Is he all merciful? Will Ziriel ever find salvation? Or is creation a snake primeval crawling with evil? How can I tell? I'm still only a minor devil." The candor is disingenuous, whether in an imp or in Singer. But we may prefer stories that leave the questions less explicit.

Despite such moments Singer's greatest achievement is the convincing authenticity with which he handles the supernatural as a real but different dimension in human experience. Hence the occasional stickiness is instructive. It tells us something about the toughness and recalcitrance of his materials and why his triumph over them gives us Singer at his characteristic best. Certainly he has the problem faced by every visionary writer, that of convincingly representing the supersensual world with the data of the apprehensible one. Poets and mystics tend to work in this medium with symbolic systems and their powers of allusive evocation. Singer does too, although since the frame of reference he uses is generally unfamiliar the reader may only sense the solidity it gives his work without knowing what it is or how it works. On the other hand, as a novelist Singer uses a very credible psychology — one is almost tempted to say a psychopathology — to develop characters and situations susceptible of producing a visionary or transcendental resonance. "The Black Wedding," for example, is obviously written with a fine understanding of sexual hysteria, but just as clearly the subjective hallucinations of the girl in the story read like a case of demonic possession. Here as in other instances in Singer's fiction, archaically primitive and sophisticated modern premises are presented as simultaneously plausible.

At his best, such techniques produce an atmosphere within which human action seems timelessly isolated and acquires an astounding resonance of meaning. At his worst, they lead to mere portentousness. Some of the reasons are not far to seek. Singer's premises, irrational without being conventionally religious, are loosely aligned with Kabbalism, whose essential appeal is its promise of a key for revelation of secrets, divine secrets concerning providence, destiny, the future, and, more particularly, the mysteries of good and evil. But no such esoteric system ever does reveal more than the insights an artist or ecstatic devotee is capable of articulating, which may indeed be considerable but remain "natural." On the other hand, with supposed access to the very source of all wisdom and spiritual energy, Kabbalists — or occultists — often find themselves tempted to announce "supernatural" revelations, and to demonstrate their powers by miracles; the wine tapped from the walls by magic, for example, to which Singer so frequently refers.

Hence, while Singer seems to have no such prophetic or magical pretensions he frequently hints at a kind of special "inner" knowledge. The question is, do such intimations legitimately grow out of his fables? When he intimates something beyond what a fable actually communicates, even the most accommodating reader is left baffled, half distrusting the limitations of his own understanding, and half suspecting that Singer is pulling his leg. On the other hand, the thing that continually threatens — the dissolution of the veil between the two worlds — is artistic-ally credible when the two worlds in response to human need dovetail and the essential psychic force is recognizable in its contours under a familiar aspect. Thus the disinte-gration of reality in "The Gentleman from Cracow" and in *Satan in Goray,* related in these instances to mass hysteria, appears objective.

To the extent that Singer's fables are almost invari-ably constructed so as to resonate with both pathological and supernatural overtones he resembles Thomas Mann. Like Mann, Singer expresses a thoroughgoing dualism tending to bring into polarized relationships characters and events which begin by being at first indistinctly bal-anced between stability and instability, disease and health, good and evil. Like Mann, whom he has translated into Yiddish, Singer sees human types as the expression of in-calculably complex but distinct historical traditions. And, like Mann, Singer is the master of the ironic suspension of judgment.

More than once in both Mann and Singer, however, such ironic suspension seems decadent and smacks of diab-olism. The fact that good and evil cannot be known except by their consequences encourages an ambiguity that is artistically suggestive but morally questionable. Generally Singer moves in this treacherously delicate area with grace and vigor, as in "The Man Who Came Back." In this story a relatively mild and inoffensive epicure apparently dies and having been resuscitated refuses to reveal what he found on "the other side." His subsequent life, however, is sinisterly suggestive, for he progressively becomes vicious and degenerate, being in the end cut down like a mad dog by Cossack troopers. But Singer is not always so felicitous in his effects. Sometimes there is a queer awkwardness, as if he was trying to solve a moral problem technically, by a literary device. This awkwardness is of a piece with the occasional awkwardness he shows in trying to deal effec-tively with the supernatural.

Singer's latitude in representing the supernatural is wide, ranging from pure fantasies of imps and demons to conventionally realistic fiction where the supernatural is only allusively invoked or there by inference. He is generally least successful in dealing with either extreme, strongest in a broad range of middle ground where there is room for suggestive rather than mystifying ambiguities. The term "irony" is inadequate to describe the nuances of tension and detachment with which he conveys human involvement in shifting realities. Lacking a better term, "irony" may have to be overworked. But with Singer's most realized characters there is less difficulty of identification. They bear psychological or temperamental dispositions — faith, guilt, disease, or simplicity — which enable them to *see through* phenomenal reality. Sometimes it is a kind of innocence, like that of Gimpel, or Singer himself in his memoirs of his boyhood, *From My Father's Courtroom,* where he tells us his childhood was spent among pious Jews for whom the supernatural was so real that it was almost negotiable. Such innocence is not trivial but is indispensably an element of religious strength. Singer's brother, the novelist I. J. Singer, once wrote of a crisis in their childhood when they and the whole community waited for the Messiah to appear. There was a time when waiting for the Messiah to appear was common among Jews. For better or worse they have grown up.

For some, however, faith remains the evidence of things unseen. But faith in what? For Singer the answer to that gives us a key to the complexity of his work. His dualism seems theologically a sort of Jewish Manicheism, a type of belief going back to Jewish Gnosticism and some aspects of the Kabbalistic compendiums. In modified forms it was a part of Hasidism and of the rich Yiddish folklore now rapidly disappearing. Martin Buber particularly has tried to incorporate elements of this nonrationalistic, ultimately dualistic tradition into a viable Jewish theology. The elements being originally syncretic, deriving from a variety of traditions, and bearing today on the general collapse in theology of rationalism, Buber's work has significantly struck a sympathetic chord throughout the gentile world. For the same reason Singer's success in translation is evidence not merely of his considerable talent but also of the general appeal today of undogmatic theology, a theology accepting as its starting point divine uncertainties.

Reflecting these tendencies, Singer's work poses special problems. It is often sufficient that the mystery in which his fables develop mirrors a vision that corresponds to our uncertainties about the benevolence or malevolence of the forces behind life. But the mystery is deepened by the fact that we do not immediately grasp the specific tradition in which Singer works. In a sense he both profits and suffers from the unfamiliarity of his "mythology." He profits in that his work is capable of an almost universal appeal (such as few or no Yiddish writers before him have ever enjoyed) to the extent that its almost uniquely Jewish preoccupations do not overtly dominate his productions. He suffers seriously to the extent that the rich implications of his work, divorced from the precise sense of its connections with elemental Jewish preoccupations, are often missed, leaving the underlying unity of his work unrealized.

Almost every writer ultimately has to cope with metaphysical ambiguity; at some point he will decide whether he believes his characters are free or determined. Here Singer's mythology is most interesting. Being dualistic it assumes a certain kind of metaphysical balance, unstable though that might appear to be in human experience. In Kabbalistic tradition this unstable dualism acquires a vast, interlocking significance. Going back for a moment to the perplexed devil in Singer's "The Mirror," it can be said that if he had his limitations so apparently does God. In parts of the Kabbala there is the suggestion that the problems and contradictions inhering in human existence are inexplicable purely in their own terms and must be referred to a seminal flaw in the process of creation — the process whereby divinity reduced itself to a material imperfection. The Jews by perfecting themselves may redeem evil, not by fleeing from it but by submitting to its necessities. To that extent they redeem as much of God as is involved in creation. For that end have the Jews been chosen. This idea is related to Mann's idea in *The Holy Sinner* (in German called interestingly enough *Der Erwählte*, the chosen or elected one), namely that the truly spiritual person creates God out of his own guilt. Now, in the realm of God-creation or God-redemption it is pointless to talk either of the absolute freedom of the human will or of the illusion of freedom in a deterministic universe. God depends upon neither of these.

Rather, what we find in Singer's work is the crucial role played by obscure psychic forces of a kind that seem to have to do with what the Kabbala terms *kavana*, the force of an intention independent of the limitations of action, but ultimately controlling it. Essentially this means that not only are all consequences unforeseeable, but their effects in the other world, where Shaddai and Samael contend eternally, are incalculable. When some intimation of the power of *kavana* reverberates back into experience the results are startling. The miserable pauper of Singer's story "Fire," like Peretz's Bontche Shweig, has suffered as only a Yiddish orphan can suffer, and like Bontche has thereby laid up a power in heaven far greater than anything he can imagine. But unlike Bontche the pauper becomes the victim of a grim psychic joke as his own power backfires upon him. His *kavana* in effect operates to make real the pauper's unfulfilled determination to stand no more and to revenge himself by arson upon his wickedly successful brother. Before he can start the fire it starts itself and the amazed pauper ends up by saving his brother and being blamed for the fire.

With such dualistic premises and his sense of psychic forces keyed in supernatural modes Singer could not really follow the drift of Yiddish literature into realism. Perhaps his brother's influence, perhaps his journalistic experience (he is and has been for years on the staff of New York's Yiddish *Daily Forward*), or, as is more likely, his stint as a script writer for Yiddish soap opera on Station WEVD in New York, led him to publish as his second novel *The Family Moskat,* a long, uneven dynastic saga in the realist mode. The work originally appeared serially on WEVD (which says a great deal about the relative quality of Yiddish soap opera), but it is not Singer's most characteristic or his most successful work. Yet even *The Family Moskat* differs from the conventional dynastic novel in which the subjects are identifiable with a declining or ascending class. It deals rather with the psychic forces that determine the destiny of a people. Taking the whole world of Polish Jewry on the eve of its dissolution the novel attempted, I think, too much, and only by bringing it into line with his other works do its underlying pattern and its motifs become clear. In that continuity the novel clearly has a place, being concerned not with a family really but with the spiritual community of Israel which in one form or another is Singer's major subject. For either his novels deal with a community, or else they deal with individuals who in modern terms are archetypes — or antitypes (reversability still implies an essential identity here) — of the Jewish community. His theme is the mystery of the covenant, the blessing which is a curse, and the curse which is a blessing.

Satin in Goray, The Family Moskat, The Magacian of Lublin, and most recently *The Slave* deal with a period of history bounded at either end by the great massacres that mark off from its first glimmerings to its collapse the 300 years of the Jewish adventure with the Enlightenment.

Satan in Goray, The Family Moskat, The Magician of ground of the Chmielnicki Massacres of the seventeenth century. *The Magician of Lublin* is set in Poland some time before World War I, and *The Family Moskat* closes with the Nazi occupation of Warsaw. Historically the whole period marked a stage in the Diaspora which witnessed a wide variety of unprecedented stresses and strains upon the basic Jewish conviction of Messianic destiny, stresses and strains which are reflected profoundly in the psychological development of Singer's characters.

And for related reasons the beginning of this period was marked by a development that crystallized the Kabbalistic habit of mind among Jews from Amsterdam to Aleppo, and which enables Singer to understand them in a way, for example, inconceivable to Sholem Asch who, in *Kiddush Ha'Shem,* also wrote about the Chmielnicki Massacres. The spread of Kabbalism in the seventeenth century was phenomenal. The frame of reference for the messianic hysteria of *Satan in Goray* is Kabbalistic, and Jacob the central figure of *The Slave,* is also a Kabbalist. Nor are the other novels untouched by this habit of mind. Yasha Mazur the magician, in *The Magician of Lublin,* while not a Kabbalist, has occult powers and reacts specifically to Hasidism, that romantic child of Kabbalism. *The Family Moskat,* for all its realism, also chronicles the degeneration of Hasidism and is the most exhaustive treatment Singer devotes to the perversion by fragmentation of the Jewish messianic faith.

In balancing the perspectives of his theme against the autonomy of each work, Singer throughout uses essentially only two patterns. The first and more frequent one shows the spiritual destiny of the Jew frustrated and deflected into the demonic. The other shows the spiritual destiny of the Jew succeeding despite the encumbrance of evil he has necessarily taken on. A common element is the invariable presence in his characters of the sense of destiny, of existing for a purpose, even when — as in *The Family Moskat* — the purpose for the "enlightened" Jews seems bafflingly perverse. In the first of his novels, *Satan in Goray,* and in his two superb novellas, "The Gentleman from Cracow" and "The Destruction of Kreshev," Singer develops with an almost archaeological particularity the theme of redemptive delusion. The root of the error in every case is the illusion that freedom is possible; that it is possible miraculously to be redeemed from the burden of the past, from the burden of the intolerable present, or from the burden of self. In short, the mistake is what leads one to believe that one is destined to be redeemed instead of being destined to be a redeemer.

Singer's psychological finesse is here, as in all of his works, unobtrusive. There is no apparent projection back into the seventeenth and eighteenth centuries of the conceptual sophistication of the twentieth. Yet by suspending many of the conventional appearances of causal relationships and sequences, by minimizing narrative commentary, by emphasizing patterns that seem to develop irrationally and impulsively, by exposing the power which systematic deceptions have of producing a totally unexpected reality, Singer produces effects which are both strikingly archaic and modern. For example, the pathological condition of the Chmielnicki survivors, the crippled community of Goray, is symbolized by the lame, half-demented Rechele and the Dionysian butcher, Reb Gedaliya. Upon them principally falls the bizarre impact of the news of Sabbatai Zevi, the historical false Messiah of Ismir. But through them the community is literally possessed — erotically, diabolically — by its ecstasy to free itself of history, of law, of everything but the unearthly promise of divine redemption.

Similarly, in "The Destruction of Kreshev" the impulse of its chief character is simultaneously to redeem and defile or desecrate. Here too a follower of Sabbatai Zevi (whose cult after his apostasy encouraged deception and perverse inversions of messianic beliefs) has a grim power that twists its way through the lives of the whole community. The Kabbalist Shloimele comes as a bridegroom to Kreshev and soon convinces his mystically inclined bride that they were atavisms, destined to relive the sins of King

David's children in order to prove that, being chosen, sin for them had no more existence; in short, that they had redeemed evil. Having corrupted his bride, Shloimele spurs his religious and sexual inversions by having her describe the details of her adultery with their coachman. Her sexuality finally asserts itself independently and she is almost toppled by a goat in heat. When she pushes her husband aside altogether for the coachman, Shloimele has a penitential breakdown and confesses in the synagogue. The revelation is electrifying and is followed by a memorable cross-examination. Why? Reb Ozer asks. And the demoralized Shloimele ironically provides the right answer in the inadequate language of talmudic legalism. He didn't know. He had "committed a grave error."

"'An error?' Reb Ozer demanded and raised one eye. It seemed as if the single eye held a laughter not of this world."

Shortly thereafter the young wife hangs herself and in the epilogue Kreshev, like Sodom and Gomorrah, is destroyed by fire. No moral is drawn, but one is plain. Whatever power the Jew has is not exerted upon himself or for himself alone.

For Singer such an eyebrow-raising notion as the power of the Jew is devoid of all arrogance. In fact, all concepts of power, it is implied, must reckon with power's incalculable nature. But one thing seems clear. When a power degenerates it is not exhausted but becomes dangerously inverted. Most particularly this development is seen in the second and third of Singer's novels, *The Family Moskat* and *The Magician of Lublin*. Here too the spiritual destiny of the Jew is deflected into the demonic. In *The Family Moskat* the force or the momentum evidently comes from the atrophy of the source of Hasidism's spiritual energies, the pure joy of the Hasidic ecstasy. Perhaps the most significant moment of that vast novel comes with the ironic frenzy of Reb Abram — lecher, profligate, skeptic, and idealist, all in one — at the feast of *Simhas Torah*

(The Rejoicing of the Law) , where like another Dionysian satyr he leads the Hasidim in their drunken dancing. Enthusiastically a clapping onlooker remarks that, well, for all his faults Reb Abram is one of their own, a real Hasid of the Hasidim. Not only Reb Abram's restless lechery but also the relentless intellectualism and the nihilism of the enlightened Jews of the novel is a consequence of the atrophy of this joy, the inversion of the redemptive hope. At the end all of Singer's insight into the essential condition of thwarted Jewish destiny is summed up by one character as the Nazis close in on Warsaw. "Death," he announces, "is the Messiah. That's the real truth."

A similar insight is presented at the climax of *The Magician of Lublin,* which deals with the dramatic conversion of an amoral libertine to the life of a medieval ascetic. "Twice in one day," Yasha Mazur realizes, "there had been unveiled to him things which are best concealed. He had looked on the faces of death and lechery and had seen that they were the same." The final turn of the screw that Singer gives to his insight is that it is for Yasha the source of his ultimate delusion. This marginal Jew, equally at home and equally an alien in both the Jewish and gentile worlds, grasps the insight with the intensity of a Faust or of a Don Juan. Like them he turns from the quest for knowledge and mastery in all conceivable experiences of the body and mind to the realization that the quest had been an error. Truth and salvation are other-worldly. So in the epilogue, like a medieval saint — a Catholic saint, as his ecstatic gentile inamorata makes us realize — he walls himself in a doorless cell, becoming outwardly a shrine for superstitious veneration and inwardly a tormented fanatic, assailed by all the sexual phantasmagoria of a St. Anthony.

Yasha had chosen his role in European myth, and in doing so he had curiously revealed himself as the antitype or parody of the central Jewish messianic myth, what Buber called the myth of "the perfect man who perfectly fulfills." Yasha's life is ironically a *drasha,* a moralistic homily on such a theme as his antithesis, the *tsaddik* Jacob, in Singer's next novel, *The Slave,* meditates: "The Jew does not tempt Evil by denying the body but harnesses it in the service of God." As may be suspected from this, *The Slave* is Singer's first major work that has as its theme the successful realization of the destiny to which the Jew is born. As such, and because it is at once the most revealing and the most recently translated of his novels, it is worth considering more carefully.

The Slave is in the main the least oblique and mystifying of all Singer's works. It makes no effort to disguise the theme it illustrates, even insists repeatedly that we see it. And upon it too Singer has expended some of his greatest gifts; notably in the evocation of atmosphere, the creation of a suspense almost as breathtaking as in *The Magician* (based in both cases on the intricacy of deception and the inevitability of exposure), and finally in the general economy of characterization, balance, development, and so forth. Yet for all that *The Slave* is Singer's most imperfect novel, being marred by a flaw so great that one can only conceive that some wholly extraneous consideration almost at the end seized hold of Singer's imagination and made him spoil his own work. Like an irrepressible atavism, when Singer deals with Jewish fulfillment there is resurrected the familiar ghost of Yiddish sentimentality. The taint is not always destructive. In "The Little Shoemakers," for example, and even in "Gimpel the Fool" the reversion to traditional Yiddish themes makes the presence of such sentimentality both expected and welcome. But somehow in *The Slave* the case is otherwise.

As the title of the work indicates, redemption for the Jew is not an escape into freedom but an acceptance of servitude. A text of the Lurianic Kabbala might almost have served as the novel's epigraph: "This is the secret why Israel is fated to be enslaved by all the Gentiles of the world: In order that it may uplift those sparks [of the broken divine effulgence] which have also fallen among them. . . . And therefore it was necessary that Israel should be scattered to the four winds in order to lift everything up."[1] The gentiles the archetypal Jacob (Israel) redeems are real, and he is their real slave. In the Chmielnicki Massacres he had been carried off and sold to a peasant in the most Godforsaken (literally) region of the Polish mountains. It was a place where "he could reach out his hand and actually touch the darkness of Egypt, the void from which God's face was absent." Here Jacob arraigns not his degenerate captors but God who had so abandoned them. On their behalf and his own he is forced to recreate Torah, not just as the law of God for man but as the moral law which God himself must somehow respect. Meanwhile a love affair develops between Jacob and Wanda, his master's daughter, which recalls the Kabbalistic symbolization of the gentiles as a woman Israel must redeem. Himself redeemed from slavery without Wanda, Jacob becomes "a man at war with himself." It is he who must redeem, but he can think of his return to Wanda as only another servitude, this time to his passions. In submitting to the evil he cannot escape he remembers, in entirely the opposite sense in which the same thought had occurred to Shloimele in Kreshev, the teaching of the Lurianic Kabbala; that "coupling was the universal act underlying everything," and that hence "all lust was of divine origin."

With Wanda he takes the precarious course of leading a double life. She becomes Sarah, a Jewish wife, disguised as a deaf-mute to conceal her telltale accent, for their situation could bring terrible reprisals. In the manorial village where they settle, Jacob assumes certain traditionally significant roles; teacher, steward of his lord's estate — in short, he becomes head of the Jewish community. There is a succession of intricate complications ringing with biblical echoes until finally the inevitable exposure catastrophically overtakes them. In the agony of an unusually difficult labor Wanda-Sarah betrays the truth and dies on the eve of the Day of Atonement, having brought into the world a Jewish man-child. With this child Jacob escapes.

Here I momentarily thought the novel ended, and maybe it would have been better if it had. At this point Singer clinched the identification of Jacob with his archetypal namesake and set the man, as was schematically appropriate, on his wanderings again. "Everything remained the same; the ancient love, the ancient grief," Jacob reflects. "Well, but the Redemption has to come. All this can't last forever." But in the same breath he submits. "Lead, God, lead. It is thy world." At this point the fable seemed rounded, complete. With a natural and delicate irony Jacob has not been able to see that in fact redemption had already come — that eternally it must come in this way. Or so Singer seems to tell us.

Then there is a very brief epilogue for which nothing in the novel has prepared the reader. After nearly twenty years (and after an incredible series of adventures hurriedly packed up in a synopsis) Jacob returns for his wife's bones, finding them only when he is laid to rest beside them in a grave that had been unmarked and up to that point unconsecrated. Over them a tombstone is set with engraved lovebirds and an eye-misting inscription. Singer's characteristic ambiguity is again evident: natural or supernatural coincidence? But this time it seems rather to ask: sentimental manipulation, or minor miracle? If miracle, to prove what? That Wanda had indeed been redeemed and sanctified? That had been unmistakably made clear earlier. The real defect, however, is that the sentimentality and mystification detract from what must have been the central point, the one Jacob made as he began again the cycle of his wandering: "not death but suffering was the real enigma." It would have been worth keeping that clear.

It would almost seem that mystification and ambiguity are so automatically part of Singer's techniques that at times — and here seriously — the mannerism takes over, while with a puzzling lack of artistic tact Singer seems to forget what it was that he was writing about. This is a fault. But it is a blemish in an otherwise impressive achievement. Even *The Slave* somehow survives its inept ending. Up to that point it is close to being a really great novel.

One last troublesome question remains when Singer's accomplishment has been surveyed. Perhaps in a way it relates to the flaw in *The Slave*. The vision that underlies Singer's work is powerful, one to which every Jew in some way can respond, and to which, as the paradigm of redemptive destiny, many in the Western Christian tradition can also respond. But is the vision dead? Is it ultimately only anthropological, or archeological, or historical? There is no doubt that Singer's psychological insights are alive. But that's not the point. He insists, in effect, upon a vision. Yet he writes of that vision exclusively in terms of the past. Jewish destiny may have been, may indeed be redemptive or demonic. But somehow the questions seem academic after Auschwitz. It is hard, in other words, to find a proper climax for the paradigm of redemptive Jewish destiny. The Christians found it in the crucifixion. Singer sees no conclusion and has Jacob start to wander again. Then he wavers and gives us a confusedly sentimental ending that is really irrelevant. So the question remains, despite Singer's great artistry. Is the vision dead?

One can reflect that on a recent occasion when Singer gave a public lecture in Boston, he began humorously by answering a question he said that people always asked him. Why does a writer of his stature continue to write in Yiddish, now almost a dead language? Why indeed? Because, he answered — and one felt the irony cresting — he really wrote, despite all other appearances, about ghosts. And what better language for ghost stories than a dead language? To which might be added: what better language for a dead vision than a dead language? But how lively the dead seem!

Note

[1] Cited by Gershom Scholem, *Major Trends in Jewish Mysticism* (Schocken Books, 1961), p. 284.

J. S. Wolkenfeld

6.

Isaac Bashevis Singer: The Faith of His Devils and Magicians

I.

One of the best writers of prose fiction in America today is Isaac Bashevis Singer, who was born in Poland in 1904 and now lives in New York, and who writes in Yiddish. His four novels and two volumes of short stories, all translated into English, avoiding both the sentimentalism and the exoticism his settings might have led into, present a meaningful vision of reality consistently moral and beautifully individual. The nature of this vision may become clearer if we follow one theme which runs insistently throughout his work — the theme of faith.

"Gimpel the Fool," Singer's best known story, is perhaps the clearest case in point. Gimpel is a fool because he is gullible; he is unwilling to disbelieve any assertion. He will not disbelieve the fantastic tales of pranksters; he will not even disbelieve his wife, the town prostitute, when she explains away the man in bed with her, or when she insists that Gimpel is the father of her illegitimate children.

To this point the story is a splendid retelling of folk material — but it is vastly expanded when the Devil appears in the final section to force Gimpel into a clearly moral choice. The devil insists that there is no God, no reward for good, no punishment for evil, and that there is thus no reason to choose good over evil. For a moment Gimpel is unwilling to disbelieve this assertion too, but he recovers in time and though he remains the gullible fool, teller of stories and butt of jokes, he becomes a heroic figure of faith, unwilling to disbelieve that God exists, that there is a moral necessity in life, and he awaits a death which will lead him into a world where all things are not only possible but also true.

As in this story, Singer asks repeatedly not what is true, but rather what a man can believe to be true. In his most recent novel, [The] Slave, the central character, Jacob, virtually creates his Jewish faith in the face of a series of forces — the lust and weakness of his own nature, the paganism, deprivation and persecution of the non-Jewish world, and the greed, fear and narrowness of the Jewish world. In The Family Moskat Asa Bannet never solves his basic problem: how to relate his deistic, Spinozist convictions to the Jewish world in which he lives. Moreover he is set in the full context of Jewish life in Poland, and thus he is juxtaposed to such a wide variety of Jewish approaches to life that one is very nearly convinced they are all the possible ones — Zionism, Chasidism, hedonism, socialism, as well as middle class concern for success in society, in the family, and in business. Significantly the book ends by leading into those events which have presented the modern world with its most horrible challenge to faith — the Nazi occupation of Europe.

In Satan in Goray and The Magician of Lublin, which I want to examine more closely, a question which is implicit in the other works becomes more explicitly central: what happens when there is a crisis of faith, when faith is threatened? In these two books, as in his others, Singer establishes as a framework what might be called the standard Jewish faith. Primarily this includes belief in the Jewish God, personal, omnipotent, who imposes after death rewards and punishments according to man's virtues and sins. The way to serve God is through *halacha*, the code of law which is essentially a code of behavior, controlling man's communal and private actions, his objective relations to society, to family, to God.

This framework serves as a standard which is taken for granted in the Jewish communities Singer's characters live in. The novels neither support nor approve it, but use it rather as a background before which the crises of faith operate, and in terms of which they can be understood. In *The Magician of Lublin* the opponent of faith is partly the Spinozist view which plays so important a part in *The Family Moskat* and which holds that there is a Creator but that He is distant and unconcerned with the individual and that after death there is nothing. But faith is more basically opposed in this book by the demands of freedom. In *Satan in Goray* the standard Jewish faith is directly opposed by another, more absolutist and less human, kind of faith.

II

Satan in Goray begins with a violently shocking description of a pogrom which in 1648 lay waste Goray, a small town in Poland almost entirely inhabited by Jews:

> They slaughtered on every hand, flayed men alive, murdered small children, violated women and afterwards ripped open their bellies and sewed cats inside. . . . For weeks after the razing of Goray, corpses lay neglected in every street, with no one to bury them. Savage dogs tugged at dismembered limbs and vultures and crows fed on human flesh.

This opening, which brings us firmly into a moral universe — that is to say, a universe in which we are forced to make moral judgments — poses first the same question to faith that the Book of Job poses, and second, makes the families who return to Goray some years later begin their community on the primary fact, on death. When they build a home it is on the ruins of one destroyed; they walk on streets very recently covered with the bones of their murdered relatives. Catastrophe lies behind them, and catastrophe is their test. But the horror which the survivors of Goray have lived through does not diminish their desire for faith. On the contrary, the horror only increases their belief that God does rule the world, that God does enter into the affairs of everyday, that no action stands by itself but is rather in a chain of spiritual causation. It is, ironically, their very need to believe that allows Satan to enter Goray, because they are led to a faith which hopes to leave behind its necessary conditions, which ignores the human situation.

This improper faith may be called Shabsaism, after Shabsai Zvi, who plays such an important role in both Jewish history and the novel. According to cabbalists it was in 1666, the year in which the bulk of *Satan in Goray* is set, that the Messiah was to be revealed. In the East, Shabsai made claims to being the Messiah, and he convinced an enormous number of Jews that he was about to usher in the Messianic age. In this same year, 1666, however, Shabsai was converted to Mohammedanism. Some of his followers returned disillusioned to their older way of life; some became Christians; others refused to give up an impossible belief. These divided into two groups. The one believed that the Messiah would come only to a perfectly righteous generation; they became pious ascetic penitents. The other group believed that the Messiah would come only to a perfectly guilty generation; they committed all sorts of public and private abominations, especially in secretly causing others to sin. The novel makes fine use of this material, controlling both its supernatural and its dangerous sensational elements.

Three characters essential to the Shabsaist movement in Goray explain its rise to us and show us how Satan enters Goray. The ascetic Itche Mattes paves the way and lets us see how, in the given evil of the world, a desire to do good and to find truth leads to self-destruction. The sensual Gedaliya is the real leader of the movement and lets us see the actual dynamics — the politics, so to speak — of the Satanic invasion. The disturbed girl, Rechele, is both the embodiment of Shabsaism and its victim.

Itche Mattes is a peddler who never asks for money. He is amazingly even-tempered and speaks in a whisper. He is learned in cabbalism. He hardly ever sleeps but rather spends his nights mortifying his flesh. On the night before his wedding to Rechele he purifies himself by rolling in the snow, recounting his transgressions, and even "begging forgiveness for the pains he had given his mother when he lay in the womb." Itche Mattes does not seek power; he doesn't demand comforts; he bears no grudge. On the contrary he seeks only to subjugate himself, to cause no evil, and to serve God. But his heroic will to believe and to serve is betrayed. The nature of this self-betrayal is indicated in his commitment to Rechele at the very moment when, in a casual phrase, she calls on Satan. Later when he lies in bed with her on their wedding night, he has a vision of Lillith which pleases him, and he compares Lillith to his bride. His attraction to Satanism is clear, whatever his other reasons for marrying, and it stems from something integral to the man and to his cabbalistic faith. Through its undifferentiating monism he views everything as stemming from God, both good and evil, a view which lends itself easily to a confusion of the two, to the possibility of serving a good God through evil actions. Itche Mattes never goes this far, but partly because of him, others do. Furthermore, Itche Mattes is impotent, perhaps as a result of his ascetic practices, and this serves to emphasize the sterile, unfruitful nature of his faith.

If Itche Mattes does the work of Satan it is in a preparatory way; in emphasizing cabbalism over *halacha,* private virtue over public and communal responsibility, and above all in setting up a general feeling of expectation for the Messiah, he prepares the way for Gedaliya. Where Itche Mattes is frail and ascetic, Gedaliya is tall, heavyset and luxury loving, and where Itche Mattes hopes and prays for the coming of the Messiah, Gedaliya sets the exact date for his revelation. Gedaliya becomes immediately necessary to the town. He is a healer; he exorcises spirits; he directs all community affairs; he collects taxes and sees to the poor. He jokes and sings and brings joy. He is also the only ritual slaughterer in Goray, so that the town depends on him for kosher meat. And it is here that we see the nature of the man, for it is his way to be lax in the examination of the animals and he never considers any animal non-kosher and unfit to be eaten. In his primary position in the community, then, his power lies over the material not the spiritual; he provides meat for the belly. In other ways, too, Gedaliya is lax in the observance of *halacha,* and a great deal of the money that passes through his hands pays for his luxurious ways. At the same time, Gedaliya's healing depends more on superstition than on medicine; his sermons are based more on tales than on Scripture or rabbinic writings. His appeal in general is one of easy promises and easy comfort, and his faith is a faith of ease. Under his direction part of the town acts in direct violation of *halacha,* notably in sexual looseness; all of the town publicly and privately gives up expectation of the future in awaiting the revelation of Shabsai as the Messiah, and this too at the time of the High Holidays, the period of spiritual preparation, and the Day of Atonement. After the apostasy of Shabsai, Gedaliya is predictably one of those who choose the way of sin. He marries Rechele, Itche Mattes' wife, without a proper divorce and after having

previously lived with her, and he encourages both adultery
and incest, and worships satanic idols. Overlooking for the
moment the clear suggestion that Gedaliya is himself the
Satan in Goray, we may say that he has been led to this
excess of sin, and later to the ultimate evil of apostasy,
through his love for power, and above all because in his
powerful vitality he indulges the self instead of following
the law which restrains.

The most interesting of the characters in *Satan in
Goray* is Rechele. Partly a psychological study of a disturbed woman, partly a study of a possessed woman in
terms which accept possession as simple fact, she is, like
Goray itself, primarily a victim. Born into violence shortly
before the pogroms of 1648, she first watches her mother
die, and then is terrified by an uncle she is sent to stay with,
and by his mother-in-law. Like Gedaliya the uncle is also
a ritual slaughterer. She watches him sharpen his knives;
she watches bloody slaughtered chickens, calves, goats. The
superstitious mother-in-law screeches at her wild tales of
beasts and witches. The coal black chimney sweep is to her
an actual visible devil. After watching the old lady die,
slowly and painfully, and after staying alone in the house
on the eve of the Day of Atonement, thinking herself surrounded by the dead, Rechele is found in a trance unable
to speak, her knees pulled to her chest, her eyes glazed. Although she improved, she always walked with a limp.
When she returns to Goray at eighteen she is, though
lovely, strangely disturbed. Her objections to marrying
Itche Mattes are virtually the last utterings of her conscious will. After his cabbalistic utterances, his failure as
a husband, and his identification of her with Lillith, she
becomes completely willess, completely possessed. She has
prophetic dreams and allows herself to be taken over by
Gedaliya. She is now all disturbed unacting spirit, he all
dynamic body.

Indeed she remains as an image of Goray, the community tortured by its position in history, by its desire

for a meaningful spiritual life, by an inner, perhaps unavoidable, weakness. Rechele's early wealth is parallel to
the rich early life of Goray; the violence which terrifies
her is parallel to the violence of the pogroms, of life; disturbed by superstition and terror, the town, like Rechele,
is made captive by cabbalism, by an unfruitful mysticism,
and by a hope for a complete and effortless salvation. The
town, like Rechele, is seduced by Gedaliya. As she lies in
bed in Gedaliya's house, tortured and seemingly exalted,
not eating, not attending to her bodily needs, her body pale
and luminous, she is Goray, suffering, seemingly spiritual
but actually playing a parody of spiritual life. Like Rechele
the town has been possessed by Satan, finding at the end
horrors reminiscent of those it had tried to escape.

The only figure who opposes the Shabsaists, though
his efforts are ineffective, is Rabbi Benish Ashkenazi, who
is alone in looking only to the law and purification through
the law, to the requirements of *halacha*. Insofar as Shabsaism is the loser in this competition of faiths, it is only
because its failure was, as it had to be, so publicly plain.
Rabbi Benish, indeed, leaves Goray before Gedaliya appears. Rabbi Benish is weak as a character and as a formal
element in the book because of the nature of his faith.
Sufficient as a way of managing, it yet cannot answer the
questions it has been posed. Rabbi Benish wanders about
asking, "How will it end? What does God want?" He is of
necessity always in doubt, at one point even afraid he
might abjure his faith. He is thus always in the middle
of the fight between good and evil. The paradox here is
that Rabbi Benish's kind of doubt, his weakness, requires
enormous strength, but though it can withstand, it cannot
overcome the easier but more vital strength of Gedaliya's
faith. The paradox reverberates into our own lives. What
we are left with at the end is that the way of law and restraint, the way of Rabbi Benish, which accepts the world
with its desperate problems, is insufficient to cope with the
horrors of reality. The other way, the way of total faith,

reacts to catastrophe by looking forward to another catastrophe, to a complete overturning, to a final solution; it reacts to problems by a desire to replace the world which created them. And we find that those who, to use the terms of the novel, bought from Satan the luxury of total faith, had to pay, with sin and with calamities. We remain, then, fixed in the human situation, needing to act, wishing to believe, confronted by horror.

III

The Magician of Lublin is, in form and in tone, much more the sort of a book we are used to. Its discussion of faith leads more directly, though not more pertinently, into the modern situation. It shows us two connected dilemmas — one, that freedom ultimately becomes a trap like any other and two, that all human actions lead eventually to death and to evil.

The plot is comparatively simple. The time is the late nineteenth century. There is a single main character, Yasha Mazur, a non-believing Jewish magician — that is, a circus performer, a Houdini-like escape artist who also walks the tightrope, does card tricks, has an animal act, hypnotizes. When the novel opens Yasha is at home in Lublin with his wife, Esther, for the holidays. On his way back to Warsaw, where he is about to open a new season, he picks up his assistant, who is also one of his mistresses, Magda, a Christian girl. On the way too he chats with some cronies who belong to a fraternity of thieves, and stops to visit another mistress, Zeftel. In Warsaw he is involved with Emilia, a Christian widow of a professor, who has a daughter, Halina, and who wishes to marry him. Their plan is to go to Italy, where Yasha's talents, not properly rewarded in Poland, will bring him great fame and wealth. Two major problems face him: to marry Emilia he will have to be converted to Christianity after breaking with his wife, and to take her to Italy he will need a great deal of money. He decides to resolve the second of his problems by stealing, and in this attempt his life seems to break down. He doesn't get the money; he injures his leg so that he can no longer perform; Magda commits suicide; Zeftel takes up with a pimp; and finally Emilia sends him away. In an epilogue Yasha has become an ascetic penitent, bricked up voluntarily in a bare cell, with a single window and no door.

It is an extraordinarily useful plot. To take the escape artist who can pick locks, escape from chains, and put him into a self-imposed — therefore escape proof — prison, is daringly right. As we shall soon see in detail, making Yasha a magician at all allows Singer to control a great number of themes in a very simple way. Furthermore, the novel gathers up a number of issues around the problem of marrying Emilia. Eventually the novel focusses on a single act, stealing. The structure of the novel, then, is precisely what it ought to be, and even this brief description should show how neatly it serves up the point: personal freedom against self-subjugation through faith.

Yasha exists in the book on two levels, the realistic and the moral. In the sense that he is limited by physical reality as a circus performer, he is limited by moral reality as a free agent. He can be totally free no more than he can fly, though with his skills he gets close to both achievements. As he open locks in his professional capacity and frees himself from chains, so he is not bound by the domestication which restricts other men. He has no children. He travels freely from town to town. Related to his skill as hypnotist is his success as a lover. He looks younger than his forty years. He adapts freely to the personality of all; with thieves he speaks like a thief; with Jews like a Jew; with cultured people like a cultured man. In the same way, he knows Russian and Polish, besides Yiddish and some Hebrew. In his religion, too, he is free. Though ethical and charitable, and conscious of his responsibility to those who depend on him, he has long ago given up the practices of the Jewish religion. He goes to the synagogue only twice a year, and that is for the sake of his wife, who is an observant Jew. Not an atheist, Yasha believes that there is a Creator, "but he revealed himself to no one, gave no indication of what is permitted or forbidden. Those who speak in his name are liars." He ends all religious discussion with a question: "When were you in Heaven, and what did God look like?" Without a religion, and without the roots of home and family, he finds himself everywhere a stranger, neither Jew nor Christian. Where others act as if they knew, he has only doubt. At the same time he finds within himself many possibilities, toward the heretical and the religious, toward good and toward evil, toward the false and the sincere. Indeed he sees himself, both in and out of the circus, "as if walking a tightrope, merely inches from disaster." This seems as good an image for freedom as any other, and Yasha Mazur walks his tightrope with ease and grace.

Yasha is also balanced between two other views of himself. He sees himself as potentially all-powerful, always growing stronger, asserting himself more and more on the universe. Professionally he is trying to perfect a new and daring trick — he plans to do a somersault on the tightrope. He dreams also of learning to fly. From his women he would like to have complete faith; "whatever happens, always be true to me," he tells them. He wants greater fame and more money than he can get in Poland, and this is connected with his desire for the upper class Emilia, which in turn demands divorce from Esther, a break with his other women, and, as he puts it, a little conversion. At the same time he has wilder, Faustian dreams of great power, through hypnosis and magic controlling armies, healing the sick, becoming emperor of the world; and also indulging in pleasures of intelect and lust.

On the other hand he sees himself also as utterly insignificant with no values strong enough to build his life on. In this view the goods of the world seem all vain.

Understandably this feeling has its origin in the awareness of death. As a tightrope walker, Yasha is always conscious of the possibility of falling; the fear of death is always with him. One of his girl friends extends the notion: "... recently I even thought of suicide," she says, "... just because I was tired and there was a rope nearby . . . you yank the rope and it's all over." Yasha continues the theme with two questions: "How long does one survive in this rotten world?" And, "What is life's purpose if we don't know why we live or die?" He also has a Conrad-like vision of Warsaw: "In every street and alley lurked murderers, thieves, degenerates." Life, for the moment, becomes an idle game over the grave, whether it is Jewish life or Christian, in Poland or in cultured France. And all belief becomes desperate pretense, because of fear or shame of ignorance.

These two opposed strands in Yasha become intensified, through his desire for Emilia, until he reaches a choice of absolutes. It is as if the tightrope walker is forced to jump first to the one, then to the other side of the rope, to pass through as it were two ways of life, two possible commitments. The first is the Jewish world, the world of faith. While running from pursuit after his crime, he escapes into a synagogue, and that the synagogue is connected for him with the idea of escape is significant. Yasha has been in synagogues before in the novel, and each time he acknowledges the call they make on him, but now he undergoes a temporary conversion. He sees first the Ten Commandments on the Holy Ark; in the prayers of the congregants the words he is able to hear clearly, acknowledge God as Creator and as supporter of the weak. He puts on a prayer shawl and phylacteries — that is, prayer thongs — and he too prays, suddenly with meaning, devotion and full faith. He accepts the existence of a personal God and concludes, "I must be a Jew! . . . A Jew like all the others!"

After he leaves the synagogue, however, he sees that

the street, the world let us say, and the synagogue deny each other. If one is true, the other is certainly false. And now he is brought into the essence of this world. Wandering to Emilia's house, he tells her what he has done. Not without reason somewhat afraid of him, and essentially a woman without compassion, she sends him away. This closes one retreat. When he finally goes back to his own apartment, he find that Magda, who previously had broken with Yasha when she called him "dirty Jew," has hanged herself, closing another retreat. With nowhere else to go, he wanders to his last resort, to see Zeftel, who followed him to Warsaw. He finds her naked in bed with a man called Herman, a card shark and procurer.

> Twice in one day there had been unveiled to him things which are best concealed. He had looked on the faces of death and lechery and had seen that they were the same. . . . The last twenty-four hours were unlike any previous day he had experienced. They summed up all his previous existence, and in summing up had put a seal upon it. He had seen the hand of God. He had reached the end of the road.

The book is now finished. Yasha Mazur has been changed from a man strong in freedom to a man caught in freedom, a man forced by freedom into one of two impossible paths. In an Epilogue, Yasha Mazur, having chosen, desperately, the way of the synagogue, is bricked up in his penitent's cell, still tormented by doubt though fully committed to his faith.

IV

That in one book total faith is seen as leading to evil and in another as a necessary choice should cause no difficulty. The books each work out their own situations and the faiths are, after all, of different kinds. In the long run the approved way of life is that which causes least harm to others, a way wide enough to include Gimpel and Yasha as well as Asa Heshel and Itche Mattes. They all know, each in his own way, that what they must avoid above all else is causing suffering to other human beings, and to avoid this each has in one way or another to remove himself from life. All four of the novels, indicating thus that there is no ultimate answer in any way of life, call at the end on the Messiah to come; "there is no other way," says Yasha.

Whatever we think of such a conclusion, we cannot but see as valid Singer's investigation of our moral situation, the conflict in us and our society between peace and achievement, between the demands of the inner and the outer man. In its relentless insistence on the lonely necessity to decide how one is to live, what to believe, and especially in its conclusion that while man must choose, the best he can hope for is commitment and never certitude, Singer's work is enormously meaningful for man today, Jew or non-Jew. But this would count for little were it not for the actuality of presentation, the reality of scene and the reality of character which Singer achieves. It is not just that Singer's craftsmanship is meticulous; it is that his books become alive. For example, the bare narration of *Satan in Goray,* with its effect somewhere between chronicle and epic, and which never lets us identify but always forces us to look and understand, makes the book a *tour de force.* But our belief in Rechele's exorcism scene, our acceptance that every one of her groans is significant, and therefore true, makes the book a work of art. In Singer the statement, the fictional reality, and the language interact in just the right way to bring us delight and to make us forget the delight in a new awareness of what lies inside of us, of men.

7.

I. B. Singer

— *Would it be fair to say that you are actually writing in a somewhat artificial or illusory context, as if none of the terrible things that have happened to the Jewish people during the last two decades really did occur?*

SINGER: Yes, very fair. There was a famous philosopher, Vaihinger, who wrote a book called *The Philosophy of "As If"* in which he showed that we all behave "as if." The "as if" is so much a part of our life that it really isn't artificial. . . . Every man assumes he will go on living. He behaves as if he will never die. So I wouldn't call my attitude artificial. It's very natural and healthy. We have to go on living and writing.

— *But do you agree that at the heart of your attitude there is an illusion which is consciously sustained?*

SINGER: Yes.

No other living writer has yielded himself so completely and recklessly as has Isaac Bashevis Singer to the claims of the human imagination. Singer writes in Yiddish, a language that no amount of energy or affection seems likely to save from extinction. He writes about a world that is gone, destroyed with a brutality beyond historical comparison. He writes within a culture, the remnant of Yiddish in the Western world, that is more than a little dubious about his purpose and stress. He seems to take entirely for granted his role as a traditional story-teller speaking to an audience attuned to his every hint and nuance, an audience that values story-telling both in its own right and as a binding communal action — but also, as it happens, an audience that keeps fading week by week, shrinking day by day. And he does all this without a sigh or apology, without so much as a Jewish groan. It strikes one as a kind of inspired madness: here is a man living in New York City, a sophisticated and clever writer, who composes stories about places like Frampol, Bilgoray, Kreshev, *as if they were still there.* His work is shot through with the bravado of a performer who enjoys making his listeners gasp, weep, laugh and yearn for more. Above and beyond everything else he is a great performer, in ways that remind one of Twain, Dickens, Sholom Aleichem.

Singer writes Yiddish prose with a verbal and rhythmic brilliance that, to my knowledge, can hardly be matched. When Eliezer Greenberg and I were working on our *Treasury of Yiddish Stories,* he said to me: "Singer has to be heard, to be believed." Behind the prose there is always a spoken voice, tense, ironic, complex in tonalities, leaping past connectives. Greenberg then read to me, with a fluency and pith I could never capture in my own reading of Yiddish, Singer's masterpiece, *Gimpel the Fool,* and I knew at once (it took no great powers of judgment) that here was the work of a master. The story came as a stroke of revelation, like a fiction by Babel or Kleist encountered for the first time.

Singer's stories claim attention through their vivacity and strangeness of surface. He is devoted to the grotesque, the demonic, the erotic, the quasi-mystical. He populates his alien sub-world with imps, devils, whores, fanatics, charlatans, spirits in seizure, disciples of false messiahs. A young girl is captured by the spirit of a dead woman and goes to live with the mourning husband as if she were actually his wife; a town is courted and then shattered by a lavish stranger who turns out to be the devil; an ancient Jew suffering unspeakable deprivations during the first World War, crawls back to his village of Bilgoray and fathers a son whom, with marvellous aplomb, he names Isaac. Sometimes the action in Singer's stories follows the moral curve of traditional folk tales, with a charming, lightly-phrased "lesson" at the end; sometimes, the spiral of a quizzical modern awareness; at best, the complicated motions of the old and the contemporary yoked together, a kind of narrative double-stop.

Orgiastic lapses from the moral order, pacts with the devil, ascetic self-punishments, distraught sexuality occupy the foreground of Singer's stories. Yet behind this expressionist clamour there is glimpsed the world of the *shtetl*, or East European Jewish village, as it stumbled and slept through the last few centuries. Though Singer seldom portrays it fullface, one must always keep this world in mind while reading his stories: it forms the base from which he wanders, the norm from which he deviates but which controls his deviation. And truly to hear these stories one must have at least a splinter of knowledge about the culture from which Singer comes, the world he continues to evoke as if it were still radiantly alive: the Hasidim still dancing, the rabbis still pondering, the children still studying, the poor still hungering as if it had not all ended in ashes and death.

Isaac Bashevis Singer was born in Radzymin, Poland, in 1904. Both his father and grandfather were rabbis, in the tradition of Hasidism, a kind of ecstatic pietism, though on his mother's side the *misnagid* or rationalist strain of Jewish belief was stronger. "My father," recalls

Singer, "always used to say that if you don't believe in the *zaddikim* [the "wonder-rabbis" of Hasidism] to-day, tomorrow you won't believe in God. My mother would say, it's one thing to believe in God and another to believe in a man. . . . My mother's point of view is also my point of view."

Raised in a poor neighbourhood of Warsaw, on Krochmalna Street, Singer received a strictly traditional Jewish education. He studied in a rabbinical seminary which was "a kind of college" providing secular as well as religious studies. During his adolescence he spent three or four years in his grandfather's *shtetl*, Bilgoray, which would later show itself as a strong influence upon his work. Bilgoray

> was very old-fashioned. Not much has changed there in generations. In this town the traditions of hundreds of years ago still lived. There was no railroad nearby. It was stuck in the forest and it was pretty much as it must have been during the time of Chmielnicki. . . . I could have written *The Family Moskat* [a novel set in Warsaw] without having lived in Bilgoray, but I could never have written *Satan in Goray* [a novella dealing with 17th-century false messianism] or some of my short stories without having been there.

A decisive example was set by Singer's older brother, Israel Joshua, who began to write in his youth and became a leading Yiddish novelist, author of *The Brothers Ashkenazi* and *Yash Kolb*. Throughout a distinguished career, I. J. Singer remained pretty much within the main lines of the Yiddish tradition, both as to moral and social attitudes, even though he was strongly influenced by contemporary Western writing, especially the kind of large-scale family novel popular in Europe at the turn of the century. Controlling the older Singer's fiction is the Jewish community, both as social framework and source of values; his style, fluent, relaxed and smooth, can be

taken as a model for cultivated modern Yiddish. The older
brother represents that which I. B. Singer learned from,
struggled with, and then mostly left behind.

In the Jewish world of Warsaw during the time Singer
was growing up, a decision to become a secular writer
meant a painful conflict with family and culture, a symbolic break from the paths of tradition:

> It was a great shock to my parents. They consid-
> ered all the secular [Yiddish] writers to be heretics,
> all unbelievers — they really were too, most of them.
> To become a *literat* was to them almost as bad as be-
> coming a *meshumed,* one who forsakes the faith. My
> father used to say that secular writers like Peretz were
> leading the Jews to heresy. He said everything they
> wrote was against God. Even though Peretz wrote in
> a religious vein, my father called his writing "sweet-
> ened poison," but poison nevertheless. And from his
> point of view he was right. Everybody who read such
> books sooner or later became a worldly man, and for-
> sook the traditions. In my family, of course, my
> brother had gone first, and I went after him. For my
> parents, this was a tragedy.

In these early years of the century Warsaw was a lively
if troubled city, the main centre of Jewish cultural life.
The binding tradition of Yiddish literature had already
been set by the pioneer generation of writers: Mendele
Mocher Sforim, Sholom Aleichem, I. J. Peretz. It was a
literature strongly devoted to problems of communal
destiny and survival; characterised by a high, sometimes
consuming ethical intent; closely tied to folk sources;
drawing profoundly upon, even as it kept moving away
from, religious tradition; resting upon a culture that
might still be described as "organic" and certainly as coherent; and yet displaying many signs of the influence of
European, especially Russian, writing. In Warsaw the
major social and cultural movements of East European

Jewish life found their most sophisticated versions: Yiddishism, the effort to create an autonomous secular culture based on the language of *galut*; Bundism, the organisation of a distinctively Jewish socialism, and Zionism, potentially of great importance but at this point still weak. Peretz's home became the gathering-place for young writers fresh from the provinces where the majority of Jews still lived; here, in this cosmopolitan haven, they could begin planning their novels and stories about the overwhelming memory of the *shtetl*. And the religious community, though now challenged from several directions and past the high point of its power, remained a major force within the world of the East European Jews.

Growing up in this feverish but immensely stimulating atmosphere, the younger Singer carved out a path of his own. He was not drawn to any of the Jewish movements: indeed, he has always been sceptical of the political messianism which, as a partial offshoot of the earlier religious messianism, runs through 20th-century Jewish life. He edged away from formal piety, yet remained close to the Jewish religious tradition, especially its more esoteric and cabbalistic elements. And while a master of the Yiddish language — he is second only to Sholom Aleichem in his command of its idiom — Singer was neither a programmatic Yiddishist nor notably at ease in the world of Yiddish culture, which has in the main been secular and rationalist in stress.

As a youth Singer began to read in forbidden tongues, discovering E. T. A. Hoffman and Edgar Allan Poe in the libraries of Warsaw. The exotic romanticism of these writers stirred his imagination rather more than did the work of most Yiddish writers, who were then in a realistic or even naturalistic phase, and with whose materials he felt all too familiar. An even stronger alien influence was that of Knut Hamsun, the Norwegian novelist, who enjoyed an international vogue during the years before World

War II. Hamsun's novels, especially *Pan,* impressed upon the younger Singer the claims of the irrational in human existence, the power of the perverse within seemingly normal behaviour. Now, several decades later, it is hard to see much evidence of Hamsun in Singer's work: perhaps it was the kind of influence that does not leave a visible stamp but instead liberates a writer to go his own way.

A still more alien influence — for a young Jewish writer fresh from the *yeshiva,* an influence downright bizarre — was that curious body of writings known as spiritualism or "psychic research," which Singer somehow came upon in Warsaw and would continue to follow throughout his life. Could anything be more distant from the tradition of Yiddish literature or, for that matter, from the whole body of Jewish religious thought? Fortunately for his career as a writer, Singer has preserved a keen Jewish scepticism — in that department he is entirely traditional! — towards this branch of "knowledge," taking the sophisticated view that belief in the reality of spirits provides his fiction with a kind of compositional shorthand, a "spiritual stenography." As he remarks: "the demons and Satan represent to me, in a sense, the ways of the world. Instead of saying this is the way things happen, I will say, this is the way demons behave." Which is precisely what any cultivated sceptic, totally unconcerned with "psychic research," would also say.

In 1935, convinced that "it was inevitable after Hitler came to power that the Germans would invade Poland," Singer emigrated to the United States. He joined the staff of the *Jewish Daily Forward,* a Yiddish newspaper, in which he printed serious fiction under his own name and a large quantity of journalism under the pen name of Warshofsky. His first major work, the novella *Satan in Goray,* appeared in Yiddish in 1935. Since then he has written full-scale novels, one of which, *The Family Moskat,* was published in an English translation in 1949, as well as a number of short novels (in English: *The Magician of Lublin* and *The*

Slave) and several collections of stories. His best work has been done in short forms, the novella and the story: exciting bursts and flares of the imagination.

Isaac Bashevis Singer is the only living Yiddish writer whose translated work has caught the imagination of a Western (the American) literary public. Though the settings of his stories are frequently strange, the contemporary reader — for whom the determination not to be shocked has become a point of honour — is likely to feel closer to Singer than to most other Yiddish writers. Offhand this may be surprising, for Singer's subjects are decidedly remote and exotic: in *Satan in Goray* the orgiastic consequences of the false messianism of 17th-century East European Jewish life; in *The Magician of Lublin* a portrait of a Jewish magician-Don Juan in late 19th-century Poland who exhausts himself in sensuality and ends as a penitent ascetic; in his stories a range of demonic, apocalyptic, and perversely sacred moments of *shtetl* life. Yet one feels that, unlike many of the Yiddish writers who treat more familiar and up-to-date subjects, Singer commands a distinctly "modern" sensibility.

Now this is partly true — in the sense that Singer has cut himself off from some of the traditional styles and assumptions of Yiddish writing. But it is also not true — in the sense that any effort to assimilate Singer to literary "modernism" without fully registering his involvement with Jewish faith and history is almost certain to distort his meanings.

Those meanings, one might as well admit, are often enigmatic and hard to come by. It must be a common experience among Singer's readers to find a quick pleasure in the caustic surfaces of his prose, the nervous tokens of his virtuosity, but then to acknowledge themselves baffled as to his point and purpose. That his fiction does have an insistent point and stringent purpose no one can doubt: Singer is too ruthlessly single-minded a writer to content himself with mere slices of representation or displays of the bizarre. His grotesquerie must be taken seriously, perhaps as a recoil from his perception of how irremediably and gratuitously ugly human life can be. He is a writer completely absorbed by the demands of his vision, a vision gnomic and compulsive but with moments of high exaltation; so that while reading his stories one feels as if one were overhearing bits and snatches of monologue, the impact of which is both notable and disturbing, but the meaning withheld.

Now these are precisely the qualities that the sophisticated reader, trained to docility before the exactions of "modernism," has come to applaud. Singer's stories work, or prey, upon the nerves. They leave one unsettled and anxious, the way a rationalist might feel if, waking at night in the woods, he suddenly found himself surrounded by a swarm of bats. Unlike most Yiddish fiction, Singer's stories neither round out the cycle of their intentions nor posit a coherent and ordered universe. They can be seen as paradigms of the arbitrariness, the grating injustice, at the heart of life. They offer instances of pointless suffering, dead-end exhaustion, inexplicable grace. And sometimes, as in Singer's masterpiece, *Gimpel the Fool,* they turn about, refusing to rest with the familiar discomforts of the problematic, and drive towards a prospect of salvation on the other side of despair, beyond soiling by error or will. This prospect does not depend on any belief in the comeliness or lawfulness of the universe; whether God is there or not, He is surely no protector:

> He had worked out his own religion [Singer writes about one of his characters]. There was a Creator, but He revealed himself to no one, gave no indications of what was permitted or forbidden.

Things happen, the probable bad and improbable good, both of them subject to the whim of the fortuitous; and the

sacred fools like Gimpel, perhaps they alone, learn to roll
with the punch, finding the value of their life in a total
passivity and credulousness, a complete openness to suffering.

Singer's stories trace the characteristic motions of human destiny: a heavy climb upward ("The Old Man"), a
rapid tumble downward ("The Fast"). Life forms a jour-
neying to heaven and hell, mostly hell. What determines
the direction a man will take? Sometimes the delicate
manoeuvres between his will and desire, sometimes the
heat of his vanity, sometimes the blessing of innocence.
But more often than not, it is all a mystery which Singer
chooses to present rather than explain. As his figures move
upward and downward, aflame with the passion of their
ineluctable destiny, they stop for a moment in the *shtetl*
world. Singer is not content with the limitations of mate-
riality, yet not at all indifferent to the charms and powers
of the phenomenal universe. In his calculus of destiny,
however, the world is a resting-place and what happens
within it, even within the social enclave of the Jews, is not
of lasting significance. Thick, substantial, and attractive
as it comes to seem in Singer's representation, the world
is finally but lure and appearance, a locale between
heaven and hell, the shadow of larger possibilities.

In most Yiddish fiction the stress is quite different.
There the central "character" is the collective destiny of
the Jews in *galut* or exile; the central theme, the survival
of a nation deprived of nationhood; the central ethic, the
humane education of men stripped of worldly power yet
sustained by the memory of chosenness and the promise of
redemption. In Singer the norm of collective life is still
present, but mostly in the background, as a tacit assumption; his major actions break away from the limits of the
shtetl ethic, what has come to be known as *Yiddishkeit,*
and then move either backward to the abandon of false
messianism or forward to the doubt of modern sensibility.

(There is an interesting exception, the story called "Short Friday," which in its stress upon family affection, ritual proprieties and collective faith, approaches rather closely the tones of traditional Yiddish fiction.)

The historical settings of East European Jewish life are richly presented in Singer's stories, often not as orderly sequences in time but as simultaneous perceptions jumbled together in the consciousness of figures for whom Abraham's sacrifice, Chmielnicki's pogroms, the rise and fall of Hasidism and the stirrings of the modern world are all felt with equal force. Yet Singer's ultimate concern is not with the collective experience of a chosen or martyred people but with the enigmas of personal fate. Given the slant of his vision, this leads him to place a heavy reliance upon the grotesque as a mode of narration, even as an avenue towards knowledge. But the grotesque carries with it a number of literary and moral dangers, not the least being the temptation for Singer to make it into an end in itself, which is to say, something facile and sensationalistic. In his second-rank stories he falls back a little too comfortably upon the devices of which he is absolute master, like a magician supremely confident his tricks will continue to work. But mainly the grotesque succeeds in Singer's stories because it comes to symbolise meaningful digressions from a cultural norm. An uninstructed reader may absorb Singer's grotesquerie somewhat too easily into the assumptions of modern literature; the reader who grasps the ambivalence of Singer's relation to Yiddish literature will see the grotesquerie as a cultural sign by means of which Singer defines himself against his own past.

It is hardly a secret that in the Yiddish literary world Singer is regarded with a certain suspicion. His powers of evocation, his resources as a stylist are acknowledged, yet many Yiddish literary persons, including the serious ones, seem uneasy about him. One reason is that "modernism" — which, as these people regard Singer, signifies a heavy stress upon sexuality, a concern for the irrational, expressionist distortions of character, and a seeming indifference to the humane ethic of Yiddishism — has never won so strong a hold in Jewish culture as it has in the cultures of most Western countries. For the Yiddish writers, "modernism" has been at best an adornment of manner upon a subject inescapably traditional.

The truly "modern" writer, however, is not quite trustworthy in relation to his culture. He is a shifty character by choice and need, unable to settle into that solid representativeness which would allow him to act as a cultural "spokesman." And to the extent that Singer does share in the modernist outlook he must be regarded with distrust by Yiddish readers brought up on such literary "spokesmen" as Peretz, Abraham Reisen, and H. Leivick. There is no lack of admiration among Yiddish readers for Singer's work: anyone with half an ear for the cadence and idiom of that marvellous language must respond to his prose. Still, it is a qualified, a troubled admiration. Singer's moral outlook, which seems to move with equal readiness towards the sensational and the ascetic, is hardly calculated to put Yiddish readers at their ease. So they continue to read him, with pleasure and anxiety.

And as it seems to me, they are not altogether wrong. Their admiring resistance to Singer's work may constitute a more attentive and serious response to his iconoclasm than the gleeful applause of those who read him in English translation and take him to be another writer of "black comedy," or heaven help us, a mid-20th-century "swinger."

The death of Satan was a tragedy for the imagination.

By and large Singer has been fortunate in his translators, but no translation, not even Saul Bellow's magnificent rendering of *Gimpel the Fool,* could possibly suggest the full idiomatic richness and syntactical verve of Singer's Yiddish. Singer has left behind him the oratorical sententiousness to which Yiddish literature is prone, has abandoned its leisurely meandering pace, what might be called the *shtetl* rhythm, and has developed a style that is both swift and dense, nervous and thick. His sentences are short and abrupt; his rhythms coiled, intense, short-breathed. The impression his prose creates is not of a smooth and equable flow of language but rather a series of staccato advances and withdrawals, with sharp breaks between sentences. Singer seldom qualifies, wanders or circles back; his method is to keep darting forward, impression upon impression, through a series of jabbing declarative sentences. His prose is free of "literary" effects, a frequent weakness among Yiddish writers who wish to display their elegance and cultivation. And at the base of his prose is the oral idiom of Yiddish, seeded with ironic proverbs and apothegms ("Shoulders are from God, and burdens too"); but a speech that has been clipped, wrenched, syncopated.

What is most remarkable about Singer's prose is his ability to unite rich detail with fiercely compressed rhythms. For the translator this presents the almost insuperable problem of how to capture both his texture and his pace, his density of specification and his vibrating quickness. More often than not, even the most accomplished translator must choose between one effect and the other, if only because the enormous difficulty of rendering Yiddish idiom into another language forces him either to fill out or slow down Singer's sentences.

By its very nature, pace cannot be illustrated, but the richness of Singer's detail can, as in this characteristic passage from *The Old Man*:

His son had died long before, and Reb Moshe Ber said the memorial prayer, *kaddish,* for him. Now alone in the apartment, he had to feed his stove with paper and wood shavings from garbage cans. In the ashes he baked rotten potatoes, which he carried in his scarf, and in an iron pot, he brewed chicory. He kept house, made his own candles by kneading bits of wax and suet around wicks, laundered his shirt beneath the kitchen faucet, and hung it to dry on a piece of string. He set the mousetraps each night and drowned the mice each morning. When he went out he never forgot to fasten the heavy padlock on the door. No one had to pay rent in Warsaw at that time. . . . The winter was difficult. There was no coal, and since several tiles were missing from the stove, the apartment was filled with thick black smoke each time the old man made a fire. A crust of blue ice and snow covered the window panes by November, making the rooms constantly dark or dusky. Overnight, the water on his night table froze in the pot. No matter how many clothes he piled over him in bed, he never felt warm; his feet remained stiff, and as soon as he began to doze, the entire pile of clothes would fall off, and he would have to climb out naked to make the bed once more. There was no kerosene; even matches were at a premium. Although he recited chapter upon chapter of the Psalms, he could not fall asleep. The wind, freely roaming about the rooms, banged the doors; even the mice left.

Or, in a more colourful vein, from *The Last Demon:*

[the last demon] came here from Lublin. Tishevitz is a God-forsaken village: Adam didn't even stop to pee there. It's so small that a wagon goes through the town and the horse is in the market place just as the rear wheels reach the toll gate. There is mud in Tishevitz from Succoth until Tishe b'Ov. The goats of the town don't need to lift their beards to chew at the thatched roofs of the cottages. Hens roost in the middle of the streets. Birds build nests in the women's bonnets. In the tailor's synagogue a billy goat is the tenth in the quorum.

Or, grotesquely, from *Blood:*

Frequently she sang for hours in Yiddish and in Polish. Her voice was harsh and cracked and she invented the songs as she went along, repeating meaningless phrases, uttering sounds that resembled the cackling of fowl, the grunting of pigs, the death-rattles of oxen. . . . At night in her dreams, phantoms tormented her; bulls gored her with their horns; pigs shoved their snouts into her face and bit her; roosters cut her flesh to ribbons with their spurs.

Or, tenderly, from *Gimpel the Fool:*

I was an orphan. My grandfather who brought me up was already bent towards the grave. So they turned me over to a baker, and what a time they gave me there! Every woman or girl who came to bake a batch of noodles had to fool me at least once. "Gimpel, there's a fair in heaven; Gimpel, the rabbi gave birth to a calf in the seventh month; Gimpel, a cow flew over the roof and laid brass eggs." A student from the yeshiva came once to buy a roll, and he said, "You, Gimpel, while you stand here scraping with your baker's shovel the Messiah has come. The dead have arisen." "What do you mean?" I said. "I heard no one blowing the ram's horn." He said, "Are you deaf?" And all began to cry, "We heard it, we heard. . . ."

To tell the truth, I knew very well that nothing of the sort had happened, but all the same, as folks were talking, I threw on my wool vest and went out. Maybe something had happened. What did I stand to lose by looking? Well, what a cat music went up! And then I took a vow to believe nothing more. But that was no go either. They confused me so I didn't know the big end from the small.

Those of Singer's stories which speed downward into hell are often told by devils and imps, sometimes by Satan himself, marvelling at the vanity and paltriness of the human creature. Singer's arch-devil is a figure not so much of evil as of scepticism, a thoroughly modern voice to whose corrosive questions Singer imparts notable force in *A Tale of Two Liars:*

> Are you stupid enough to still believe in the power of prayer? Remember how the Jews prayed during the Black Plague, and nevertheless, how they perished like flies? And what about the thousands the Cossacks butchered? There was enough prayer, wasn't there, when Chmielnicki came? How were those prayers answered? Children were buried alive, chaste wives raped — and later their bellies ripped open and cats sewed inside. Why should God bother with your prayers? He neither hears nor sees. There is no judge. There is no judgment.

Using demons and imps as narrators proves to be a wonderful device for structural economy: they replace the need to enter the "inner life" of the characters, the whole plaguing business of the psychology of motives, for they serve as symbolic equivalents and co-ordinates to human conduct, what Singer calls a "spiritual stenography." In those stories, however, where Singer celebrates the power of human endurance, as in *The Little Shoemakers* and *The Old Man,* he uses third person narrative in the closest he comes to a "high style," so that the rhetorical elevation will help to create an effect of "epical" sweep.

Within his limits Singer is a genius. He has total command of his imagined world; he is original in his use both of traditional Jewish materials and his modernist attitude towards them; he provides a serious if enigmatic moral perspective; and he is a master of Yiddish prose. Yet there are times when Singer seems to be mired in his own originality, stories in which he displays a weakness for self-imitation that is disconcerting. Second-rate writers imitate others, first-rate writers themselves, and it is not always clear which is the more dangerous.

Having gone this far, we must now turn again. If Singer's work can be grasped only on the assumption that he is crucially a "modernist" writer, one must add that in other ways he remains profoundly subject to the Jewish tradition. And if the Yiddish reader is inclined to slight the "modernist" side of his work, any other reader is likely to underestimate the traditional side.

One of the elements in the Jewish past that has most fascinated Singer is the recurrent tendency to break loose from the burden of the Mosaic law and, through the urging of will and ecstacy, declare an end to the *galut*. Historically, this has taken the form of a series of messianic movements, one led in the 17th century by Sabbatai Zevi and another in the 18th by Jacob Frank. The movement of Sabbatai Zevi appeared after the East European Jewish community had been shattered by the rebellion-pogrom of the Cossack chieftain, Chmielnicki. Many of the survivors, caught up in a strange ecstacy that derived all too clearly from their total desperation, began to summon apocalyptic fantasies and to indulge themselves in long-repressed religious emotions which, perversely, were stimulated by the pressures of Cabbalistic asceticism. As if in response to their yearnings, Sabbatai, a pretender rising in the Middle East, offered to release them of everything that rabinical Judaism had confined or suppressed. He spoke for the tempting doctrine that faith is sufficient for salvation; for the wish to evade the limits of mundane life by forcing a religious transcendence; for the union of erotic with mystical appetites; for the lure of a demonism which the very hopelessness of the Jewish situation rendered plausible. In 1665–66 Sabbatianism came to orgiastic climax, whole communities, out of a conviction that the messiah was in sight, discarding the moral inhibitions of exile. Their hopes were soon brutally disappointed, for Sabbatai, persecuted by the Turkish Sultan, converted to Mohammedanism. His followers were thrown into confusion and despair, and a resurgent rabbinism again took control over Jewish life. Nevertheless, Sabbatianism continued to lead an underground existence among the East European Jews — even (I have been told by *shtetl* survivors) into the late 19th and early 20th century. It became a secret heretical cult celebrating Sabbatai as the apostate saviour who had been required to descend to the depths of the world to achieve the heights of salvation.

To this buried strand of Jewish experience Singer has been drawn in fascination and repulsion, portraying its manifestations with great vividness and its consequences with stern judgment. It is a kind of experience that rarely figures in traditional Yiddish writing yet is a significant aspect of the Jewish past. Bringing this material to contemporary readers, Singer writes *in* Yiddish but often quite apart from the Yiddish tradition; indeed, he is one of the few Yiddish writers whose relation to the Jewish past is not determined or screened by that body of values we call Yiddishism.

Singer is a writer of both the pre-Enlightenment and the post-Enlightenment: he would be equally at home with a congregation of medieval Jews and a gathering of 20th-century intellectuals, perhaps more so than at a meeting of the Yiddish PEN club. He has a strong sense of the mystical and antique, but also a cool awareness of psycho-analytic disenchantment. He has evaded both the religious pieties and the humane rationalism of 19th-century East European Judaism. He has skipped over the ideas of the historical epoch which gave rise to Yiddishism, for the truth is, I suppose, that Yiddish literature, in both its writers of acceptance and writers of scepticism, is thoroughly caught up with the Enlightenment. Singer is not. He shares very little in the collective sensibility or the *folkstimlichkeit* of the Yiddish masters; he does not unambiguously celebrate *dos kleine menshele* (the common man) as a paragon of goodness; he is impatient with the sensual deprivations implicit in the values of *edelkeit* (re-

finement, nobility) ; and above all he moves away from a
central assumption of both Yiddish literature in particular
and the 19th century in general, the assumption of an
immanent fate or end in human existence (what in Yiddish is called *tachlis*) .

But again qualifications are needed. It is one thing
to decide to break from a tradition in which one has been
raised, quite another to make the break completely. For
Singer has his ties — slender, subterranean, but strong —
with the very Yiddish writers from whom he has turned
away.

At the centre of Yiddish fiction stands the archetypal
figure of *dos kleine menshele*. It is he, long-suffering, persistent, lovingly ironic, whom the Yiddish writers celebrate. This poor but proud householder trying to maintain his status in the *shtetl* world even as he keeps sinking
deeper and deeper into poverty, appeals to the Yiddish
imagination far more than mighty figures like Aeneas or
Ahab. And from this representative man of the *shtetl*
there emerges a number of significant variations. One
extreme variation is the ecstatic wanderer, hopeless in this
world because profoundly committed to the other. An
equally extreme variation is the wise or sainted fool who
has given up the struggle for status and thereby acquired
the wry perspective of an outsider. Standing somewhere
between *dos kleine menshele* and these offshoots is Peretz's
Bontsha Schweig, whose intolerable humbleness makes
even the angels in heaven feel guilty and embarrassed.
Singer's Gimpel is a literary grandson (perhaps only on
one side) of Peretz's Bontsha; and as Gimpel, with the
piling up of his foolishness, acquires a halo of comic sadness and comes to seem an epitome of pure spirit, one
must keep balancing in one's mind the ways in which he
is akin to, yet different from, Bontsha.

The Yiddish critic Shlomo Bickel has perceptively
remarked that Singer's dominating principle is an "anti-
Prometheanism," a disbelief in the efficacy of striving, de-

fiance, and pride, a doubt as to the sufficiency of knowledge or even wisdom. This seems true, but only if one remembers that in a good many of Singer's fictions the central action does constitute a kind of Promethean ordeal or striving. Singer makes it abundantly clear that his characters have no choice: they must live out their desires, their orgiastic yearnings, their apocalyptic expectations. "Anti-Prometheanism" thus comes to rest upon a belief in the unavoidable recurrence of the Promethean urge.

What finally concerns Singer most is the possibilities for life that remain after the exhaustion of human effort, after failure and despair have come and gone. Singer watches his stricken figures from a certain distance, with enigmatic intent and no great outpouring of sympathy, almost as if to say that before such collapse neither judgment nor sympathy matters very much. Yet in all of his fictions the Promethean effort recurs, obsessional, churning with new energy and delusion. In the knowledge that it will, that it must recur, there may also lie hidden a kind of pity, for that too we would expect, and learn to find, in the writer who created Gimpel.

Baruch Hochman

8.

I. B. Singer's Vision of Good and Evil

For some time now Isaac Bashevis Singer has played a curious role in Yiddish and American letters alike. For a decade after the end of the Second World War he figured as one of the last vital exponents of Yiddish fiction, writing of a world that no longer existed for a public that was rapidly diminishing. Then, with the publication of *Satan in Goray* in an English translation in 1956, a larger public began to take note of his work. The bulk of his writings have since become accessible in English. By now the quarterlies print his work, the weeklies praise him, and the critics are beginning to speak of him as one of the important *American* writers of the age. They find him a master story-teller whose fiction, with its animated evocation of strange, demon-ridden worlds, is not merely exotic, but the vehicle for a comprehensive vision which would seem to express something vital to the spirit of the age. There is hardness in it, and bleakness, and a sense of the problems of finding order in a world of violence and chaos.

Yet even as American critics praise him, his original public is turning its back on him. Yiddish readers used to regard him as a fine stylist who had redeemed a dimension of the ancestral world from oblivion. But now these virtues fall into the background and the Yiddish public is beginning to question both his integrity and the validity of his picture of that world. His rogues are no longer seen as imaginative creations, to be enjoyed as that, but as a reflection on the virtue of our grandmothers or the virility of our grandfathers.

What is peculiar about Singer's position amid these conflicting views of him is that neither his admirers nor his detractors seem to be concerned with either his real limits or his vital relation to the tradition from which he comes. It is immediately evident, for example, that his detractors confuse literature with life. They assume that fiction directly represents the world, and, overlooking the highly stylized, idiosyncratic quality of Singer's tales, speak as though he is "doing" the *shtetl* as it really was. It follows that he must be willfully distorting a known reality. And if the distortion is willful, then it must also be malicious, misrepresenting the *shtetl* with a view to cashing in on the public taste for the lurid and grotesque.

Such confusion on the part of the Yiddish-reading public is partly a matter of defensive self-consciousness. Jews perennially have an image to worry about. It happens that in America at this time it is not a bad image at all, but there remains nevertheless the sense that one must beware of sullying it. Nor is this solely a question of the image as perceived by others; there is also the matter of a self-image. The Yiddish-reading public wants to look back fondly upon nobler days — meager and oppressive days, to be sure — but pious and full of dignity. For the most part, Yiddish literature has nourished such wishes, conditioning its public to expectations that Singer's work violates at every turn. It is a literature that came into being as a latter-day Enlightenment endeavor, which sought to reform and improve the Jewish masses of Eastern Europe, and to inculcate an affirmative self-consciousness among them. Populist in character, Yiddish literature latched directly onto the prevailing modes of response among the masses to whom it was addressed. In their classic introduction to *A Treasury of Yiddish Stories,* Irving Howe and Eliezer Greenberg have pointed out that it was a sentimental literature, one that affirmed the possibility of goodness, the inviolability of feeling, and the unproblematical reality of character as a substantial entity in the world.

Unlike most nineteenth-century fiction, the Yiddish did not probe character but postulated it, and assumed that the reader would fill in the gaps. Behind the great tradition of the European novel stands the Romantic absolutization of individual existence, the assumption that individuality is an autonomous entity which is at odds with the bourgeois and the emergent industrial world. Yiddish fiction, on the other hand, assumes a solidarity of feeling between the individual and his community. It has no articulated sense of a highly developed, relatively coherent social structure that must be confronted. If it exposes social abuses, it does so, not from the vantage point of the autonomous individual, but rather from that of an ethical tradition, on the one hand, and of what may loosely be termed "the folk," on the other. What it lacked in its capacity for rendering individuality in tension with the highly particularized social world, it gained in its vaunted qualities of intimacy and humanity. There is truth in the widely held view that the major writers of Yiddish fiction assume a warmth and a communality in human relationships and in the relation of man to God that is absent, except as an abstract ideal, in the literature of Western Europe in the nineteenth and twentieth centuries.

But Singer is strikingly deficient in these qualities; he even defies them, flying in the face of the deeply ingrained expectations of his Yiddish readers. The protagonists of his longer tales verge on misanthropy; the process of their development involves a decisive movement of alienation from the folk and its ways. They tend to be men who vex questions of faith and reason, and confront the abstruse theological implications of the troubles that beleaguer them. It is no accident that they are often named Jacob; like their Biblical namesake, they wrestle with angels, but their angels are wayward and diabolical agents of impulse who threaten to drive them from the traditional ways of their forefathers.

Even in their rebelliousness, however, the God-problem and the God-idea pervade their being. The protagonists of the longer tales are great sinners, but their very sinfulness is an expression of their sense of the Absolute. They are massive egotists, Job-like men, whose sense of God's existence is rooted in their awareness of the value and scope of their own identity. When, like Jacob of Zamosc in *The Slave*, they reaffirm the divine order of a seemingly disorderly Creation, they find that their absolute, almost saintly, sense of God and their submission to Him is incompatible with the makeshift pieties of mere conventional men. All of Singer's works, with the exception of *The Family Moskat*, are parables of conversion, in which the primary relationship is between man and God, not between man and man. The pattern is one of conversion from defiance, sin, greed, lust, and doubts to submission, virtue, chastity, and selfless faith in God. Since only the radical sinner can undergo a dramatic conversion of this sort, Singer's protagonists cannot, in the nature of things, be other than they are. They do indeed violate the expectations of the Yiddish reader in their initial arrogance and lack of charity toward their fellow men, yet they must violate them if Singer is to write the sort of fable that engages him. It is, in fact, one of the ironies of Singer's relationship to his "natural" audience that the end toward which his fables move is a total affirmation of what his heroes grasp as the Jewish deity and His way. Their way is one of traditional holiness — involving earlocks, ritual fringes, abstinence, charity, fasting, and prayer.

Yet, if in the end the way that they choose is the traditional Jewish one, the path to it is a somewhat deviate one. Singer's heroes mistrust their fellows, and the novels in which they figure are singularly lacking in an affectionate sense of people and objects. The world of a Singer novel is alive with *things*; it is sharply pictorial, and vibrates with the energy of observation. Yet the primary emphasis is not upon the actual, desirable world of people and things, but upon the principles and problems that confronts Singer here. These are always radical manifestations of highly polarized principles: good and evil, God and the devil, life and death, love and hate. And this dualistic world is apprehended above all by desire, which elicits only the demonic, willful, and oppositionist elements of the self. Hence, the movement toward conversion in the novels, though it is a movement toward God, takes place within a peculiar field of consciousness. It is a highly eroticized field, where desire and its renunciation exist in intimate relation with each other, and where, given the perversity of the instincts, desire itself leads man toward a highly ascetic renunciation of the world and the flesh.

Now, such renunciation is alien to the mainstream of the Jewish religious tradition and still more alien to that of Yiddish literature. For I. L. Peretz, Mendele Mocher S'forim, and Sholem Aleichem the religious element is mainly a *given* framework of experience within which their characters move. The everyday, this-worldly emotions of Tevye the Dairyman, for example, are especially poignant in the context of his purehearted relationship with a transcendent but not essentially other-worldly deity. The point of Tevye's religiosity, such as it is, is his capacity to argue with God about the mundane conditions of his existence. Singer, on the other hand, not only moves toward ascetic resolutions, but far from depicting a simple pietism, invokes an esoteric strain of Cabalistic thought as the framework of his fiction. Jacob of Zamosc invokes the Cabalistic doctrine of *tzimtzum*, which posits a temporarily absconded deity to explain how evil got into the world, and he affirms sin and suffering as the only medium through which God can exercise his highest powers, those of love and mercy. By placing this Cabalistic dualism, raised to a higher synthesis, into Jacob's mouth, Singer uses the ideas involved as a goad and a prop to his own imagination. Affirmation is achieved in his novels only through a deep identification with the subversive agencies of sin and negation that lurk beneath the surface of the normal and the respectable. On the other hand, *The Family Moskat* — the most conventional of his novels — would seem to be the relative failure it is because it lacks the fantastic dialectic of good and evil to be found in the more stylized fables.

In fact, Singer come into his own only with his vision of the grotesque, often macabre world of the archaic *shtetl*. Within this world he makes no effort at strict historical verisimilitude, but rather reformulates that world to suit his own artistic needs. And within it, he makes Puckish identifications with the repressed energies of a ritual-bound folk culture that speaks directly to his own imagination. But he deals with impulses one suspects were indeed there, and he does so with authority and integrity — though in modes of stylization that confound his more traditional readers. This, of course, is the final irony of his relation to the official custodians of Yiddish culture in America. For if Singer deviates from the normal expectations of Yiddish *literature*, his achievement is nonetheless rooted in modes of thought, feeling, and speech native to an authentic folk *culture*. Approaching his work without prejudice, one is struck first of all by the power with which Singer, like no one else before him, animates a valid strain of the folk imagination.

To be sure, Singer revels excessively in the purely demonic. But at his best he taps with consummate mastery an unfamiliar stratum of his culture. His language itself is informed by a gusto that seems to draw its liveliness directly from the resources of the spoken tongue. The peculiar power of Singer's demonology and of the narrative form in which it is unfolded would seem to be rooted in the world from which it stems. One senses that the condition for its creation is a complex relationship between Singer's personal preoccupations and very real qualities of language and feeling in the world he represents. In this sense, Singer's style, like his subject matter, does not seem arbitrary. It is his unique creation, but it has the inevitability of all styles distilled from an actual tradition of speech.

This impression of stylistic and structural inevitability is furthermore reinforced by one of the strong historical determinations of his vision. Singer has survived a civilization all but annihilated in the Holocaust, and one feels that the dark vision of his fiction is the product of a deeply felt experience of all that was implied by that event. Singer rarely treats the Holocaust directly, and his work touches only obliquely upon the actualities of life in the Nazi period. *The Family Moskat,* to be sure, concludes with the bombing of Warsaw by the Nazis, and the sense of doom that pervades the novel would seem to arise in part from a fully contemporary sense of the implications of that event. But elsewhere Singer tends to turn away from the contemporary scene, to revel in the remote, the exotic, and the legendary. And yet, within the confines of seventeenth-century Goray or nineteenth-century Lublin, one glimpses the moral actualities of the twentieth-century world. It would seem that Singer's very personal sense of the psychically and erotically subversive is compounded by his sense of the horrors of recent history, and that he resorts to the familiar rhetoric of pogrom and persecution in order to represent a set of moral and psychological problems analogous to the modern ones.

That Singer is in touch with the vital experience of the age is suggested by the underlying affinity of his apparent dualism with that of other writers who have tried to come to grips with the Holocaust. André Schwarz-Bart places this event in the perspective of the legend of the thirty-six saints who redeem the world by the suffering they willingly undergo — a legend grounded in the notion of atonement and the perception of the scope of evil in the world. Schwarz-Bart's rendering is sentimental, but it arises from the need to vindicate the world in the face of suffering so great that only atonement within a transcendent scheme can make any sense of it. Singer is more oblique, but his obliquity is possibly more trenchant. Posing his problem at a great distance with a nearly inhuman detachment, he probes the frailty of the individual soul as well as of the historical reality. The domestic and parochial schemes are as problematical as the political and cosmic ones. Every man is open to assault from his neighbor, but also to incursions from his own impulses, which feed into the overreaching negativity of the world. Singer's world is as skewed as that of Yakov Lind, with the difference that Lind calls upon us to exercise our imagination of the particular horrors of the Nazi era, while Singer asks us to fall into a fabulous realm of betrayals and bedevilments wholly abstracted from the particulars of the times. What Singer's world contains that Lind's does not, is the explicit question of the meaning of it all, and a consciousness of an order within which affirmation is still conceivable.

Yet if Singer poses questions that are essentially contemporary, he nevertheless poses them in terms that are so abstract as to render all of his longer work extremely problematical. Singer works, for all his unconventionality, as a Jewish writer, within the framework of an essentially traditional theodicy. Without a real concrete interest in history, he resurrects doctrines and attitudes that belong to a dead world, and presents its solutions without comment or judgment, as though they have immediate relevance to him — and to ourselves. Yet he clearly does not believe them and he affirms them only sentimentally. Nor does he enter into the process through which these affirmations become humanly meaningful. At the same time, his highly stylized world, with its radical alternatives, does not point to other modes of thought or feeling, or other frames of moral or metaphysical reference, through which we could adapt them to our own circumstances and beliefs. As a result, his solutions — or rather, those of his protagonists — have a kind of archeological interest, as ways that men could once take in grappling with the problem of evil; and even so they are not psychologically credible. Such a process as he can represent is so abstract and so wholly formal that it suggests the *forms of* experience rather than its contents. Hence his world, though it does indeed reflect issues that we apprehend, and though it poses terms for formulating them, remains a more hypothetical construct.

This is the greatest difficulty of Singer's more ambitious fiction. And once this problem is so defined, other difficulties are soon to follow. His extreme polarization of fantasies and impulses, together with his extreme "inhuman" objectification of people and things, is troubling. His vision has power, and it has a certain integrality, but it is at its best only in short tales like "Gimpel the Fool," in which he plays out one term of a tension, and does so briefly. In the longer tales, in which a process rather than a condition must be rendered, the governing scheme of ideas tends to be too simple and the concepts too abstract to be convincing. Singer renders marvellously well a limited range of psychological states, and the shorthand in which he represents them is remarkable for its swiftness and its fidelity to the situations which give rise to them. It is the perfect instrument for parable, especially since, for him, psychological and intellectual processes are always meshed. The characters think as they feel, and reason even as they observe themselves and their worlds. But the limitation is striking, and while it makes for occasional perfection in the single parable, it is a great handicap for the writer who is trying to project a more comprehensive vision.

There are two signs of this limitation. One is the fact that the tales, and especially the longer tales, begin far better than they end. They are characterized by a rich animation of a static condition, so that characters are presented through the things and the thoughts that constitute their being for us. The nature scenes, which have a haunting beauty, are always woven into the experience of characters who are communing with nature or with the Being that inhabits it; the human and social scenes are done through a calm but vivacious enumeration of the things, acts, spirits, gestures and thoughts which fill them. But within such scenes people themselves seem only to have the quality of things. One would venture the notion that the very identification of evil with matter implied by the Cabalistic dualism entails for Singer a withdrawal of human energy from the material, social, and historical world. The human agent is overwhelmed within the "diabolical" material and instinctual reality just as Singer himself is virtually overwhelmed as a speaking, feeling, judging voice within the nightmarish atmosphere of his tales.

A second, related symptom, then, is the peculiar place of sexuality in the longer tales. Singer not only revels in the phenomena of sexuality, but tends to align the human will in general with the sexual will. His self-assertive characters are always seen in terms of some relation between their desire for omnipotence — their longing, like Yasha Mazur, to be "as God" — and the problematics of sexual potency. This is most clear in the figure of Yasha Mazur, the magician of Lublin, for whom the prideful wish to be as God exists in direct relation to the strength of his lust. At the novel's climax he submits in utter passivity to the omnipotent Deity, but his submission comes only after he — the arch magician and fabled fornicator — has failed as a man with the woman of his choice. But we are unable to grasp the meaningful process of this transformation, being afforded only the primitive pattern of regressive fear and anxious reversion, with no exploration of the further meaning and dimensions of the experience.

Hence, it is a rather circumscribed vision that Singer projects, one that palls as we encounter it in tale after tale. He feels much about love, and about the tenderness, violence, and treachery that figure in love. He apprehends the obstacles to a full realization of love and tenderness, and grasps with rare firmness the ways in which these obstacles are the work of human and cosmic spite. But his work, in the last analysis, is concerned with a dialectic of longing and spite rather than one of love and hate; the demons of perversity that inhabit his world do not touch or express the deeper dynamics of *eros* and *thanatos* that inform the world he sees and evokes. When one attempts to go beyond the longing and the spite, one moves onto a plane of abstraction, of quasi-philosophical transcendences that are grounded novelistically either in conceptions that bear little relation to the world of our experience, or that point back to a blatant, infantile longing for wholeness and unity.

The terrible abstractness and rootlessness in Singer's fiction would seem to account in part for the critical success he has enjoyed in America over the past decade. Since Joyce, at least, it has been held that the novel, in its classical, realistic forms, is dead or dying. While the novel seems peculiarly sturdy for a moribund genre, it certainly has lost the rootedness in immediate social and personal experience which was the strength of the form in the nineteenth century. More and more, modern fiction has rendered a receding world, a world in which social surfaces no longer reveal human depths, in which subjectivity tends to be divorced from the political and moral grounds of its existence. As our century has worn on, it has increasingly tended to conceive of the world of action as dead or demonic, as a world to which no life-giving relationship can be conceived. From the nineteenth century novel of manners and morals, the twentieth century novel has moved to the realm of physics and metaphysics to elaborate frames of reference that allow experience to be regarded from idiosyncratic and even solipsistic points of view. And, significantly, the novelistic interest has turned from long, elaborated actions set in a socially concrete "world" to more limited actions, exquisitely executed in lyric or symbolic modes, or to longer actions oriented to more abstract imaginative issues.

Singer satisfies just this kind of interest. His one "real" novel is a failure, and his shorter novels are really elaborate parables, not nearly so effective as the very short tales, which evoke a single, haunting, obsessive mood and reveal a single, simple insight or experience. His work, to be sure, is formulated in terms of the traditional questions of evil and justice, and it leans upon a stable frame of traditional folkways to contain its vision. Yet it is suffused with the prevailing contemporary sense of isolation, disintegration, alienation, and dread, and it provides a further spice of the exotic, on the one hand, and of transcendent solutions grounded (though ambiguously) in a primitive craving for love, on the other. Moreover, the sense of the inefficacy of the human will that pervades his work accords with the sense of human possibilities, or rather impossibilities, that has increasingly beleaguered us. And his erotic concerns sort well with our own public concern with the erotic. It is not surprising, therefore, that within American fiction, he has easily found a place with the masters of the Gothic and the macabre; those who admire him tend also to admire Carson MacCullers and William Faulkner, Tennessee Williams and William Styron — that is, the Southern writers who have rooted their vision of nightmare, loneliness, and death in the finely sifted actualities of a moribund "traditional" world. Add to this the readiness with which his work, like that of his indigenous counterparts, falls into the ready existentialist terms of discourse, and we have all the ingredients of acclaim.

Obviously, there is no necessary connection in literature between fashion and value. Singer is clearly a writer of value; what he achieves in some of the short tales is both rare and eloquent, and this will doubtless outlast the exaggerated admiration he has recently elicited. Yet one can only regret the wrenching of values that comes of thoughtless acclaim. Among other things, it makes for demands and gives rise to judgments not wholly relevant to a man's best work. Singer, as his recent memoirs suggest, is not a man to grapple heroically with his own experience; he is beset with vanities and sentimentalities that obviate final confrontations. What is most engaging in him is the gift of casting the imps of his own perversity in the mould of a tradition, which has had a meager literary existence outside his work, but which nonetheless binds him in the coils of its obsessions. That Singer can speak to a public beyond his natural one and outside his tradition is an outcome partly of his gifts, partly of Zeitgeist. But in the end, the qualities which ally him to certain trends in contemporary American fiction are far less interesting than those which align him with his own tradition.

Singer is a very different sort of writer from S. Y. Agnon, and his moral and human commitments are widely different from his. Yet, as writers in the decline of a culture with the knack of catching characteristic strains of feeling within that culture, they are linked by striking affinities. Both of them, the one in Hebrew, the other in Yiddish, carry to an extreme a variety of tendencies implicit in the self-directed literature of modern Jewry. Both of them lack real interest in the conduct of common life; neither has any concern with the nuances of character in and for themselves. Both of them, moreover, have the trick of cutting themselves loose from the moorings of the everyday world, within which character is ordinarily forged and honed, and of clinging valiantly to the finely spun, silken thread of fantasy, letting it carry them into realms of experience that often elude the more reality-bound literatures of the West. Both of them do so within modes of feeling felt to be generic in their community; even at a great distance from the everyday, they catch the immediate strains of discord within it. In both, moreover, there is an underlying craving for harmony, for conciliation of all discords under remembered modes of religious feelings.

Agnon, to be sure, confronts the impossibility of resurrecting such modes in the modern world; his late work is an elaborate consideration of the problems attendant upon the wish to restore them or return to them, and is replete with elaborate irony that cuts two ways: against the dreamer and against the dissonant experience that drives him back to the dream. Singer never attempts such a confrontation. He is less self-conscious, almost primitive by comparison, and realizes himself artistically only in an untrammeled indulgence in a certain kind of fantasy. His strength, in fact, lies in a remarkable immediacy, in the sense conveyed of his being *there,* in the work, lustily enjoying the perversity that beleaguers his "world," even while seeking to transcend it. His trouble lies in the falsification, in the novels, of the way to transcendence and reconciliation — a falsification which fortunately fails.

What is interesting in the juxtaposition, however, is not the difference, but the affinity between these two writers. The qualities of feeling and stylization — or fantastication — that they share seem characteristic of a moment in the history of their civilization. They have a further interest owing to the way they have highlighted the continuation of those qualities in some of the Jewish practitioners of fiction in America today — in Malamud and Bellow, at the highest level, and in Friedman and Roth many notches below them. What people speak of today as "American Jewish" writing has startling affinities with Agnon and Singer; certain stories by Malamud might seem, on first sight, to be the work of either. And the affinity is the more intriguing because it is clearly not the product of imitation. It would seem to have been transmitted through obscure cultural channels that lend themselves to some definition in relation to these two last major representatives of the East European Jewish literary tradition.

Max F. Schulz

9.

Isaac Bashevis Singer,
Radical Sophistication,
and the Jewish-American Novel

I wish in this paper to offer a generalization about the
current Jewish-American novel, using as my major illustration the admittedly special case of Isaac Bashevis Singer.
The arbitrariness of this procedure, since Singer would appear to occupy a peripheral position in relation to the
American novel, will, I hope, become less objectionable as
I go along. Because he is imbued with old-world Jewish
habits of thought more thoroughly than his American
counterparts, while also continuing undeniably to be a
new-world Jew, the radical sophistication of his creative
imagination lends itself uniquely to the attempt to isolate
the sources, and to define the achievement, of contemporary Jewish-American fiction.

Singer's is a twentieth-century sensibility attempting
an imaginative recreation of the social and religious milieu
of Polish Jewry of the previous three centuries. The unique
— and now vanished — circumstances of this society confront Singer's historical consciousness with special irrefraga-

bility. Tolstoy could revert in *War and Peace* to the time
of the Napoleonic invasions without risking intellectual
dislocation, for his society still assented essentially to the
assumptions of his grandfather. Tension of a profound philosophical order, however, affects the moral pattern of
Singer's stories as a result of the radically different *Zeit-
geists* of the author and his dramatis personae. One of the
central paradoxes of Singer's fictional world is that even as
he pays loving tribute to the value system of a back-country
Jewry, dirty, ignorant, but firm in a simplistic faith in what
Dr. Yaretsky in "The Shadow of a Crib" calls "a seeing universe, rather than a blind one," Singer questions such a
world picture with the narrative structures he composes for
them. His rabbis and pious matrons may think and act in
unquestioning accord with a Jewish cosmic vision but their
lives present the absurd pattern familiar to the modern
sensibility. It is not without significance that in at least
three of Singer's novels the historical setting is that of a
catastrophe wrought upon the Jews by external circumstances, and that his protagonists are caught beween rival
claims of the Jewish and non-Jewish worlds. As in a Greek
tragedy impersonal fate and individual responsibility
merge ambiguously in his stories.

The symbolic overtones implied in the title *The Slave*
underscore this ambiguity. Jacob is carried off into slavery
in the aftermath of the Chmielnicki pogroms of the second
half of the seventeenth century. Yet even as he struggles,
in captivity among the Polish peasants to whom he is sold,
to retain his Yiddish tongue, to observe his religion, and in
effect to recreate the Law, he falls in love with Wanda, the
daughter of his master. Rescued after many years by elders
of his village he is driven by his love to return furtively for
Wanda, and against the laws of both the Jews and the Poles
to introduce her into the *shtetl* as a true daughter of Israel.
Thus Jacob is enslaved by man, society, religious law, spiritual fervor, human desires, and earthly passions. Who can
discriminate between Jacob the individual who is person-

ally accountable for his actions, and Jacob the victim who is determined by historical, social, and biological forces? Between the Jacob who observes the historic role of the Jews by bringing Wanda to God and who fulfills in his life the return to Palestine, and the Jacob who is profoundly alienated from village and synagogue because of these deeds?

Similarly, the enlightened and richly human integration of Yasha Mazur, *The Magician of Lublin,* into the freethinking, mobile habitat of Warsaw contrasts inexplicably with the escalation of his conscience, the lapse of his skill at lockpicking and gymnastics, and the reversion of his beliefs to the Jewish faith of his forefathers. Three underlying patterns of theme and image provide an ironic commentary on the narrative of Yasha's progress from Pole to Jew. (1) The higher Yasha soars as profane tumbler the deeper he plunges as sinful man into "the bottomless pit." Only after his body has fallen from the balcony of the house he has tried to rob — his ankle sprained and subsequent flight arrested — can his soul begin to levitate. The controlling metaphor here is that of Icarus, with Yasha's rise and fall treated dualistically as both grace and damnation. (2) The more freely he roams from mistress to mistress the more he feels his body to be imprisoned within Poland and his soul within the embraces of women. Only after he quits both roaming and whoring can he hope to be free. Here, the controlling metaphor is that of a prison and of a spider spinning its web to entrap. (3) The more he dissembles the more he is threatened by disclosure. Only when he renounces deception of his loved ones can he dare to be honest and open with all men. Here, the controlling metaphor is that of a magician or master dissembler. All three patterns underwrite the change in Yasha as one of religious casuistry. Despite the skill with which they are used, however, Singer is too responsible an artist and too economical a storyteller to indulge in such hackneyed paradigms humorlessly. They reflect rather the skeptical half of his response to his story, supplying us with an ironic measure of Yasha's transformation into a saintly person celebrated (as Emilia's letter is meant to corroborate) all over Catholic Poland. Yasha may have turned his back on his former amoral circus life for the Jewish religious ethos of the *shtetl* but the mode and consequence of his gesture hardly reassure us of its efficacy. His un-Jewish, antisocial adoption of the monastic ideal, walling himself off from the world as a way of serving both God and society, gives no greater moral illumination or meaningful pattern to his life than had his previous consorting with the thieves of Piask and his roaming of Poland as a performer. The temptations from within and from without of evil talk, slander, wrath, and false flattery in the form of supplicants who look upon him as a holy man, continue to assail him and to interrupt his meditations. He remains in body and spirit earthbound, imprisoned, reserved and secretive; radically alienated from his pious wife and friends, his former associates, and the *shtetl* community; a sainted man holding daily audience to "entertain" the people as the magician in him had done in happier days.

Singer is seriously concerned with the complicated moral and ethical relationships of man to his God and to his society — with the degree to which human conduct describes a moral pattern affecting that of the community and with the extent to which man's actions lurch in pointless arabesques to the indifferent push and pull of historical and psychobiological forces. In *The Family Moskat,* for example, Asa Heshel Bannett and the Warsaw Jews are portrayed as bringing about their own dissolution. Reb Meshulam at the age of eighty lecherously marries for the third time, introducing into the Chassidic community a Galician widow with modernized Western habits. With devastating vividness the deterioration of the old pious solidarity of the Warsaw ghetto is depicted in the drunken cynicism, lust, and avarice of the Channukah Ball, an auspicious place for Asa Heshel, ex-Yeshiva student, to meet his next mistress, the atheistic communist Barbara. "More sex and fewer children. The bedroom is the key to all social and individual problems," he tells Barbara. And in its marriage of Spinoza and Malthus, and its aimless, fruitless wanderings, his life passes moral judgment on himself and the Warsaw Jews as a society bent on self-destruction. In the concluding scene of the book he waits resignedly for the Nazi to fulfill his wish to die. He refuses to accompany Barbara, who elects to "keep on fighting for a while," and stands with Hertz Yanovar, religious scholar turned table-tipping occultist, the two quoting to each other in Polish rather than Hebrew, the "real truth" of the Bible that "Death is the Messiah." Yet the advent of the Nazi is a jarring note, for in no moral or historical sense can the Warsaw Jews be held responsible for the Second World War and the Nazi pogrom. The same can be said of the historical phenomenon of the Enlightenment, which claims as victims Asa Heshel, sundry members of the Meshulam family, and Eastern European Jewry in general, diverting them from the paths of righteousness and tradition into the dead end of alienated self-seeking. And there is a sense in which the many chance turns that Asa Heshel's life has taken — for example, his introduction to the libertine Abram Shapiro at the Chassidic synagogue where he had gone fresh from a country *shtetl* for guidance in attending a university — make him as much a victim of cosmic irony as any of Hardy's characters. This positivist rendering of Asa Heshel's comings and goings on earth denies the contrary structure of meaning in the novel, that is, that there was a moral pattern to his life. With the insistence that there was possibly no coherent relation between him and the world, his life is robbed of moral significance, its events reduced to incoherent moments of sensation.

Clearly, Singer does not find it easy to fix the blame for personal catastrophe, as an older Judaic dispensation would have — and as Reb Abraham Hirsh, in I. J. Singer's *The Brothers Askenazi*, does, when he is replaced as gen-

eral agent of the Huntze factory by his son Simcha Meyer,
consoling himself with the words of King Solomon, "there
is a time to plant and a time to pluck up that which is
planted, a time to build up and a time to break down."
"Nothing happens," he sighs, "without the will of God, not
even the breaking of a little finger." No such easy comfort
is available to Isaac Bashevis Singer, despite the tender sympathy that he on occasion expresses for unaffected Jewish
ritual and piety, as in the Jewish Cotter's Saturday-Night
story, "Short Friday." But even in this story there is the
inexplicable twist of fate, which prompts the pious couple
to copulate following the Sabbath meal and then lets them
suffocate in their sleep because of a defective stove. I suspect that it is this divorce of his religious sensibility from
precise religious beliefs, this drift of his thought away from
the ethical certainties of the Judaic Law, that allows Americans to read Singer with an understanding and sympathy
unavailable to the Hebrew writer S. Y. Agnon and to such
Yiddish writers as Sholem Aleichem and I. L. Peretz. Such
stories as "A Tale of Two Liars," "The Destruction of
Kreshev," "Skiddah and Kuziba," and "The Shadow of a
Crib" dramatize the ambiguous hold on Singer's mind of
belief and skepticism. His use of an Arch-Devil narrator
simultaneously demonstrates the notion of a seeing will,
purpose, and plan in the everyday affairs of the *shtetl,*
while underscoring the capriciousness of the forces man-
ipulating human actions. At other times, in even more explicit fashion, Singer often parallels, as in "The Black
Wedding" and in some of the stories just mentioned, a
pious account of the protagonist's actions with a psychological or naturalistic explanation which denies the moral
cohesion of that world. In the story "Cunegunde," for example, he explains the strange noctural torments of abused,
demented Cunegunde in her hovel from the viewpoint of
her demon-obsessed mind and from that of naturalistic
fact: "At night imps came to her bed, mocking her, wetting
her sheet, calling her names, poking and biting her, braid-

ing her hair. Mice dung and vermin remained after they had gone." The danger in this strategy is real, for the coherence of Singer's fictional world depends on his maintaining a perilous tension between irreconcilables. If he relaxes an instant, his story is threatened with fragmentation. The endings of *The Slave* and *The Magician of Lublin* are painful instances of such falls into disunity. Miraculously to transform Wanda the Polish peasant into a Jewish Sarah and Jacob into a righteous man, or to metamorphose Yasha Mazur from circus prestidigitator to holy *Zaddik*, is to sentimentalize their lives under the intolerable pressure to give some kind of meaningful construct to them.

Singer's mind seems to rejoice in dichotomies. In his autobiographical account of his boyhood he refers to his home as a "stronghold of Jewish puritanism, where the body was looked upon as a mere appendage to the soul." One day, he tells us, while visiting his older brother's atelier, he discovered the artist's healthy respect for the flesh. "This was quite a change from my father's court," he remarks, "but it seems to me that this pattern has become inherent to me. Even in my stories it is just one step from the study house to sexuality and back again. Both phases of human existence have continued to interest me." The ambivalence of this intellectual position is pervasive in much that Singer writes. Like the tightrope walker Yasha Mazur, he balances between contrary modes of thought, his *modus operandi* at once archaic and modern, preoccupied with angels and demons and with Freud and Spinoza. He is drawn to the simple piety of his ancestors who never doubted the moral importance of life. He is also a man of the twentieth century, an uprooted European transplanted to America, seized by the contemporary vision of an absurd world — and his artistic integrity will not let the comfortable climate of divine reward and punishment remain intact. In the tension between moral cause and effect which his divided mind creates, his protagonists act out the unwitting drama of their lives. That these stories do not fragment into their unresolved elements attests to the remarkable narrative skill of Singer. That Singer has persisted despite the absence of an answer in posing again and again the question of the moral meaning of human experience attests to the radical sophistication of his vision.

It is fashionable these days to see the Jew as the perfect symbol of the Camusian man. Although not as viable a fact in the fifties and sixties as in earlier periods, the Jew's lot of perpetual exile is a convenient symbol of alienation and hence of what one segment of contemporary thought conceives of as the essential consciousness of being man. Yet only in a highly qualified sense can what I have called the radical sophistication of Singer's vision be considered existential. As a Jew he appeals, however hesitantly, to a construct of beliefs that makes sense of the human experience. Nor does he, like the Christian, reject earth because of the expulsion from paradise. The Jew has historically been God-intoxicated and man-centered. His relationship with the world reveals itself simultaneously as *eros* and as *agapé*. " 'Mazeltov,' " Shifrah Tammar greets her daughter the morning after her wedding in Singer's "The Destruction of Kreshev"; " 'You are now a woman and share with us all the curse of Eve.' And weeping, she threw her arms about Lise's neck and kissed her." Like the holy men of Chassidism bent on the hallowing of each day, she acknowledges the edict that love of man is a prerequisite to adoration of Jehovah. In short, the Jew does not pursue the Christian pilgrimage from this world to the next, but performs the miracle of merger of the other world with this one.

During more than two thousand years of Diaspora the Jews have learned to breathe amidst the incertitude that is the daily air of a persecuted minority. A tenuous equipoise of irreconcilables is the best they could hope for, and it pervades their world picture. One could hardly expect otherwise with a people who have persisted for several milleniums in the belief that they are chosen, with a divine mission, when the contrary has been the fact of their daily lives. Out of this knowledge has grown a philosophy — anchored at one end by the teachings of Isaiah and at the other by the realities of this century — which conceives of the Jew as redeemer of the world through his acceptance of God's servitude. But the encumbrance of evil — even when put to the service of God — is an uncertain business, never quite relieving the mind of inquietude. Christianity has stumbled over this legacy of sin since its inception. The Age of Enlightenment could only palely affirm with Alexander Pope that "Whatever is, is right," "All partial evil, universal good." Among Western men the Jew has accepted most completely the ambience of this mixed blessing, this gift of the gods to man. The wisdom of the Jew's tragic passiveness is underscored by Singer in stories of what happens to a town when its people covenant with the Arch-Fiend in the interests of God, e.g., in "The Destruction of Kreshev" and *Satan in Goray*. Grounded in the harsh realities of this life, the Jew retains unshakable conviction of man's spiritual destiny.

This capacity for belief in the face of "uncertainties, mysteries, doubts" is a radical sophistication that the Jew, with a culture historically of long standing, is currently giving to a century convinced in its existentialist isolation of the incoherence of existence. Today's intellectual, like the Coleridge whom Keats characterized as "incapable of remaining content with half-knowledge," clutches at any "fine isolated verisimilitude caught from the Penetralium of mystery." To him the contemporary Jewish novel has much to say. It is a commonplace among Jews that Judaism is not in the habit of disowning its great heretics completely. Rather it accommodates with worldly wisdom what is worthwhile in Spinoza, Maimonides, Freud, and Kafka. This willingness to accept the world on its own terms — disorderly, incoherent, absurd — "without any irritable reaching after fact and reason" and yet without losing faith in the moral significance of human actions underlies the confrontation of experience in the best of the contemporary Jewish-American novels.

The radical sophistication that I refer to here should not be confused with the open-ended artifact as defined by Robert M. Adams in *Strains of Discord: Studies in Literary Openness* or by Alan Friedman in *The Turn of the Novel.* In one sense, Mailer's, Malamud's, Bellow's, and Salinger's novels conform to the unresolved pattern of assertions that Adams has in mind. That is, their ambiguous endings raise unanswered questions. Do O'Shaugnessy and Rojack make good their rebellious impulse toward existential individuality or do they merely escape the conformity of mass society by fleeing it? Are Hobbs, Alpine, Levin, and Bok triumphant as Grail fertility heroes or badly compromised as human beings? Do Henderson and Herzog achieve loving integration with their fellow man or do they continue as subtle instances of social and intellectual disinheritance? Is Seymour a modern saint or isn't he? Unlike the open-ended fictional creations discussed by Adams, however, these characters do not have a weak sense of life as pattern. On the contrary they reflect their authors' convictions about the moral significance of man's actions. Nevertheless, a sense of fractured and divided consciousness paradoxically occurs because these writers are formulating human experience into patterns of conduct at an historical moment when disorder, opposition, and the absurdity of existence have acquired philosophical respectability. It is not then the fictional character — who may inhabit an earlier century of faith as in Singer's stories — but the author who knows with a sophistication radical in its simplism that faith and skepticism comprise less an either/or equation than complementary additions to an indefinite whole. Hence the inconclusiveness of these novels as structures of meaning, despite the motive and direction of the protagonist. A difference in openness of a like sort also marks these novels when they are compared to the experiential openness that Friedman explores. Although their conclusions do not conform to the conventional novel's "tapering experience" but instead, like the novels that Friedman examines, end on a new beginning or continuing ethical experience, the openness of this new moral action — unlike the expansive undefined experience which Friedman contemplates — *has been shaped* and we are led to believe *will continue to be shaped* by a moral attitude or standard. The paradox here is that whereas the moral inner direction of the protagonist is known, his future experience remains uncertain because he is part of a larger modality of experience, encompassing contradictory concepts with which he is not fully in rapport. The protagonist may have realized a moral stance through his previous confrontation with the existent ethics of society, yet he continues to resist containment by that society. Thus, in spite of his moral growth having reached thematic climax, his experiential rapport with society remains open ended. Hence, Friedman is not wholly accurate when he interprets the "flux of experience" in a Bellow novel as being brought to a "balanced irresolution." This may accurately enough describe the sensibility of Bellow but does not do justice to the moral and intellectual resolution with which the Bellow hero comes to terms with his world. Neither Moses Herzog nor Tommy Wilhelm is "poised at the end between two (or three) worlds," as are the irresolute equilibrists of John Crowe Ransom's poem. Each accepts the fundamental prerogative of his heart, even though recognizing its obsolescence in a society managed according to the materialistic and ratiocinative assumptions of mass science. Hence the relationship between him and society is not static but open to future modification or expansion — and just to that extent is he "poised . . . between . . . worlds" of knowing. As embodiment of a sophistication radical in its illusion, he (and the protagonists of Mailer, Malamud, Wallant, and Salinger) are portrayed as inhabiting like Tennyson's Ulysses a limitless world of open-ended happenings devoid of causality, where yet their every action has moral significance.

The Jew seeks to make everything systematic, logical, sensible, subject to law. So Samuel Talmon rails at his relatives and in-laws in Dan Jacobson's novel *The Beginners*. "When you believed in God, he was a God of laws," he adds. "What is Judaism if not a system of laws, of rules how to live, from one day to the next — even from one meal to the next, if you please? And what do you call Moses, why was he the greatest Jew who ever lived? Because he was Moses the Lawgiver. And you try to carry on in the same spirit now, even though you're modern people and don't believe in God any more. So you try to live by other laws: you still look for reasonable arrangements, orderly developments, clear understandings, settled, sensible ways of living." The radical sophistication of the Jew, then, like most of the great constructs of Western thought, is inherently dualistic. The patterns that this attitude takes in the novels of the contemporary Jewish-American writers vary, but most can be reduced to an antinomy which presumes some form of socioreligious determinism, while insisting upon the existential will of the individual. The dilemma — which appears to have become almost a Jewish problem, particularly for the American Jew since the end of the Second World War — is defined by Lionel Trilling in *The Middle of the Journey*. "How much the idea of personal responsibility had been shaken by modern social science," Laskell muses. "Educated people more and more accounted for human action by the influence of environment and the necessities and habits imposed by society. Yet innocence and guilt were more earnestly spoken of than ever before." Thus Malamud may involve his protagonist simultaneously in a mythic and a private quest. Salinger may portray the Glass progeny as hoisted on the petard of their own Zen ideals, by contradictory psychological determinants. Mailer may urge his hero to seek the American dream of illimitable power through sexual release. Wallant may define full spiritual growth of the individual in terms of *caritas*. Fiedler may dance his minority American through a *pas de deux* of cultural betrayal. Bellow may torture his protagonist in a lonely war of mind and heart. Still, these ambivalences are all reducible to the conflict between human autonomy and divine purpose, and its corollary conflict between personal desires and communal needs.

That this version of human experience should suddenly dominate the American literary scene is, of course, one of those cultural mysteries, like the creative outbursts of the Elizabethans and the Romantics, which defies ultimate comprehension. Yet there is discernible a convergence of literary and historical forces that makes the contemporary Jewish-American novel a logical heir of the central tradition of the American novel. This tradition, Richard Chase has defined in part, in *The American Novel and Its Tradition*, as the discovery of "putative unity *in* disunity" or willingness "to rest at last among irreconcilables." The Jewish imagination similarly has been stirred by the aesthetic possibilities of a radical sophistication, which simultaneously entertains contrary intellectual systems: the secular view of man alienated in an absurd universe and the religious view of man enthroned by divine fiat in God's earthly kingdom. A corollary factor is the historical parallel between the American frontier and the European *shtetl*. Both environments raised similar questions about individual rights. The American experience continues to grapple with a political and social system, defined by the tension between private freedom and public restriction. Marius Bewley, in *The Eccentric Design*, has brilliantly shown that the conflict over the rights and the powers of the one and the many has been a persistent preoccupation of American thought. The American dream of a freely roving Adamic man was disrupted by the reality of legal restraint almost as soon as the first Puritans put foot ashore on the new land, long before Natty Bumppo clashed wills with Marmaduke Temple. Old-world Judaism, in an effort to submerge the individual in the social whole, for internal purposes of psychic and spiritual continuity as much as because of external forces beyond its control, has wrestled with the obverse side of this problem. Seemingly living always as a minority in one Pale or another, threatened perpetually by extinction from without and from within, the Jew developed in survival a strong identification of personal observation of the Law with continuation of the community. An individual in the sight of God, he was also a member of an embattled group. His actions affected not only his salvation but also the group's survival. Thus in Singer's stories the *shtetl* defines a moral and ethical principle as much as a physical place and social entity. Both frontier and *shtetl* versions of human aspiration meet in the Jewish-American novel of the past two decades, deepened and universalized by accommodation with the religioscientific antinomies of old-world Judaism and of new-world skepticism.

Note

1 A somewhat different version of this essay appeared in *Southern Humanities Review.*

Karl Malkoff

10.

Demonology and Dualism: The Supernatural in Isaac Singer and Muriel Spark

Linked to distinct religious traditions and possessed of sharply contrasting literary temperaments, Isaac Singer and Muriel Spark occupy common ground in their dealings with the supernatural. This commerce with unseen worlds does not in either writer proceed from a consciousness of man's solid relation to a divine hierarchy, but rather from its absence; in fact, in their works, the miraculous is at best on the fringe of orthodox theology, and sometimes completely independent of it. God is seen through a glass darkly, if — for his existence is never conclusively demonstrated — at all. And so, for Singer, Jewish, and Spark, Catholic convert, the light of the supernatural is used chiefly to transfigure the commonplace. Like the seventeenth-century cosmogonist Thomas Burnet, they contemplate the demonic "lest the intellect, habituated to the petty things of daily life, narrow itself and sink wholly into

trivial thoughts." That Singer or Spark may literally believe in the supernatural is irrelevant; suspending belief,
they seek appropriate literary symbols with which to communicate their visions of the human condition. It is not in
the least surprising that they emphasize the irrational and
the primitive; with Dostoevsky's Underground Man,
Singer and Spark refuse to concede that human behavior is
entirely accessible to reason, that logic provides either a
basis for moral choice or a way of understanding the
universe.

For Singer, the sources of the irrational are usually to
be found within the deep recesses of the mind. Possession
by devils and dybbuks, crucial to much of his fiction, depicts the perverseness in man's nature that leads him insistently to destruction. The Babas and Dziads that inhabit
the Polish countryside in *The Slave* embody the pagan's
sense of intimate relation to the natural world. But although it is possible to justify Singer's demons psychologically, there is no need to do so.[1] Explaining sexual hysteria in demonic terms is inefficient in curing illness; but it
is a powerful and direct expression of the moral crisis induced by the parts of the self beyond conscious control.
Rituals designed to dispose of the Baba will not save crops;
but they do formalize views of the vitality of all being, even
the inanimate world.

The irrational in Miss Spark's novels is generally more
closely associated with man's existential predicament.[2] In
Momento Mori, for example, a group of elderly folk receive mysterious telephone calls reminding them that they
must die. The caller, or callers — the voice seems to change
according to the recipient — is never identified, but two of
the most level-headed characters in the novel think it is
Death itself. Meaningless when intellectualized, death,
honestly confronted, leads to a fuller commitment to life.
By dramatizing death's presence rather than simply talking
about it, Spark avoids the rationalist trap of pigeonholing
death instead of encountering it with one's total being.

It should not be supposed that Spark ignores the irrational within (indeed, Freudian allegory is of the greatest importance in *Robinson* and *The Mandelbaum Gate*[3]) , or that Singer is unaware of the absurdity of the human condition (as, for example, in the nihilistic conclusion of *The Family Moskat*) . But the direction of emphasis in the work of each is reflected by their use of the supernatural, which, as I have suggested, is not indiscriminate, but restricted to the illustration of a special bias. It is also reflected in the writers' techniques, the forms by which they convey their ghostly visions.

Miss Spark, viewing man's relation to the universe with a measure of detachment, writes with wit and sophistication. Her sensibility leads her to withhold judgment on the apparently supernatural events in her novels, which abound in unresolved problems:[4] whether the voices in *The Comforters* that seem to be dictating a novel in which Caroline Rose is a character are Caroline's hallucination or evidence of a "higher novelist"; the identity of the caller in *Momento Mori;* whether the bumps on Dougal Douglas' head in *The Ballad of Peckham Rye* are indeed vestiges of diabolical horns; whether *The Bachelors'* Patrick Seton, a fraud in his worldly life, is a legitimate medium. In each case, the bulk of evidence supports a supernatural interpretation that is never confirmed. To insist on the supernatural would suggest taking it more seriously than Miss Spark, in the witty context of her work, is prepared to do; that would emphasize the apparatus by which vision is achieved at the expense of the vision itself. On the other hand, altogether to deny the possibility of the supernatural would give the world back to the logicians, to deprive it of final mystery.

Singer takes what seems to be an opposite tack in his treatment of the demonic. Artfully naïve, he enters the world of the folk tale, in which the supernatural is very much part of the texture of reality. In short fiction such as "The Mirror" and "The Last Demon," demons not only definitely exist, they are the stories' narrators; in *Satan in Goray*, the presence of evil spirits, impregnation by Satan, and possession by a dybbuk are essential to the novel; telepathic communication and messages from the grave motivate Jacob in *The Slave*, and the former phenomenon is important to *The Magician of Lublin* as well.[5] This magical world, usually associated with child or primitive, is indeed far removed from Spark's more "civilized" detachment. Where Spark's constructs require largely intellectual apprehension, Singer appeals to man's inherent, if often repressed, sense of awe at the powerful forces influencing his life. However, the final goals of these approaches are similar. What both Singer and Spark seek is a shift in perspective violent enough to force a reexamination of the human condition; although they seem opposites, uncritical naïveté and witty sophistication provide equally detached points of view from which to attack the rigid, logically consistent systems that traditionally have been used to evaluate experience.

The supernatural in Singer and Spark, then, is used to represent the irrationality of man's fate, to symbolize his moral dilemmas; however, the unseen world has ontological and epistemological implication that may in fact provide the basis for psychological and moral perception. For both authors, the dichotomy of natural and supernatural is simply one manifestation of a fundamental split in the nature of reality. The great chain of being ripped in two by this at least apparent duality, matter is cut off from spirit, man from God; conscious and unconscious are at odds with each other, mind with body, good with evil. In the novel of Singer and Spark, two broad areas of difficulty crystalize: first, as we have already seen, the conflict of warring opposites, be they psychological or moral; second, the problem of knowing, of understanding one world in terms of another, in short, of faith.

In the responses of Spark and Singer to this fragmented universe the differing emphases in their work may well originate. Spark usually declares for "unity of being"; if her characters are not always able to achieve this unity, they can at least be said to recognize it as a good.[6] Singer, however, responds to schism with ambivalence, or at least ambiguity. Warning frequently against the dangers of polarizing experience and rejecting part, he is nonetheless clearly fascinated by the possibilities of dualism and often convincingly demonstrates the position he attacks. It is sometimes possible to say that Singer decries a dualism of flesh and spirit, but accepts, with an awareness of its pitfalls, one of good and evil; but even this qualification does not consistently describe the world of his novels. If *Satan in Goray*, *The Slave*, and the more "realistic" *The Family Moskat* and *The Manor* seem to reject commitment to an extreme, *The Magician of Lublin's* Yasha, after a life of worldly desire, renounces the world completely by walling himself into a small doorless house, without any internal evidence of irony on the part of the author.

Possibly, Miss Spark's intuition that duality of being is illusory leads to her ironic mode, in which human perception is transfigured by a broader perspective, while Singer's inner conviction that existence is defined by the tension of conflicting universals results in mythopoeia. But this is as far as generalization can take us. To understand without oversimplifying the crucial distinctions that emerge from these similar preoccupations, it is necessary to examine the works thmeselves, a task facilitated by some remarkable coincidences of theme and structure in two sets of novels by Singer and Spark: I am speaking of *Satan in Goray* and *The Ballad of Peckham Rye,* and *The Slave* and *The Bachelors.*

The resemblances between the first pair are especially striking. Both novels concern the intrusion of a diabolical visitor — or visitors — on closely knit communities; in each case the mysterious strangers bring news of a "new morality" that destroys many of those who come in contact with it; and in each the communal bias of the narration views the fate of the individual in a distinctly social context.

Singer's novel is set in the village of Goray in seventeenth-century Poland. Barely in the past looms Chmielnicki's brutal massacre of Polish Jewry, leaving in its wake a sense of apocalyptic expectancy. Symbolically, the unity of being, embodied in the uneasy Jewish-Gentile relationship, has broken down, creating a world in which, to use Yeats's phrase, "the center cannot hold." Europe is alive with rumor: the Messiah has come. In the person of Sabbatai Zevi he will lead the exiled Jewish people to the land of Israel. Even Goray is aware of the imminence of some awful event. And to this village come a series of "legates," who give more precise form to the rumors, culminating in Reb Itche Mates, the packman, and Reb Gedaliya, the ritual slaughterer. These last two, proclaiming the sect of Sabbattai Zevi, successively marry the orphan Rechele. Hysterically paralyzed in one leg and subject to mysterious ills (and possibly possession by several varieties of demons) as a result of an adolescence spent in terror with her uncle, still another ritual slaughterer, she is an appropriate apex for this triangle of fanaticism.

Rechele is first wed by Reb Itche Mates. A cabalist and an ascetic, he utterly rejects the sensuous, indulging himself in what has apparently been a continuing orgy of fasting, self-denial, and mortification of the flesh:

> All day he sat swaying over the appendix to the Zohar, and working out numerical combinations of the names of Yaweh. At night, when everyone else was asleep, he ... went to the bath house. ... The scorched stones lay cold and scattered near the oven. Reb Itche Mates took off his clothes. His body was covered with a heavy growth of yellow hair. It was scarred by the thorns and thistles on which he had mortified himself. ... Two and seventy times did he immerse himself, according to the numerical signification of the letters Agin and Beth.[7]

Because of these very excesses, Reb Itche Mates, tangible evidence of the approaching messianic climax, is held in the greatest esteem; but when, after marriage, a mystified Rechele remains a virgin, the resulting gossip begins the fall, and replacement, of Itche Mates. His dualism itself has twofold implications. Most obviously, rejecting the flesh and committing himself thoroughly to the spirit, he ceases to function effectively in this world; and, similarly, by devoting himself to the mysterious and mystical teachings of the Cabala, and neglecting the orthodoxy of the Law, Itche Mates repudiates the morality of the here and now. He is in fact a prototype of what the town of Goray itself will become. Accepting the impending advent of the Messiah as fact, the villagers abandon as pointless their quotidien obligations. The single most powerful voice of reason, Rabbi Benish, departs half way through the novel, in part rejected by his congregation, but also forsaking them. Opposed to the study of hidden or potential worlds, seeking strength in the clarity of the Law, this solid, moderate leader of the community deserts Goray just before Itche Mates' wedding; the town has given itself over to the world to come at the expense of the present.

Coincidental with Itche Mates' later decline is the rise of Reb Gedaliya. Like Itche Mates a cabalist, Gedaliya is in most other respects his complete opposite. Corpulent rather than emaciated, a ritual slaughterer instead of a vegetarian, Reb Gedaliya is totally devoted to the pleasures of the flesh. While Itche Mates emphasized the coming of the Messiah as the conversion of body to pure spirit, Gedaliya prefers to insist on the necessity of immersing oneself in sensuality, of giving onself over to absolute evil in order to attain the supreme good.

Furthermore, the prophet Isaiah had foretold this. "And he shall be reckoned with the sinners." According to those who supported this interpretation, the generation before redemption had to become completely guilty; consequently, they went to great lengths to commit every possible offense. They were secretly adulterous, ate the flesh of the pig and other unclean foods, and performed those labors expressly forbidden on the Sabbath as most to be avoided (p. 134).

The orgy of denial has been succeeded by an orgy of indulgence; all perverse desires are given free reign.

Told with the simplicity of a folk tale, the power of *Satan in Goray,* and of a good deal of folk material, can probably be traced to correspondences between microcosm and macrocosm. On the ground of Goray opposing forces fight for man's soul; the fate of the village parallels the fate of the individual. There is first, after Rabbi Benish's flight, the conflict between Reb Itche Mates' asceticism and Reb Gedaliya's sensuality. And finally, when the rumor arrives that Sabbatai Zevi must, to save his life, become a Mohammedan, the frantic struggle between the Faithful and the disillusioned. Rechele, whom we have already located at the center of this upheaval, is of special interest: it is through her that Singer reveals the mechanics of Satan's triumph. Her susceptibility established in the years spent at her uncle's, Rechele is exposed first to the extreme embodied by Reb Itche Mates. It is important to recognize that without this first marriage, she could not have fallen under the influence of Gedaliya, for Rechele is driven by her "spiritual" husband to the hysteria of prophecy, and only then is she noticed and desired by the newly arrived slaughterer (the second butcher in her life). When Gedaliya imposes his will upon her, when she is induced obscenely to violate the Law, she is impregnated by Satan and possessed of a dybbuk.

However great the temptation to substitute the terms of modern psychology as we read of Rechele's disintegration, it should remain clear that Singer is at least as concerned with moral or religious hysteria as he is with sexual hysteria; that is, the physical self-indulgence preached by

Gedaliya and acquiesced to by Rechele is the equivalent of Goray's fanatical disregard of the Law in favor of personal communication between God and man — or at least God's mysteries. The lesson is as clear as it ever gets in Singer's work. Like Abraham in Kierkegaard's famous exegesis *Fear and Trembling*, man, finite in being and understanding, cannot directly know the absolute; he cannot distinguish between God and the Devil. But unlike Kierkegaard, Singer seems to reject the "absurd" leap that bridges this gap. Salvation, in *Satan in Goray*, appears attainable only with one's eyes on this world, not the next, and through obedience to the Law, not supersedure of it. As the tale of "The Dybbuk of Goray," a supposedly traditional account of Rechele's possession, with which Singer ends his novel, concludes: "Let none attempt to force the Lord." But even here, the law of the Cabala, which certainly fascinated Singer in the course of his education,[8] is not completely rejected.

In the tale, Gedaliya has the villain's role to himself; Reb Itche Mates, who passionately studies the Cabala, is praised (ironically, since he has clearly paved the way for his successor). More important, the novel's strength lies not in its condemnation of excess, but in its sense of an unseen world filled with dybbuks, demons, and perhaps, hidden manifestations of God, all of which invite, even demand, investigation. Man, like the world, is split into opposing principles: in Freudian terms, the struggle between Gedaliya, the Id, and Itche Mates, the repressive Superego, overwhelms Rechele, the Ego; metaphysically, pure spirit contends with matter; morally, good contends with evil. The balance is at best delicate, and once the superficial unity is broken by catastrophe — on a racial scale, Chmielnicki's butchery, personally, Rechele's uncle's — the ceremony of innocence is drowned.

The title of Muriel Spark's *Ballad of Peckham Rye* itself suggests folk materials, a suggestion reinforced in the first chapter by allusion to several possible versions.

However, the bulk of the novel bears little relation to this mode; the working class community of Peckham Rye (in South London) is not a magical world mysteriously influenced by unseen creatures. And yet the Devil may very well be present, for Miss Spark's novel seems to be based on the same archetypal pattern as Singer's.

Economically, the roles of Reb Itche Mates and Reb Gedaliya (and probably Satan himself) are played by Dougal Douglas, the Arts man from Edinburgh, hired by nylon manufacturers Meadows, Meade and Grindley "to bring vision into the lives of the workers." [9] However, the nature of his "vision" is questionable. A humpback, Dougal also has a less noticeable physical deformity: two bumps on either side of his head, which he claims are the remains of horns removed by a plastic surgeon. Together with dreams in which he appears as the Devil, this feature openly hints at infernal origins. But Dougal is complex. As suggested by his simultaneous employment (in the same capacity) by Meadows' rival firm, Drover Wilson, this time under the name Douglas Dougal, his identity is dualistic. Although he insists it is not incompatible with being a devil, Dougal claims powers of exorcism, the art of casting out devils. And, walking through a cemetery with a female employee, he poses "like an angel-devil, with his hump shoulders and gleaming smile" (p. 34).

Dougal differs from Itche Mates and Reb Gedaliya, who are so completely defined by the forces they represent that they almost become universals, in his ironic self-consciousness. Always joking about his demonic attributes, Dougal sees himself with a certain amount of detachment. Hardly as fanatical as Singer's protagonists, Dougal, like Falstaff, is capable of fabrications that are acts of creative imagination rather than lies: typical are his invented versions of the life of retired actress Maria Cheeseman, whose autobiography he is ghostwriting, and his later adventures in Africa selling tape recorders to witch doctors.

Dougal has in a sense created his own satanic mask, in which neither he nor the reader can completely believe nor disbelieve. Like the intruders of *Satan in Goray,* Dougal brings with him a new "morality," a new way of looking at the world. And, like the Polish villagers, his converts in Peckham Rye are led to destruction. Dougal's employer murders his mistress, Dougal's friend jilts his fiancée, the entire community is set into a turmoil that subsides only with Dougal's hasty departure. For, again like the visitors to Goray, Dougal is an enemy of the "Law," of conformity to standards endorsed by the community; he is above all an apostle of self-expression. To a certain extent this resembles the self-indulgence encouraged by Reb Gedaliya: although employed to reduce absenteeism, Dougal systematically urges workers to take a day off whenever they feel like it; he helps free people from confining relationships; his "fatal flaw," he insists, is the inability to tolerate illness in others, to give anything up in order to take care of them.

But Dougal's attack on conventional values, which often seems nihilistic, is not at all without point. His analysis of Peckham Rye's morality is instructive:

> Take the first category, Emotional. Here, for example, it is considered immoral for a man to live with a wife who no longer appeals to him. Take the second, Functional, in which the principal factor is class solidarity such as, in some periods and places, has also existed amongst the aristocracy, and of which the main manifestation these days is the trade union movement. Three, Puritanical, of which there are several modern variants, monetary advancement being the most prevalent gauge of the moral life in this category. Four, Traditional, which accounts for about one per cent of the Peckham population, and which in its simple form is Christian (pp. 93–94).

What each of the first three moralities have in common is a response to other human beings as objects subordinate to other concerns: personal psychological needs, class consciousness, and materialism. The gap between self and other has become absolute and, paradoxically, there is therefore no true access to the self. Confronted by these perversions of morality, Dougal's own position is given moral significance. He seeks to have everyone dispense with the rigid, and often externally imposed, patterns that dominate their lives, and discover what they really want, who they really are. This is the beginning of moral sensibility; self-respect is the prerequisite of respect for others. And to this extent there is an "angelic" component in Dougal's dual nature.

However, unfortunately for Peckham Rye, Dougal goes no further. To his disciples he offers self-expression, he offers freedom; but, his response to reality an attitude rather than a system of thought, he provides no guides to action. Freedom, at least to Peckham Rye, is chaos, and there is a general sigh of relief when Dougal leaves (although, as in Goray, there are still converts to the discredited prophet).

We may conclude, then, that the ambiguity of Dougal's identity derives from the fact that he is neither good nor evil in himself, but only insofar as he affects those around him; he is a catalyst, he removes the scales from people's eyes, but his commitment is to neither God nor Devil. The point to be emphasized in comparing him with the Satan (or satans) of Singer's novel is that the dualism Dougal represents is only apparent. Always obsessed with the threat of dualism, Spark usually emerges as a good monist. The world, and therefore the individual human soul, are not transformed into battlegrounds on which good and evil struggle for dominance. For good and evil are understood not as principles of being, but results of specific actions in particular contexts; they do not reside in human beings (like dybbuks), but rather emerge from conditions and situations, and are ultimately invoked by moral choice.

The contrast and its significance become clear when we examine the "new behavior" elicited by the intruders in each work. In *Ballad,* the results are not uniform: Mr. Druce, reexamining his affairs, does indeed kill his mistress; Humphrey Place, however, realizes his fiancée is a penny-pinching, soul-deadening bitch. In this case the reader disapproves only when, after Dougal's departure, it appears that Humphrey ultimately does marry her. Dougal does not bring on the inevitable; he simply forces decisions. In Singer, the Devil works on firmer ground. There is an evil principle (or a core of libidinous desire) in all men; Satan's task is merely to wear through the veneer of civilized behavior. Gedaliya leads his wife into increasingly degrading perversions until the perverse in her own nature takes over; the Devil has gained ascendancy. Freed from convention, Peckham Ryers can choose for better or worse, usually, though not necessarily, worse; freed from the Law, the inhabitants of Goray are immersed in sin.

While *Satan in Goray* and *The Ballad of Peckham Rye* emphasize the moral implications of a dualistic view of reality, *The Slave* and *The Bachelors,* not in the least ignoring these implications, give proportionately more time to the nature of reality itself. Less spectacularly similar than the first pair, these novels nonetheless display important relations in theme and structure.

Like *Satan in Goray, The Slave* is set in Poland in the years following the Chmielnicki massacres. His wife and children killed in the pogrom, the Jew Jacob is sold into slavery in a remote Polish village that is almost more pagan than Christian. Tending animals on the mountainside, he is frequently visited by Wanda, his master's daughter, whose advances he is finally, after great conflict, unable to resist. Suddenly ransomed by the Jews of his community, he resists resettling until he is uncannily summoned by a dream "sent" by Wanda. He goes back to carry her off, teaches her the Jewish religion, and takes her to Pilitz, where he is unknown. Wanda, now called Sarah, poses as a deaf-mute to conceal her Gentile origins. Here Jacob later becomes caretaker of the manor for Pilitzky, the perverse (in a Dostoevskian sense) lord of the village. When Sarah dies in childbirth, Jacob goes to the Holy Land, falling temporarily under the influence of Sabbatai Zevi, and, in an epilogue, returns to be buried with Wanda-Sarah, whose unmarked grave is miraculously discovered.

The heart of this novel, however, is not its plot, but rather its consistent perception of reality as a boundless series of dichotomies, opposites yoked together in uneasy tension, of which the following are probably the most significant:

1. *Master/slave.* Jacob's (Israel's) bondage is the bondage of the Jewish people. He is first enslaved like the Hebrews in Egypt — the "dark of Egypt" is often alluded to — and in fact imitates Moses by trying to carve the Law into a stone on the mountain. In the second part, he becomes a second Joseph, managing the land for a Gentile ruler and resisting the temptations of his master's wife. Finally, in the brief third section, after a false start as follower of Sabbatai Zevi, Jacob roams the promised land in the service of God. He serves "without hope," but the novel's conclusion suggests that through this final bondage alone can man arrive at true freedom, the liberation of the spirit. It is in fact against the so-called "free will" made possible by God's voluntary withdrawal from complete control of creation that Jacob most bitterly rails: "Yes, Free Will was necessary, and Your Face had to be hidden, but there has been enough of concealment. We are already up to our necks in water." [10]

2. *Good/evil.* Jacob attempts to avoid "Manicheism" in much the same way as the Christian Augustine: "Jacob remembered from his readings in *The Tree of Life* that evil, synonomous with absolute emptiness, only arose be-

cause God had contracted and hidden his face" (p. 162).
Thus dualism is intellectually avoided. But Jacob's instinc-
tive belief in the struggle between good and evil makes
itself felt, especially in his efforts to resist the almost con-
tinual temptations which he believes have been placed in
his path by Satan.

   3. *Spirit/matter.* A good cabalist, Jacob subscribes
to a theosophical system of correspondence. "If so much
could vanish from the physical eye, how much more could
elude the spiritual. . . . Infinite worlds, angels, seraphim,
mansions and sacred chariots surrounded man, but he did
not see them because he was small and sinful and immersed
in the vanities of the body" (p. 55). Although he tries to
find importance in the physical world, which is, after all,
part of God's creation, Jacob clearly suspects that reality
lies in the invisible. The temptation to emulate Itche
Mates must be formidable, but he resists, and searches for
ways to unify being.

   4. *Male/female.* This polarity must be understood
not simply in its superficial sense — very few novels indeed
do not concern the relations of men with women — but as
a principle of existence, used by Jacob to justify his lust
and lend respectability to the merely physical. "His in-
vestigations of the Cabala since his return had uncovered
the doctrine that all lust was of divine origin. . . . Coupling
was the universal act underlying everything; Torah, prayer,
the Commandments, God's holy names themselves were
mysterious unions of the male and female principles"
(p. 111).

   5. *Jewish/Gentile.* Most concrete of the dichotomies
we have examined, this pairing becomes symbolic of all
the others; Chmielnicki's massacres usher in a time of universal schism. Jacob, in spite of his fierce grip on Judaism,
has little in common with the Jews, most of whom he
finds, in this post-Chmielnicki context, strange and superficial; he is forced into relationships with the Gentile community which keeps him as a slave, with Lord and Lady

Pilitzky, and, most important, with the Gentile-Jewess Wanda-Sarah, who in herself embodies all schism.

The reader, however, is probably most aware of the gap between nature and supernature, between man and God. Jacob certainly is, brooding incessantly over the evil and injustice in the universe of a totally good God, and he is driven by this paradox to seek the true nature of being through the Cabala. He pursues the unseen to make sense of the seen. Nonetheless, Singer's insistence that the reader accept the supernatural is not especially strong. Less intimately related to the folk genre than *Satan in Goray* and many shorter works, *The Slave* is about primitive tradition rather than an imitation of it. Here, at least, Singer's methods begin to approach Spark's. His novel contains one reasonably unchallenged instance of the supernatural, the telepathic dream by which Wanda summons Jacob; one definitely bogus event, the "dybbuk" possessing Sarah, who is unable to maintain the disguise as deaf-mute in the pain and fear of her childbirth; and, finally, the kind of ambiguous occurrance Spark delights in, the communication of the dead Wanda-Sarah with Jacob, never established as definitely miraculous or debunked as hallucination. Most important, as in Spark, is the sense of a world of infinite possibility in which finite man must make his way.

Just as the title of *The Slave* introduces Singer's ambiguous symbol of man's relationship to God, Spark's *The Bachelors* announces her symbol of man alienated — from God, from other men, even from himself. Gone is the unity of being so important to Miss Spark; the "wedding" does not take place.

Out of her world of bachelors, three in particular begin to dominate the reader's attention: the medium Patrick Seton (his name is probably pronounced s̄atan), whose allegiance is clearly with the supernatural; Matthew Finch, who, reconciled to the flesh, ultimately marries; and his friend Ronald Bridges, an epileptic and a handwriting expert, who attempts to span the dangerous gap between two worlds.

Seton, accused of fraudulent conversion (the deceptive appropriation of a widow's money for his own purposes), plans to "liberate the spirit" of his pregnant and diabetic mistress with an overdose of insulin as soon as he is acquitted. Fiendish as he is in name and action, Seton is not the incarnation of evil or immorality. His problem, as Matthew Finch perceptively remarks, is his total commitment to the spiritual, his failure to develop a morality of the flesh taking into account the totality of human nature. That Seton's commitment is indeed sincere only one or two envious rivals doubt. In worldly matters completely false — a forged letter, exposed by Ronald Bridges in court, symbolizes his duplicity — few contest his abilities as a medium. If spirit is the only reality, Seton rationalizes, then worldly transgression, including the killing of the body, is no sin at all. "What do you expect of a spiritualist?" demands Matthew Finch. "His mind's attuned to the ghouls of the air all day long. How can he be expected to consider the moral obligations of the flesh? The man's a dualist" (p. 87).

Finch does not, however, limit his condemnation to Seton alone; Jesuit-trained, he extends it to include all bachelors. "I'm afraid we are heretics . . . or possessed by devils. . . . It shows a dualistic attitude, not to marry if you aren't going to be a priest or a religious. You've got to affirm the oneness of reality in some form or another" (p. 87). Finch, who affirms oneness by marrying Seton's fiancée after the medium's conviction, is like Jacob in his attempt to find a place for lust in God's universe. But in spite of Matthew's feelings of guilt, which lead him to forestall sexually seductive situations by eating raw onions, he is on far better terms with his body than the tormented Jacob; we must turn to Ronald Bridges, the novel's focal point, to find a comparable sense of conflict.

Almost a priest (his epilepsy has eliminated this alter-

native) Ronald has also had a love affair, which he himself terminated. Unable to marry, like Matthew Finch,
or to renounce the world completely, like his former mistress, who enters a convent, Bridges is plagued by a keen
vision which does not allow him to ignore part of reality.
"It is all demonology and to do with creatures of the air,"
he comments, brooding on the world of bachelors, "and
there are others besides ourselves. . . , who lie in their
beds like happy countries that have no histories" (p. 219).
His charm to cast out devils (Philippians 4:8) is ineffective
because he himself is part of the demonic world; aware of
duality of being, his history is tormented.

In fact, although he at first seems antithetical to
Patrick Seton, a closer look reveals that Ronald is in some
ways his double. "There are only two religions," says
Ronald, "the spiritualist and the Catholic," and he and
Seton are in their own ways faulted priests of the spirit.
Less diabolical in action than his rival, the epileptic
Bridges is alternately described as possessed by the Devil
or suffering the Devil's revenge. In addition, Ronald's fits
look exactly like Seton's trances, so that when the handwriting analyst has a seizure during the trial, the judge,
dazed by the jargon of spiritualism, desperately asks, "Is
this man a medium?"

Attuned, then, to demons and creatures of the air,
Ronald seeks his own vision of unity. As in *The Ballad
of Peckham Rye,* Spark tries to remain a good monist.
The conflict between good and evil is merely apparent.
The Devil is not at odds with the drama of salvation, but
rather an essential part of it. "The Christian economy,"
says Ronald, "seems to be so ordered that original sin is
necessary to salvation" (p. 88). Like Jacob in *The Slave,*
Ronald struggles to incorporate deceit and evil into a
coherent vision of divine order. Less obsessively dualistic
than Jacob, he is nonetheless not completely successful —
nor can he be — in his search for unity; the novel's conclusion is an uneasy one.

While *Satan in Goray* and *The Ballad of Peckham Rye* serve to emphasize the important distinctions between Singer and Spark, *The Slave* and *The Bachelors* find them each approaching the position and, occasionally, even the methods, of the other. The differences remain crucial, but they are sometimes overshadowed by the common assumptions involved in using the supernatural: that there is a pervasive irrationality in human experience, and that this irrationality is in some way traceable to man's dualistic perception of reality and the consequent limitations on his understanding.

Notes

1. Most criticism of Singer's work inevitably deals with the supernatural. The following essays are among those whose interpretations of his demons are most relevant to this study. Michael Fixler, "The Redeemers: Themes in the Fiction of Isaac Bashevis Singer," *Kenyon Review,* XXVI (Spring 1964), 371–86; Irving H. Buchen, "Isaac Bashevis Singer and the Revival of Satan," *Texas Studies in Literature and Language,* IX (Spring 1967), 129–42; J. S. Wolkenfeld, "Isaac Bashevis Singer: The Faith of His Devils and Magicians," *Criticism,* V (Fall 1963), 349–59.

2. Among the essays dealing specifically with Spark's use of the supernatural are Frank Baldanza, "Muriel Spark and the Occult," *Wisconsin Studies in Contemporary Literature,* VI (Summer 1965), 190–203; Carol Murphy, "A Spark of the Superatural," *Approach,* No. 60 (Summer 1966), 26–30.

3. See Carol Ohmann, "Muriel Spark's *Robinson,*" *Critique: Studies in Modern Fiction,* VIII (Fall 1965), 70–84; and my own *Muriel Spark* (New York, 1968 scheduled publication).

4. There are short stories, however, which center on the definitely supernatural, e.g., "The Portobello Road," "The Seraph and the Zambesi." Nonetheless, it is by the techniques developed in her longer works that her solidest achievements stand.

5. There is also a more "sophisticated" side to Singer's fiction. Told from a more conventional point of view, *The Family Moskat* and *The Manor* exclude the demonic or treat it with skepticism.

6. Miss Spark's passion for unity of being, at least implicit throughout her work, is clearest in the nondemonic world of *The Mandelbaum Gate,* a book about a divided city and divided religious traditions. See discussion in *Muriel Spark.*

7. *Satan in Goray* (New York, 1963), p. 60. Subsequent references to this novel will be followed by page numbers in parentheses.

8. See "An Interview with Isaac Bashevis Singer," *Commentary*, XXXVI (November 1963), 368.

9. *Two by Muriel Spark: The Ballad of Peckham Rye; The Bachelors* (New York, 1964), *Ballad*, p. 17. Subsequent references to these novels will be followed by page numbers in parentheses.

10. *The Slave* (New York, 1964), p. 41. Subsequent references to this novel will be followed by page numbers in parentheses.

Jules Chametzky

11.

History in
I. B. Singer's Novels

I

The novels specifically under consideration are *The
Family Moskat* (New York, 1950; reissued 1965) and *The
Manor* (New York, 1967). The first is a complex weaving
together of the fortunes of scores of Polish Jews whose
lives touch those of the Moskat family from around 1900
to 1939. Until the First World War and its aftermath the
presence and spirit of the irascible, powerful and wealthy
patriarch Meshulam Moskat presides as the unifying center
of this large, Warsaw-based family. After his death the
disintegrative forces of that time and place, and within the
family, forcefully display themselves. The story ends with
the family and the larger Jewish community of which it is
a part at the brink of destruction by the Germans. The
second novel, of which only part one is at present in
English, deals with a slightly earlier period. It begins in
1863, the date of a failed Polish insurrection against Russia, the point at which Poland began its emergence as an
industrial nation, and concludes at the end of the nineteenth century. It too centers largely on the fortunes of
a family, that of Calman Jacoby, a pious, honest Jew who

prospers in this period by responding sensitively to the new direction of events. Part One ends with Calman in despair over his no longer simple life. Although rich, he considers his situation — with a deceitful wife, an apostate daughter, envious and malicious neighbors — a living hell; he is in retreat from the modern secular world.

Both novels, as can be guessed from even this cursory summary, display many similarities in method, tone, point of view and, on a deeper level, philosophy. It is quite proper to consider them together, and to consider them separately from his other novels. Broad in scope, epic in their intention to trace historical movements and the destiny of a whole people over the course of many decades, uncomplicatedly realistic, even-handed and steady in the writing, they seem to stand apart from *Satan in Goray, The Slave,* and *The Magician of Lublin.*

As I have argued elsewhere (*The Nation,* October 30, 1967), however, there are important connections among all his works, so that even the most dissimilar reveal the constant presence of Singer's peculiarly dualistic sensibility. His dedication of *The Family Moskat* to his older brother I. J. Singer should be applied even more to himself: "a modern man [with] all the great qualities of our pious ancestors." That is, significant themes and, more importantly, Singer's attitude toward his material (the "matter," after all, whatever the form of the fable or narrative, is, fundamentally, a concern with the meaning of human life) can be shown to be repeated and essentially unchanged from work to work. What I have to say will, I hope, bear upon the questions of history and myth that are central to my concern with Singer's novels.

II

Satan in Goray seems to me to be only in part a study of demonology: it shows quite plausibly how the process of possession of various souls by diabolical forces works. The scene is the small town of Goray in the aftermath of the Chmielnicki massacres of 1648 and the effects upon the town of the hysteria induced by hopes that the legendary Sabbatai Zevi was the new Messiah. Actually, the focal point of the book is the opposition of images of order and disorder. An old rabbi, Benish, leaves the disorder of Lublin for the calm of Goray, there to help establish an orderly life for himself and the surviving remnant of Jews based on a strict but not unkind observance of the traditional Law. God-Father-Rabbi in the quintessentially Hebraic dispensation is an assurance of an orderly and harmonious life. In a simple structural plan, the book first displays and celebrates this order, then shows the downfall of Rabbi Benish and the assumption of power over the town's life by the zealots, messianics, and mad sowers of discord.

It is a frightening and wholly convincing presentation, based upon an historically accurate portrayal of folk customs, traditions, and actualities. Singer is not to be seen as of the party of demonism — I suppose that goes without saying — nor, and this does require saying, is he necessarily of the party of the traditional order. What he is concerned to do is to present within the framework of Jewish experience, perhaps within that experience above all others because it transcends the normal categories of history (about which more later), the perennial struggle between order and chaos.

The same concern is evident in *The Slave,* that superbly articulated love story between a pious (but profoundly questioning) Jew sold as a slave after the Chmielnicki massacres and a Polish peasant girl (Wanda) whose family he serves. After deliverance from bondage by the Jewish community, he goes back for Wanda, whom he converts and marries secretly in defiance of both communities. Despite the hardships she must now endure, the contrast for Wanda (now become Sarah) between a life of near animality as the wife of a drunken Polish peasant and the light and grace into which she is brought as a Jewess ("the image of a lady" as she sits in prayer among the other women) is near miraculous.

Ultimately Joseph, the central character, comes to a resolution and way of life that eludes Rabbi Benish and many of the other venerable sages in Singer's work. He believes, finally, that the inner spirit of the Law is more important than outward observances, holding in contempt those Jews who meticulously observe the fine points of ritual while in their personal relations displaying only small-mindedness, meanness, and self-interest. Yet, and this is important, he does not abandon ritualistic observances, at least not in the course of the book's action. For a while, we are told expositorially, after the loss of Sarah and his expulsion from Poland, Joseph believed in the false Messiah and the "unnatural" practices encouraged by some of Zevi's followers, but at the end he has come away from that sort of total abandonment. Just as the observances of traditional Jewishness saved him morally in the days of his captivity, when he lived, slept, ate literally among the beasts, so he returns to them at the end as a necessary (but not the only or even the essential) element of an ordered existence.

This return is paralleled in *The Magician of Lublin,* another novel that is not strictly speaking "historical," but that is, like the historical novels, thoroughly grounded in a given historical circumstance. The time and setting are closer to our time, its central character Yasha Mazur as modern as any existential hero. The story is at once a parable of the artist and of modern man — amoral, skeptical, playing at God — whose end is more than likely only lechery, death, despair. All of Yasha the Magician's finely spun plans, all his formidable skill, wit, charisma, collapse into disaster. It is, from one perspective, a cautionary tale about a life lived outside traditional values and codes. In the book's epilogue, Yasha renounces the world and goes back to the old ways (and his pious wife). He devotes his days to prayers, penance, meditation and is widely regarded, despite his disclaiming the role, as sage and rabbi, Reb Jacob the Penitent.

Now, does all of this mean that Singer is advocating a return to orthodoxy as the cure for our malaise, the void of nothingness — the chaos that preceded God's order — that yawns beneath us and before us at every moment, now and forever? In the best Talmudic fashion, we can say on the one hand yes, on the other no, but, basically, I think not. What I have suggested earlier is that Singer offers us a bodying forth in Jewish terms of the ancient and scarcely to be resolved conflict endemic to human existence. The rabbis *always* struggle against discord and disorder in themselves and in the community. Those islands of light, order, and harmony (very heaven as Calman Jacoby calls them in contrast to the hell of modern secular existence) of the study hall, the synagogue, the rabbi's table are only momentary stays against Satan: clean, well lighted places in a universe of *nada*. Singer is too sophisticated to believe they are anything but an image of order, just as the dybbuks of Goray are images of disorder. In *Goray*, for example, Singer is careful as narrator to distance himself from belief in the miraculous and supernatural, very much as Hawthorne, when "mingling the marvelous" in *The Scarlet Letter,* takes care to ascribe reports of miraculous occurrences to someone other than the narrator. In short, what Singer is concerned with is myth and myth-making.

Is Singer, then, essentially an ahistorical novelist? In a sense, yes, insofar as all novelists, finally, are concerned with creating or shaping stories that give coherence and meaning to the facts of life, copulation and death and to the emotions associated with them. But in another sense, and here the Talmudic dialectic is helpful, no, for Singer's great ability at myth-making is formidably authenticated by the painstaking fidelity of his mythic elements to concrete historical events, to Jewish actualities and life. The powerhouse of history, to use Philip Rahv's provocative phrase, is not necessarily and always at war with timeless myth, at least not in the work of Singer set more within a medieval than a modern world. In his novels of a concentrated and somewhat static focus, historical events provide the ground against which persistent aspects of human experience play themselves out. Singer's Jewish perspective equips him admirably for this vision of life. It is a vision that is sorely tired, however, by recent history.

III

History is movement and change. But throughout most of European history, or parallel with it, a basically unchanging footnote, the Jews, has been carried along. Professor Toynbee has called the Jewish people a fossil, a term with unfortunate negative connotations (the term and the notion have been strikingly repudiated by Maurice Samuel and others), which nevertheless points to a useful idea: Jewish survival defies history — its very existence is, in effect, mythic. Preeminently the People of the Book, or of the Law, Jews have been the bearers of an absolute through all the vicissitudes of change. For centuries, what did Jews have to do with — except to feel, peripherally, the effects of — the rise and fall of princes, the movements of armies and peoples, diplomatic intrigues and embassies, the stuff, in short, of "history?" Their concern has traditionally been with the relationship of man and God, of a people and God. Such a view prevailed basically unchallenged among the mass of Jews until the post-Enlightenment phase of the life of the Jewish people. At that point, the powerhouse and the myth began to collide, and it is with that collision and its effects that *The Family Moskat* and *The Manor* concern themselves.

By the middle of the nineteenth century, the bulk of the world's Jews, who were Eastern European, were beginning to be caught up in the swift currents of ideological and economic change that transformed all of Europe in that century. An almost hermetically sealed world was irreparably torn open. Liberalism, socialism, nationalism, positivism, evolutionary theory, all the heady ideas of the age made inroads upon the intellectual segments of the Jewish world. In the twentieth century, with the accelerating effects of war, revolutions, emigration and rapid communications, the interplay of Jewish and modern life seemed complete. The process, Singer shows, was irreversible once begun. The Jews appeared to be entering, after millenia, the mainstream of European history. In the event, it proved, as we know, an illusion — a deadly illusion. At the least, the price to be paid was the traditional Jewish identity, at the worst, the German final solution of expunging Jewish existence altogether.

There is then a certain grim logic, but one that appeals to the emotions rather than the intellect, to the Zionist and orthodox religious positions. In entering history (as Europeans or Westerners), the Jews are in danger of losing their identity as Jews. Each camp represents the position, in its own way, that the separateness and specialness of this people, their myth about themselves, must be maintained. Each position is essentially unhistorical. Singer's work is beautifully poised between the attractions of an ordering myth and the unsettling rush of historical realities.

In these *romans fleuves,* the older images of order persist, types and modes of thought and action recur frequently, echoing from book to book. But they become increasingly less relevant as meaningful alternatives. The kind of piety and order that solace Calman Jacoby or Moshe Gabriel of the Moskat family profoundly irritate such modern, and sympathetically portrayed, men as Ezriel in *The Manor,* the skeptical rabbi's son who abandons the *capote* for medicine, or Asa Heshel Bannet, the most interesting character in *The Family Moskat.* Asa Heshel is a God-seeker and intellectual whose soul-sickness and des-

pair at the meaninglessness of modern existence are meant
to parallel the spiritual condition of Polish Jewry. Asa
Heshel is literally involved in great events: he refuses to
avoid the army in the World War, he goes through the
Russian Revolution, the subsequent pogroms and Civil
War, he is immersed in the "mainstream," the momentous
events of his era. The net effect is to leave him more at
sea than ever; it has all been bizarre, after all, and strangely
illusory. What, finally, *does* a Jew have to do with all that?
Rejected and rejecting, he is much like Joseph in *The
Slave,* with a Jewish identity despite all; but unable to
embrace Zionism, orthodoxy, or the complete historicism
of communism, what is left for him to do, in God's name,
but to die? Singer suggests that there will be a saving
remnant, to be sure, in Israel, America and Russia, but
not Asa Heshel, that peculiar, proud, and doomed flower
of two thousand years of Diaspora.

The last words of *The Family Moskat* draw a line
under the final collapse of the messianic hope that threads
its way through the Jewish faith in all of Singer's novels:
"Death is the messiah. That's the real truth." In light of
the holocaust, Singer seems to be saying that all values,
modern and traditional, any image of order snatched from
the chaos of life, are unavailing and illusory. But one's
experience of these books is by no means so negative or
pessimistic. What is the secret and the measure of Singer's
achievement?

His first achievement, as a Polish Jew and Yiddish
writer in our time, is not to be paralyzed by the horrors
of history, nor be rendered impotent by filial pieties, nor
become tendentious and overtly moralistic. Avoiding these
pitfalls, he honorably performs his function as a chronicler,
epic namer and celebrant of well lived and worthy lives.
There are in these books astonishing images of vitality of
character, place, emotion, so that while one feels the burden of sadness in realizing that this life was annihilated,
one also feels wonder and pleasure that it was truly lived,

felt, real. Indeed, this is always the effect of good biography or history: mingled sadness and awe at the spectacle of the transitoriness of human life and institutions along with the astonishing persistence of recognizable human motive, desire, and aspiration. "Histories make men wise," said Francis Bacon, and in this sense, balancing between images of order and chaos, the worlds of past and present, myths and realities, the historical novelist at his best and wisest dignifies for us the pathos of human existence.

Melvin J. Friedman

12.

Isaac Bashevis Singer: The Appeal of Numbers

"If I were in your place I'd go to see a psychiatrist."
"Then every Jew in the world would have to go to one. I mean every modern Jew." (The Family Moskat)

I

In his intriguing study of Roman Catholic literature in the twentieth century, *Maria Cross,* Conor Cruise O'Brien asks the question: ". . . why, admitting that they are disposed to be Christians, should such writers as Mr. Waugh and Mr. Greene choose to be Catholics rather than Protestants?" He answers the question himself: "Modern Protestantism, which is dead from the waist down, . . . has obviously nothing to offer to imaginations like these." He proceeds to define a "Catholic language, the *lingua franca* of suffering," with its elaborate metaphorical and rhetorical tools. By the time that O'Brien has finished discussing the work of his eight Catholic writers, he has supplied us with so convincing a set of symbols that we can readily understand a literary experience passed under the shadows of the Roman Catholic Church.

The "conversion" to Catholicism (the "going over to Rome" as many writers quaintly like to put it) is so much a part of literary experience in the twentieth century that we often think of it as essential to the inspiration of such spiritually different writers as Paul Claudel, Valery Larbaud, and Evelyn Waugh. Claudel's famous Christmas "religious illumination" in 1886, for example, is very much a part of his apprenticeship.

Conor Cruise O'Brien is quite correct in pointing out that there is no similar experience with modern Protestantism. Judaism, however, has offered convincing literary baptism to a group of writers. The demands of being part of a Diaspora, of knowing an intimate sense of exile (even after the proclamation of a Jewish national state, Israel, in 1948) have offered Jewish authors the kind of imaginative urgency that "converts" to Catholicism have had since the time of St. Augustine. And indeed some of them have had their own *"lingua franca* of suffering," Yiddish. There is a toughness about this language which has helped it survive the pogroms experienced by Eastern Europe's Jewry. Until very recently it was almost the official language of the Diaspora. Its future is now insecure because a language of suffering is no longer appropriate for a people with a vitally new homeland — successfully defended only a year ago in the heroic "Six-Day War." The final literary outposts of Yiddish are the occasional newspaper, like the *Jewish Daily Forward,* and the most famous contributor to that newspaper, Isaac Bashevis Singer.

Singer has all the credentials of the Yiddish writer: he was brought up in traditionally pogrom-ridden Warsaw, spent important formative years in a *shtetl,* Bilgoray, and finally settled in New York City in 1935. Yet there is something "offensively" heterodox about his work; the spell of Maimonides' *Guide for the Perplexed,* Spinoza's *Ethics,* and the teachings of the Baal-Shem-Tov (however different these three are) seem to have triumphed over more con-

ventional sources of Jewish inspiration. Irving Howe is
quite correct in pointing to his iconoclasm. He is also correct in separating Singer from the "ethic of Yiddishism."
Singer continues to write his stories and novels in Yiddish
and oversee an army of translators render his work into
English.[1] He remains apart, as several of his critics have
remarked, both from the American-Jewish tradition from
Daniel Fuchs and Henry Roth through Bernard Malamud
and Philip Roth and from the Yiddishist tradition of
Sholom Aleichem and I. J. Peretz. He seems to walk the
literary equivalent of the tightrope which Yasha negotiates
in *The Magician of Lublin,* except that he is never, as he
describes his hero as being, "merely inches from disaster."

Irving Malin has left Singer out of his standard work
on the American-Jewish writer, *Jews and Americans.*
Harry T. Moore has partly accounted for the omission in
his preface to the book by suggesting that "although
Singer is an American resident, he is a special case, a man
whose works usually have to be translated, a man who
writes chiefly of European rather than American experiences." We should underscore "special case."

There is also a special case among contemporary
Catholic writers. I am thinking of Flannery O'Connor.[2]
On the surface no two fiction writers seem quite as differ-
ent as Flannery O'Connor and Isaac Bashevis Singer. Miss
O'Connor's settings are mainly Bible Belt Southern while
Singer's are usually Polish ghetto. Her novels and stories
are all contemporary while his sometimes wander as far
back as the middle of the seventeenth century. Even when
they both locate their stories in midtwentieth-century New
York City (Flannery O'Connor in "Judgement Day" and
Isaac Singer in "A Wedding in Brownsville" and "The
Letter Writer"),[3] we still seem to be confronting two very
different settings and two very different eras. The sense of
place and of history could not be more different.

They are both, however, literary apostates and cause
discomfort to readers who believe that Catholic literature

must be concerned only with Roman Catholics and priests and that Jewish literature should be firmly anchored to such traditional texts as the Pentateuch, the Talmud, and their various glosses. Catholics are as suspicious of Flannery O'Connor's revivalists as Jews are of Singer's preachers of the gospel according to the Baal-Shem-Tov, Baruch Spinoza, Arthur Schopenhauer, and Martin Buber.[4] Flannery O'Connor writing about a Protestant South is quite as suspect as the Singer characters who quote with rare conviction from Spinoza's *Ethics* or Schopenhauer's *The World as Will and Idea.*

The similarity cuts more deeply. In the broadest sense both Singer and Flannery O'Connor belong to a loosely apocalyptic tradition which attempts to define a spiritual dimension. In one of her essays Miss O'Connor speaks admiringly of the authors (Christian for her) with "the sharpest eyes for the grotesque, for the perverse, and for the unacceptable. In some cases, these writers may be unconsciously infected with the Manichaean spirit of the times and suffer the much discussed disjunction between sensibility and belief." She goes on to say that the writer "may well be forced to take ever more violent means to get his vision across to this hostile audience. When you can assume that your audience holds the same beliefs you do, you can relax a little and use more normal ways of talking to it; when you have to assume that it does not, then you have to make your vision apparent by shock — to the hard of hearing you shout, and for the almost blind you draw large and startling figures." [5] The complete text is liberally sprinkled with the word Christian; otherwise, it could handsomely serve as part of a preface to the collected fiction of Isaac Bashevis Singer. Singer's stories and novels offer a constant reminder of the disproportion between the ethic the Jews have fashioned for themselves in their *galut* and the abuse it has fallen into at various moments in their history; this is his real subject — whether he chooses to etch it in reality or in myth.

Irving Howe was the first of Singer's critics to point to his use of the grotesque: "His grotesquerie must be taken seriously, perhaps as a recoil from his perception of how ugly — how gratuitously ugly — human life can be." [6] The accompanying spirit of the Manichaean "heresy," with its confrontation of good and evil (to which Flannery O'Connor also refers), is a crucial part of Singer's vision. He dramatizes it for readers of his fiction by occasionally having Satan appear *in propria persona* and tempt the Jobs (often disguised as *schlemiels*) of Singer's world. Thus he begins "The Destruction of Kreshev" (in *The Spinoza of Market Street*) in this way: "I am the Primeval Snake, the Evil One, Satan. The cabala refers to me as Samael and the Jews sometimes call me merely, 'that one.' " "Zeidlus the Pope" (in *Short Friday*) also has Satan as narrator and begins: "In ancient times there always lived a few men in every generation whom I, the Evil One, could not corrupt in the usual manner." There is always implicit warfare going on between the tempting *dybbuk,* Satan's representative, and Singer's virtuous. His first novel, *Satan in Goray,* especially allegorizes the conflict. His recent story "The Dead Fiddler" (*The New Yorker,* May 25, 1968) renders it more literally.

Singer's strategy, then, like Flannery O'Connor's, is to make his "vision apparent by shock." By giving human proportions and credibility to satanic creatures, sometimes named Lilith, sometimes named Asmodeus, he has expanded our notions of evil and has made the world of the ghetto a continuing *Walpurgisnacht.* The shocking effect of a Mephistopheles, Goethe-style, who walks freely among men and takes over their habits as well as their speech patterns (Goethe has his devil use the vernacular even in conversation with God) becomes part of the "violent means" Miss O'Connor believes that the writer must fall back on "to get his vision across to this hostile audience."

Thus far we have seen Flannery O'Connor's theory work in Singer's practice. We might clinch the argument by discussing certain fictional practices of both. Flannery O'Connor's two novels and several of her stories have a tripartite structure. I have elsewhere labeled these parts transplantation, prophecy, and return.[7] In at least one of Singer's novels we have the same structural and thematic principle at work: *The Slave*. This novel, like Flannery O'Connor's *The Violent Bear It Away*, has three parts — the first and second of almost equal length, with a very short third part. The third, in the case of both novels, acts pretty much the way a coda does in music; it offers not only a formal resolution but also a kind of vision. Miss O'Connor did not title any of the three parts of *The Violent Bear It Away* while Singer had the happy notion of calling the third part of *The Slave* "The Return."

Jacob, the hero of this novel, speaks the most authentic *"lingua franca* of suffering" we find anywhere in the Yiddish writer's work. He has been "transplanted" from his accustomed urban surroundings during the Chmielnicki massacres of 1648; he has passed into rural slavery. (For the Jew, rural existence outside of Israel is ordinarily the remotest of possibilities; he cannot imagine cultivating anybody's soil other than his own. When the Bablyonians — metaphorically, I suspect — asked their Jewish captives to "sing," in Psalm 137, the Jews replied with a question, "How shall we sing the Lord's song in a strange land?") Jacob's, in a sense, is a double exile. He not only is part of the Diaspora which has experienced dislocation since the destruction of the second temple in A.D. 70; he has also been uprooted from his familiar ghetto surroundings and been forced to live among Christians. Part I of *The Slave* describes the painful isolation of a tortured sensibility which withstands every variety of temptation. Jacob is a kind of Jewish St. Anthony and Wanda (whose name is used as the title of part I) is his Queen of Sheba — but with a difference. Jacob passes his apprenticeship as an exile by "engraving the six hundred and thirteen laws of the Torah onto a stone." [8] In the "transplantation" section of the novel he manages to hold on to his *shtetl*-taught Judaism and finally submits to Wanda who becomes his "Jewish wife."

Part II is the "prophetic" section of the novel. Jacob has been released from slavery and returns to live among Jews in a town called Pilitz. He is now accompanied by his wife who has changed her name to Sarah (the title of this second part) and pretends to be mute. Jacob now experiences something of what Sir Maurice Bowra once called, in a different context, "the troubling and unloved responsibilities of prophecy." The biblical intrudes quite heavily in this section of *The Slave:*

> He had wrestled with God as had the Patriarch Jacob, but his defeat had brought more than a dislocated thigh. He, Jacob, the son of Eliezer, had been utterly destroyed by heaven. No longer did he fear anything, not even Gehenna. He deserved no better, having cohabited with the daughter of Jan Bzik and then illicitly converted her. What did he expect? In these days justice ruled untempered by mercy (p. 191).

This final sentence has a particularly biblical cadence and even syntax. Even the events turn out to be quasi-Old Testament. Sarah dies in childbirth and the son is appropriately called Benjamin: "Like the first Benjamin, this child was a Ben-oni, a child born of sorrow" (p. 227). We are told on the final page of Part II: "Like the Biblical Jacob, he was crossing the river, bearing only a staff, pursued by another Esau. . . . somewhere, at another river, another Jacob would walk mourning another Rachel" (p. 228).

The prose thickens as the "Sarah" section comes to a close and Jacob's own prophetic position in Pilitz gains increasing assurance. It is in certain ways comparable stylistically to the final paragraphs of Part II of *The Violent Bear It Away* which describe the baptism-drowning of Bishop by Tarwater, the hero of Flannery O'Connor's novel. Singer even makes a slight concession to the Christian tradition by telling us that "nine years later he [Jacob] watched over the body of a saint [Sarah]." Singer is usually fond of the "sacred" Old Testament number seven but on this occasion startles us a bit by using the New Testament-Dantesque nine (three times three as various commentators have reasoned).[9]

The brief Part III of *The Slave* marks Jacob's return from Jerusalem, where he spent approximately twenty years, to Pilitz. He returns to be buried next to Sarah, who periodically came to him in Old Testament-type dreams in the intervening years.[10] Singer works history (the coming of Sabbatai Zevi, the false Messiah, in 1666) in with myth in this final section of the novel. The biblical echoes seem more disturbingly intrusive than in the second part; they are part of the *Drang nach Osten* which takes Jacob to the Holy Land with Benjamin, who marries a rabbi's daughter and becomes a teacher in a yeshiva. The conclusion is perhaps too pat for such a prophetically imaginative novel.

It has already been pointed out that *The Magician of Lublin* falls naturally into three parts.[11] Transplantation-prophecy-return, as a literary motif and structural device, works more loosely and erratically in this novel. In the sense we have spoken of, the third division might easily be considered a return (Singer calls it "epilogue"). Like the third part of *The Slave* it is shorter than the other two sections and forms a kind of coda.

Yasha, the magician of the title, after a brief stay at home with his wife Esther departs early in the novel for another of his erotic itineraries. This is a "transplantation" in which he engages on a regular basis and with great joy; it is quite different from Jacob's forced removal from his *shtetl*. We see Yasha on the road gently avoiding God's commandments at every turn; yet he has a kind of respect for God's power. Yasha starts out at the point where Hermann Hesse's Steppenwolf ends. To quote Harry Haller, the Steppenwolf: "I knew that all the hundred thousand pieces of life's game were in my pocket." Yasha has the most authentic *risus purus* in all of Singer's work. His life is a game in which he continues to delight.

Yasha's antics, both professional and extracurricular (he has a variety of mistresses as well as a faithful wife), fill the first part of the novel. Irving Buchen describes the middle section as "nightmarish, wild and surrealistic." The leisurely, episodic pace of the first part of *The Magician of Lublin* gives way to a more frantic, elliptical cadence. There is something of the Steppenwolf's "Magic Theatre," with its legend "For Madmen Only!" about this middle part of the novel. Yasha experiences his greatest frustration when he fails to open the safe belonging to the wealthy Kazimierz Zaruski. His long experience with locks betrays him at this crucial moment. His reaction is instructive:

> Yasha felt its presence — a dybbuk, a satan, an implacable adversary who would disconcert him while he was juggling, push him from the tightrope, make him impotent. Trembling he opened the balcony door. His perspiring body shivered. It was as if winter had suddenly arrived.[12]

Singer uses a scene very like this in two other novels, but with much less telling effect. Koppel Berman, in *The Family Moskat,* makes off with the contents of his dying employer's safe and experiences intense anxiety as he leaves the house in a droshky. The event, however, turns out not to be especially crucial. It gets lost somehow in a very crowded novel which must resort to genealogical charts to make complex family relationships clear. The scene involving Lucian Jampolski's attempts to find the miser Chodzinski's money in *The Manor* is even more blurred, less incisive.

In *The Magician of Lublin* we follow Yasha from the moment he descended the balcony and "landed too violently on his left foot" (p. 117) through his entrance in the synagogue, his visit with Emilia, his discovery of the dead Magda who has hung herself, his view of Zeftel and Herman sleeping side by side. We do not leave him for a single moment during the crucial period — highlighted by his blundering attempt at opening the safe — when he discovers, in good Hesse fashion, "yes, people are mad" (p. 140). He says two sentences later, in this "prophecy" section of *The Magician of Lublin,* "Today is my Day of Reckoning." (Notice the use of the upper case!) The incident with the safe is neatly placed at the midpoint of the novel; Singer sacrifices everything else to it and sets it off in brilliant symbolic relief. It has certain of the archetypal qualities that Prince Myshkin's cracking of the vase has in Dostoevsky's *The Idiot* or of the awkward scene of the wife and daughter departing for the theatre, leaving the dying father alone, in Tolstoy's *Death of Ivan Ilych.* Variations on the cracked vase are found in such different novels as *The Red and the Black, The Egoist,* and William Styron's *Set This House on Fire.* The Tolstoy scene has near equivalents in *Old Goriot* and even in the final pages of Proust's *Guermantes Way.* The interesting point for Singer is that he recognizes the symbolic possibilities of a man, otherwise in control of himself, recklessly risking theft at a particularly deranged moment. He concentrates all his energies on it in *The Magician of Lublin* and makes it a kind of architectonic point for his novel. He refuses it the necessary loving care in *The Family Moskat* and *The Manor* and so the scene is soon forgotten in these books. This is a matter of fictional technique and explains why Singer succeeds with the "closed" form of *The Magician* (or *The Slave* and *Satan in Goray,* for that matter) and manages less well with the "open" form of the two family novels.

After the frenetic pace of the second part, *The Magician of Lublin* slows down noticeably. Yasha has "had himself bricked up" and now lives the life of a penitent in a "small, doorless house with its tiny window" (p. 182). His "return" is in certain ways like that of Hazel Motes in Flannery O'Connor's *Wise Blood,* who also turns ascetic — except that it does not end in death.

II

The Slave and *The Magician of Lublin* have rather similar structures and fictional techniques imposed on very different historical periods and settings. Singer uses history quite precisely in *The Slave,* taking serious account of the Chmielnicki massacre and the coming of Sabbatai Zevi. The nineteenth-century setting of *The Magician of Lublin* is less crucially historical although it is still firmly anchored in reality. (It does not depend on a single nineteenth-century event the way *The Manor* is firmly attached to the year 1863, a year which has almost as much importance for Singer as 1666.) *Satan in Goray* is a different kind of work from *The Slave* or *The Magician of Lublin.* It is divided into two parts. Part I is realistically set in the messianic year 1665–1666. Cabalists struggle against more orthodox interpreters of Judaism represented by Rabbi Benish Ashkenazi. When the rabbi dies at the end of the first part to the lamenting cries of his faithful, "Holy Rabbi, why do you forsake us? Rabbi! Ho-ly Rabbi!" the hysterical voices of the Sabbataists take over and submerge the novel in phantasmagoria. It is a witches' sabbath from then on. Ben Siegel is right in saying: "The sudden insertion of demons and *dybbuk* into Goray's harshly realistic setting comes so late as to jar." [13] When we discover that the "heroine" of the novel, Rechele, is impregnated by Satan our willing suspension of disbelief seems to quite give out. We might speak of this second part as being a surrealistic fabliau, if such is not a contradiction in terms.[14] The bawdiness, earthiness, and cuckoldry are all here, but without the realism.

Singer is perhaps working in a tradition in *Satan in*

Goray which goes back to Goethe's *Faust* and has a recent exponent in Hermann Hesse. Myth and history come together in a manner to offset temporal and spatial distinctions. *Faust* begins in the realistic setting of the scientist's study and maintains relative credibility through most of the first part, despite the human dress, behavior, and speech assumed by Mephistopheles. Part II, like the second half of Singer's novel, breaks down all distinctions between illusion and reality. Hesse's *Steppenwolf* is probably even more to the point. The view we get of Harry Haller at the beginning of the novel is soberly realistic: a man approaching fifty who lives in a furnished room filled with books. His sensual urges may be a bit exaggerated but otherwise there is nothing curious about him. The novel gradually become hallucinative as Harry enters the Magic Theatre: characters tend to merge with one another; Haller has conversations with Goethe and Mozart; distinctions of space and time cease to matter. I imagine that the technique used here should be called expressionistic. *Steppenwolf* is the unusual hybrid product of essay, drama, and novel.

Satan in Goray does not go quite this far. It is in no sense a hybridization of several forms. Singer takes the novel too seriously to willingly compromise it. He makes this point in his *Commentary* interview:

> Many writers are half essayists and half fiction writers. Thomas Mann, for example. He writes a story, and in the middle of the story he inserts an essay or an article. He is himself both the writer and the critic. . . . I avoid these things. When I tell a story, I tell a story. I don't try to discuss, criticize, or analyze my characters (p. 366).

A few lines later in the interview he agrees with Flaubert's views on the "purity of the novel." Yet the differences in tone and mood between the two parts of *Satan in Goray* would probably have offended Flaubert. The nineteenth-century French novelist would very likely have written two separate novels, rather than combined them in one, as in a sense he did with *Madame Bovary* and *Salammbô.*

Singer has, however, made his "vision apparent by shock" (in Flannery O'Connor's sense). His *dybbuk,* imps, and other satanic creatures have turned men into swine, in good Circe fashion, just as they do in some of the later stories contained in *Gimpel the Fool, The Spinoza of Market Street,* and *Short Friday.* In the shorter form it is somehow less artistically offensive than in the novel which begins in Rabbi Benish's *Beth Din* and ends with *dybbuk* inhabiting ladies' souls.[15]

Satan in Goray lacks, then, a unity of tone which characterizes Singer's best fiction. What works for Goethe in *Faust* and Hesse in *Steppenwolf* (and also in *Demian*) does not work for Singer. His change from realism to fantasy is too abrupt. He even takes on interesting new stylistic habits in the second part. Thus whenever he mentions Reb Mordecai Joseph (Rabbi Benish's principal antagonist) in the final pages of the novel he attaches a Homeric-type epithet to his name. In the last chapter "Reb Mordecai Joseph (may his remembrance be a blessing)" occurs six times.

What Leslie Fiedler described as "this frantic religiosity without God, this sense of the holiness of violence," in another context, seems precisely to the point of Part II of *Satan in Goray.* This is the ambience which Singer is at pains to reproduce as he uses his tactics of shock and literary disproportion.

III

The three "closed" novels we have been looking at in various ways compromise history with myth, reality with illusion. The transplantation-prophecy-return pattern in *The Slave* and, in a less strict sense, in *The Magician of Lublin* gives these books an admirable tripartite design.

Satan in Goray turns over too much, with too little preparation, to the unreal and fantastic. It seems to thrive on Gide's famous paradoxes about the devil expressed in his *Journal of "The Counterfeiters"*: "The more we deny him, the more reality we give him. The Devil is affirmed in our negation"; and "Why should you be afraid of me [the Devil]? You know very well I don't exist."

Singer seems to be a writer for whom pattern matters a great deal. He has none of Henry James's articulate formulas, expressed in his prefaces, for composing novels. Yet he would doubtless admire the geometric shape which E. M. Forster found in *The Ambassadors*. As *Steppenwolf* seems related to music and as Virginia Woolf's *To the Lighthouse* seems related to the plastic arts, so do Singer's best efforts bear a kinship with mathematics. He finds beauty in numbers and in symmetrical shapes probably more than he finds it in words.

The right length for Singer, it seems to me, is the two-hundred-page novel. The shapelessness of *The Family Moskat* and *The Manor* seems almost a betrayal of Singer's art. The short story — even at its best in "Gimpel the Fool" and the recent "The Letter Writer" — doesn't give him enough ideological base from which to work. In the end we might say that Singer's iconoclasm, in his best work, is balanced by his careful attention to pattern and form. In this sense he is also very like Flannery O'Connor.[16] *The Slave* and *The Magician of Lublin* are among the finest short novels we have in any language. Stanley Edgar Hyman is not exaggerating when he says: "*The Slave* towers over everything else being written today." [17]

Notes

1. Singer seems never to have decided on an official translator. A collection of short stories like *The Spinoza of Market Street* has nine different translators, two sometimes combining on a single story. The late Cecil Hemley probably comes closest to being Singer's "English voice," serving him as both translator and editor.

Saul Bellow did a justly celebrated English version of "Gimpel the Fool" which helped make that story the most widely known in the Singer canon. Singer offered his own views on translation in an interview in *Commentary* (November 1963), p. 370. He said, "The same translator can do a good job on one book and a bad job on another. Nevertheless, good translation is possible, but it involves hard work for the writer, the translator, and the editor. I don't think that a translation is ever really finished. To me the translation becomes as dear as the original."

2. She happens to be excluded from Conor Cruise O'Brien's *Maria Cross,* probably only because when he published his book she had written only *Wise Blood* and some scattered stories; neither her stature nor her reputation at the time merited her being placed in the company of Waugh, Claudel, Mauriac, or Graham Greene.

3. "Judgement Day" first appeared in the posthumous collection of Flannery O'Connor's stories, *Everything That Rises Must Converge.* "A Wedding in Brownsville" was collected in *Short Friday* while "The Letter Writer" first appeared in English in the *New Yorker* (January 13, 1968).

4. See Edith Mucke, "Isaac B. Singer and Hassidic Philosophy," *The Minnesota Review,* VII, 3 1967), 214–21.

5. "The Fiction Writer and His Country," *The Living Novel: A Symposium,* ed. Granville Hicks (New York: Macmillan, 1967), pp. 162–63.

6. "Demonic Fiction of a Yiddish 'Modernist,'" *Commentary,* XXX (October 1960), 350.

7. See my introduction to *The Added Dimension: The Art and Mind of Flannery O'Connor,* ed. Melvin J. Friedman and Lewis R. Lawson (New York: Fordham University Press, 1966), pp. 1–31.

8. *The Slave,* trans. from the Yiddish by Isaac Bashevis Singer and Cecil Hemley (New York: Avon, 1964), p. 46. All subsequent references will be to this edition.

9. On the one occasion I met Mr. Singer, the evening of April 11, 1968 in Madison, Wisconsin, he indicated an enthusiasm for numbers, especially for what mathematicians call "prime numbers." He seemed fascinated by the fact that they continue to infinity (as Euclid told us) and that they are only divisible by themselves and by the number one. Mr. Singer suggested that there is something almost "mystical" about prime numbers. Seven and three happen to be prime numbers, or course.

10. Singer's handling of dreams is worth an essay in itself. Dreams are as important to him as they are to the Dostoevsky of *Crime and Punishment* — a novel which Singer tells us he read at an early age in Yiddish (see his *Commentary* interview, p. 368).

11. See Irving H. Buchen's interesting "Isaac Bashevis Singer and the Eternal Past," *Critique, VIII* (Spring–Summer 1966), 9–10.

12. *The Magician of Lublin,* trans. from the Yiddish by Elaine Gottlieb and Joseph Singer New York: Bantam, 1965), p. 115. All subsequent references will be to this edition.

13. "Sacred and Profane: Isaac Bashevis Singer's Embattled Spirits," *Critique,* VI (Spring 1963), 29. See also Michael Fixler, "The Redeemers: Themes in the Fiction of Isaac Bachevis Singer," *Kenyon Review,* XXVI (Spring 1964), 371–86, for a skillful reading of *Satan in Goray* in the context of Singer's fiction; and J. S. Wolkenfeld's "Isaac Bashevis Singer: The Faith of His Devils and Magicians," *Criticism,* V (Autumn 1963), 349–59, for a reliable explanation of Singer's fictional practices, especially in *Satan in Goray.*

14. Singer has already been called a writer for "Yiddish novels and fabliaux." See Richard M. Elman's "The Spinoza of Canal Street," *Holiday,* XXXVIII (August 1965), 83.

15. Singer handles all of this very pleasantly in his children's stories, such as the collection *Zlateh the Goat and Other Stories* and the book-length parable *The Fearsome Inn.* His respect for the number seven is especially in evidence in several of these pieces: "the celebration lasted seven days and seven nights" ("Fool's Paradise"); "For seven days and seven nights they sat wrinkling their foreheads and tugging at their beards" ("The First Shlemiel"); "They sang, danced, and made merry for seven days and seven nights" *(The Fearsome Inn).*

16. One of Singer's critics places him, in an interesting way, in the company of contemporary Roman Catholic writers, although he does not specifically mention Flannery O'Connor's name. See Lothar Kahn, "A World of Spirits and Imps: Isaac Bashevis Singer," *Commonweal,* LXXXI (January 22, 1965), 540. The first critic, as far as I know, to mention Flannery O'Connor in connection with Singer is Irving H. Buchen in an excellent book which appeared after completion of this article, *Isaac Bashevis Singer and the Eternal Past* (New York: New York University Press, 1968). Professor Buchen's study suggests grouping Singers work with that of another writer whom I have mentioned frequently in this essay, Herman Hesse. Buchen sees the atmosphere of *Steppenwolf* permeating the texture of *The Family Moskat* much as I found it suggesting certain of the techniques of *Satan in Goray.*

17. "The Yiddish Hawthorne," *Standards: A Chronicle of Books for Our Time* (New York: Horizon Press, 1966), p. 87.

Edwin Gittleman

13.

Isaac's Nominal Case: In My Father's Court

Of the nine books by Isaac Bashevis Singer published in English translation, it is the eighth which for the first time explicitly dramatizes in narrative form a problem fundamental to all his books. This problem, although an important one, has been either unrecognized by readers or else simply dismissed by them as curious but irrelevant. However, with the publication of *In My Father's Court* in 1966, it was projected in such a way that it can no longer be ignored if Singer's work is to be taken seriously and is to continue to receive responsible critical attention. It is the problem of the author's multiple names — or rather, of his multiple identities — and their significance in terms of the form, style, and substance of his work.

Several years before publication of *In My Father's Court*, during an extended interview printed in *Commentary* (November 1963), Singer himself discussed this matter, but in a guarded and defensive way. (Such caution itself signals an important disclosure about Singer's elusive art.) Questioned about his work for the *Jewish Daily Forward*, the Yiddish-language newspaper on which he had served as staff member and regular contributor for nearly thirty years, he explained his binomial career as a writer.

> Generally I sign my name in the *Forward* Isaac Bashe-
> vis, but once in a while I publish under the name of
> Isaac Warshofsky. When I write under the name of
> Warshofsky I take less care, but I never publish such
> things in book form. I use a different name to dis-
> tinguish between two different kinds of writing. Since
> I must write a great deal and I cannot work on every
> piece of writing the way I work on the stories which
> I take very seriously, I publish some pieces which I
> consider belle-lettristic journalism. It sometimes hap-
> pens that some of them come out well. In fact, one
> of my books [*Mayn Taten's Bes-din Shtub* (1956)] is
> a compilation of this kind of work, published [origi-
> nally] under the name of Warshofsky. Only later I
> adopted it, as it were, and signed the name Bashevis
> . . . after I cleaned it up and worked on it.

The "compilation" has since been translated into English as *In My Father's Court*. It is his only book so far to derive from the "belle-lettristic journalism" of Isaac Warshofsky, prepared for *adoption* as the literary child of Isaac Bashevis by being "cleaned" and "worked on."

When pressed by the interviewers to explain further, he replied that "Isaac Singer" was his "real name." But he immediately complicated this simple *reality* by giving the word "adopted" an emotional charge quite different from the playfulness conveyed by a metaphor for the culmina-tion of an editorial process of revision. "In Yiddish I sign my fiction Isaac Bashevis. For some reason this name is sacred to me, and I won't sign my journalism with it. Per-haps it's because Bashevis is derived from my mother's name. Her name was Bathsheba."

If indeed "Isaac Singer" is his "real name" in any substantive sense, its reality has been deliberately displaced by the power of the "sacred" matronymic. *In My Father's*

Court suggests that this displacement was neither sentimental gesture nor simple rejection of paternal authority.
Rather it was a son's brilliant attempt to identify himself
in terms of conflicting family loyalties. Most importantly,
"Isaac Bashevis" was an essential definition of a complex
artistic sensibility, and its operative component was the
familiar form of the name "Bathsheba."

Beyond distinguishing the professional Yiddish journalist Isaac Warshofsky from Isaac Bashevis the writer of
Yiddish short stories and novels, the *Commentary* interviewers did not pursue very far the subject of *real* names,
pseudonyms, and personal identities. Isaac-of-Warsaw was
merely the newspaper columnist, writer of conventional
reviews, boyhood reminiscences, *feuilletons,* and "all kinds
of things" not otherwise specified. By contrast, the "sacred"
Isaac-the-son-of-Bathsheba was a conscientious artist who
did something more than "just write" and then "let it go":
he attempted instead to "create [his] own tradition."

However, the relationship between Isaac Singer, the
not-so-sacred son of Rabbi Pinchos Menachem Singer, and
the distinctive literary consciousnesses designated "Warshofsky" and "Bashevis" was not clarified in the *Commentary* interview, nor was the process described by which
Isaac Bashevis was able to *adopt* the work of Isaac Warshofsky. Instead, a fourth name was introduced casually
and employed indiscriminately in the interview, the syn-
thetic name most familiar to American readers, Isaac
Bashevis Singer, author of Yiddish fiction translated into
English. This name, denoting the last of a series of
authorial personations (made necessary by the shock of
re-cognition when he migrated in 1935 to a country where
Yiddish is an alien language) belatedly affirms the continuing titular existence of Isaac the not-quite-sacrificed
son of a patriarchal father.

In My Father's Court is a book in which Isaac Bashevis Singer attempts to create his own tradition in a way
different from that of the eight volumes of fiction which

have made him an important contemporary writer. Only here is this tradition personal, being initially that of Isaac Singer; its *reality* is the psychological reality of Isaac Singer. The method used is the journalistic memory of Isaac Warshofsky, but only after that memory has been *adopted,* and thereby transfigured, by the sacralizing imagination of Isaac Bashevis. Therefore, whatever the original journalistic intentions of Isaac Warshofsky in the pages of the *Jewish Daily Forward,* the book has become a self-conscious literary experiment in the form of a fictional autobiography. It depicts the early years of Isaac Singer, during the period when his consciousness was first beginning to polarize into Warshofsky and Bashevis, and was thereby gradually losing its original Singerian identity. Accordingly, *In My Father's Court* is a book of discoveries, of prophetic discoveries, although the prophetic tones are muted. Woven into its basic patterns is a pervasive consciousness of later lives as journalist and as writer of fiction; simultaneously the book narrates a period of a boy's increasing detachment from his father and of compensatory affiliation with his mother. This reorientation of his sense of himself, a gradual rather than sudden shift, was made necessary because of pressures to which he was first exposed by his early life in Warsaw, and which later were increased during several years spent in the remote Polish village of Bilgoray where his mother had lived before her marriage.

In the "Author's Note" prefacing *In My Father's Court,* Isaac Bashevis Singer describes the book as being a "literary experiment" only "in a certain sense." The "experiment," he explains, is stylistic since the book combines the "style" of "memoirs" with that of "belles-lettres." By way of further explanation, he adds that the book's "approach to description" and its "manner of conveying situations" differ from those employed in his other writings. This *belletristic memoir,* with its uncharacteristic "approach to description" and "manner of conveying situations," is designed (he says) to tell "the story of a family and of a rabbinical court that were so close together it was hard to tell where one ended and the other began." A narrative in which journalistic reminiscence is combined with literary imagination, in which personal and official relationships overlap, facts blend with invention, history with fiction, discovery with prophecy, *In My Father's Court* subverts conventional distinctions between real and not-real events.

What, from the point of view of Isaac Bashevis Singer, justifies this "literary experiment" is that it portrays "a life and environment that no longer exist and are unique." Actually this is a journalistic and therefore too limited statement of the book's accomplishment. Its unifying focus is actually an evolving consciousness through which Isaac Singer begins to be destroyed ("sacrificed") by becoming aware of a "life and environment" which *continue* to exist. They survive partially in the reportorial memory of Isaac Warshofsky and totally in the shaping imagination of Isaac Bashevis. This constitutes their uniqueness. In this sense he succeeds in creating his own tradition for *In My Father's Court*.

Not only is it difficult to tell where the family "ended" and the rabbinical court "began," but it is also difficult to recognize the limits of fiction in such a book, a difficulty which distinguishes it from the short stories and novels of Isaac Bashevis Singer.

The book is divided into forty-nine short chapters, only seventeen of which actually involve Rabbi Singer's "Beth Din." A traditional rabbinical court, it is located in the family's shabby pre-World War I apartment on Warsaw's disreputable Krochmalna Street. If the title of the book is accurate, it must refer to more than the conferences which are overheard by the boy Isaac and recalled many years later by Warshofsky in the pages of the *Jewish Daily Forward*. During these sessions the rabbi answers questions about ritual observances, settles domestic quar-

rels, adjudicates disputes over money and commercial trans-
actions, solves problems of love and marriage, gives advice
to the emotionally disturbed, argues fine points of Talmudic law, and listens patiently to whomever requires the
purgation of talk. These seventeen recollections are sketchy
and anecdotal. They are narrated by an impatient and superficial reportorial intelligence which immediately identifies itself by delighting in novelties, by taking pride in
knowing "very strange individuals whose thoughts are
even stranger than they are" (p. 3), by expressing com-
placent "regret" to the "dear reader" when no "dramatic
climax" can be reported for an incident in which it
"eventually lost interest" (p. 10), and by believing the
questionable truism that "Things happen in life so fantastic that no imagination could have invented them"
(p. 116).

Such chapters are never fully developed narratives. As
story, they remain literate glosses and curious fragments.
Fortunately they are subordinated to the recurring appearances of rabbi, wife, and eavesdropping son. Only the
presence of these members of the family redeem such recollections. They have been provided with a validity which
is lacking in the comical, grotesque, colorful, or abject
visitors to the apartment. For this strategy Bashevis is
responsible. The Beth Din is therefore more than the in-
stitution serving the religious needs of Krochmalna Street
Jews which Warshofsky remembers; rather, it is what
Bashevis creates out of that memory, a force which sustains,
defines, confines, and ultimately releases Isaac Singer.

The Beth Din — literally a place of judgment and
discrimination — is what gives the book its narrative im-
petus and its episodic rhythm. The court is the *donnée,*
and in its terms the growth of a boy is retrospectively
measured. It is what enables the emergence and differentia-
tion of Warshofsky and Bashevis to be recognized. It is
what preserves the paternal system of restrictive Hasidic
customs, unworldly values, and puritanical habits of mind.

On this altar of traditional beliefs Isaac is almost sacrificed.

What saves him from extinction, and therefore saves the book, is the presence of Bathsheba Zylberman Singer. The daughter of an anti-Hasid talmudist, she is devout but rationalistic, pragmatic and skeptical, and therefore her faith makes her wary of the supernatural marvels and miracle-working rabbis in which her rigidly pious and scholarly husband completely believes. For both, however, if for different reasons, their home is a sanctuary, a refuge from a grim world outside: Krochmalna Street is repugnant to her because the vulgarity and greed of shopkeepers and their customers violate her genteel sense of what is proper; it is terrifying to him because Krochmalna Street is *tref,* spiritually unclean, being the secular sphere in which people daily hold intercourse with the Evil One. Hers is therefore a threatening yet liberating humanistic authority, which simultaneously challenges and confirms the commitments of the Holy Fool who is her husband and who is the Abrahamic father of Isaac.

Although the Singer home is a sanctuary, its security is precarious. It is continually assaulted by those who support the rabbi and his family by their occasional donations. Regular penetrations into the court by the Krochmalna Street residents, however well intentioned, introduce a worldly if transient atmosphere which jeopardizes the severe Hasidic discipline he insists upon preserving. Those who seek out his learned, almost oracular judgments — "Out of my father's mouth spoke the Torah, and all understood that every word was just" (p. 71) — carry into this sanctuary the dust of the street, in the form of their confessional tales. In this familiar setting, the boy Isaac becomes increasingly fascinated by what he witnesses and overhears of immorality, ritual carelessness, frivolities, dissensions, undeserved suffering, and especially sexuality.

The sanctuary is also threatened from within. The presence of a woman in the patriarchal system, however great her piety and essential her supporting role, jeopar-

ISAAC'S NOMINAL CASE: *In My Father's Court* 201

dizes the spiritual purity which is the justification for
Hasidic sanctions and prohibitions. Even her name, like
that of God, cannot be uttered. According to domestic cus-
tom, therefore, a euphemism protects the Hasidic husband
against that degree of intimacy which would transform an
equivocally sacred relationship into a sacrilegious one. Of
this practice Isaac was well aware even as a schoolboy. He
was aware too that his mother's name happened to represent mysterious sin in a form more dangerous than most
feminine names.

> Although I knew [Bathsheba] was my mother's name,
> I had never heard her called anything but "Listen
> here —," which was my father's method of gaining
> her attention since the Hasidim did not approve of
> addressing a woman by name. Bathsheba, for all I
> knew, was merely a biblical name that no one actually
> used, and although the . . . [other] boys often men-
> tioned their mother's names, I was ashamed to men-
> tion that of mine, for it seemed to me too suggestive
> of King David's sin (p. 273).

This then is Isaac's mother: a woman who cannot be
completely acknowledged by her Hasid-husband in Warsaw, and who indirectly caused her soldier-husband's death
in battle by shamefully exposing her body to the gaze
of an Old Testament king casually strolling on his palace
roof. Despite crimes potential and ancient (perhaps because of them), her biblical name is "sacred" to Isaac. In
his own way he participates in her guilt. On a balcony
high above Krochmalna Street he reenacts the Davidical
sin by coveting what he sees stretched out nakedly below
him.

Connected to the pious world of his father within
the apartment, and therefore a structural extension of the
sanctuary, the balcony is nevertheless a spiritually dangerous place. Rabbi Singer himself avoided it because it
gave unlimited access to the profane street below. "The

balcony was already part of the street, of the crowd, of the Gentile world and its savagery," and therefore threatened the integrity of Hasidism (p. 77). But Isaac is excited by the view in spite of his father's disapproval. From the balcony he can see busy shops and markets, the establishments of the world; carriages and wagons traveling swiftly toward unknown destinations; the scurryings of secular Jews committed to Zionism, socialism, territorialism, assimilation, and other worldly causes; the criminal world of thieves, prostitutes, and gamblers; the mysterious world of violence where "abominations were being committed"; and the infernal regions where the "forces of evil" freely roam (p. 171).

The balcony is the perilous resort of the biblical Bathsheba, where physical attractions exchange innocence for guilt, where abominations are fascinating, where thinking jeopardizes faith and honor. It is a state of mind where the imagination can range beyond the limits of paternal control, and where one's own tradition may be created and then examined. Here distant vision is possible, from a vantage which simultaneously is a part of and apart from the sanctuary. This is where the perspective of Bashevis is possible.

On the balcony Isaac can stand, in his satin gabardine coat and velvet hat, gaze about, and reflect upon matters he would never dare to consider inside the apartment.

> How vast was this world, and how rich in all kinds of people and strange happenings! And how high was the sky above the rooftops! And how deep the earth beneath the flagstones! And why did men and women love each other? And where was God, who was constantly spoken of in our house? I was amazed, delighted, entranced. I felt that I must solve this riddle, I alone, with my own understanding (p. 72).

Here he goes to ponder questions which he does not have the courage to discuss with his father. "Even before I learned to read or write, I was obsessed by the paradoxes of time, space, and infinity, and moreover I was convinced that only I myself could reason out such enigmas, that no one could help me" (pp. 160–61). Here too he wonders about the existence of a God who is invisible, and about the possibility of life after death. "I do not recall a time when these questions did not torment me" (p. 161). And on the balcony he comes into fleeting contact with a world more marvelous and beautiful than the sanctuary or Krochmalna Street:

> Many different kinds of flies used to alight on the railing of our balcony: large, small, dark, green-gold. Once in a while a butterfly would stray there. I would not try to catch it, but would hold my breath and stare at it in wonder. The fluttering creature was for me a greeting from the world of freedom [p. 176].

The consciousness of Warshofsky never appears on the balcony. Although derived from the experience of Bashevis, it is separate and subordinate. It too exists outside the sanctuary, but its province is beneath the balcony. Below, the sprawling world of Warsaw can be experienced, not by exercising the mind but by walking the streets of the city, or by taking extravagant rides in a hired carriage or perhaps on a milkwagon. It observes and reports on the same level as what is observed. It is concerned only with what is palpably present in the world of Warsaw, with what can be touched, with events and not significances, and therefore does not require the sharply angled vision of Bashevis. Its perceptions, accordingly, never release the imagination; they only indulge sentimentality. It is a commemorative consciousness, which tends to idealize and romanticize not only the life of Warsaw but also the Singer family, especially Isaac's rebellious and "enlightened" older brother Israel Jonah.

However, even on the street (the province of Warshofsky), whenever the location or situation provides an equivalent for the oblique view from the balcony, the sensibility of Bashevis breaks through, exposing itself in surprising ways, as during a game of "cops and robbers" which Isaac plays with children of the neighborhood:

> I remained standing on the steps leading down into the cellar, and closed my eyes. I actually *felt* that there was a holy soul inside me, a particle of the Godhead. In the darkness I beheld a fiery flower, glittering like gold, luminous as the sun. It opened up like a chalice and bright colors leaped forth: yellow, green, blue, purple — colors and forms such as one sees only in a dream.
>
> Someone tugged at my hand. I shuddered. It was a "cop" who had caught me, the "robber." Suddenly the game bored me, and I walked off alone . . . [p. 79].

For the last seven chapters of *In My Father's Court* the Krochmalna Street balcony is no longer available. After the German occupation of Warsaw, Isaac accompanies Bathsheba to the land of her birth, leaving Rabbi Singer in Warsaw. In the remote Polish village of Bilgoray, where a medieval past exists amid the present of World War I, he discovers already existing within himself a self-supporting platform which was fashioned while he was still living in Warsaw. From it he can observe his mother's relatives, formerly known to him only through family histories which she had recited in the sanctuary. By these relatives the name of Bathsheba is frequently uttered. Therefore, at the age of fourteen or fifteen, Isaac enacts and reenacts balcony experiences in Bilgoray.

> My mind filled with thoughts that were both sweet and painful. I had suddenly become aware of the female sex. My own cousins stirred in me a shameful curiosity. I recalled secrets I had heard in Warsaw, and my mind dwelt on passages in the Pentateuch and Talmud that the teacher had said I would under-

stand when I grew older. I felt that I almost knew the answer to the riddle. My dreams became frightening and pleasurable. I thought I was going crazy, or was possessed by a dibbuk. Desires and fantasies became all-consuming [pp. 294–95].

Similarly, from an unexpected source in Bilgoray, come answers to questions which had puzzled him high above Krochmalna Street, answers which make him as beautiful and free as the butterfly on the balcony railing.

As I read [Stupnicki's book on Spinoza], I felt intoxicated, inspired as I never had been before. It seemed to me that the truths I had been seeking since childhood had at last become apparent. Everything was God — Warsaw, Bilgoray, the spider in the attic, the water in the wall, the clouds in the sky, and the book on my knees. Everything was divine, everything was thought and extension. A stone had its stony thoughts. . . . God was eternal, transcending time. Time, or duration, controlled only the modi, the bubbles in the divine cauldron, that were forever forming and bursting. I too was a modus, which explained my indecision, my restlessness, my passionate nature, my doubts and fears. But the modi too were created from God's body, God's thought, and could be explained only through Him. . . .

I was exalted; everything seemed good. There was no difference between heaven and earth, the most distant star, and my red hair. My tangled thoughts were divine. The fly alighting on my page had to be there. . . . The most foolish fantasy in my mind had been thought for me by God. . . . Heaven and earth became the same thing. The laws of nature were divine . . . [pp. 305–306].

Having left behind him his father's Beth Din, but never completely forgetting it, Isaac Bashevis has now arrived *in his mother's court.* The belletristic memoir ends accordingly: "I was prepared for the turmoil that writers call 'love' " (p. 307).

From the maternal balcony, fifteen years later, he will envision his first novel, *Satan in Goray*. All that remains before the Bashevis sensitivity can be completed is for Isaac to become aware of the power that might be released by combining a sense of the historical past with a bizarre demonology of dybbuk, imps, succubi, and assorted fiends. In Bilgoray, where fragments of the seventeenth-century world of Chmielnicki and Sabbatai Zevi have been preserved, this awareness is achieved.

In My Father's Court originally may have been designed (as some disappointed readers have suggested) as a Warshofsky effort to satisfy the demands of those readers who have made a cult of Isaac Bashevis Singer. However, the *irony of familiarity* — of which the mature Bashevis is a master — interjects itself often enough to prevent the book from becoming merely a celebration of Singer family experiences. To the extent that the book is Isaac's, it is a confirmation of the evolving Bashevis consciousness. Therefore it is a creation out of memory, relying upon imaginative techniques of fiction for grasping the facts of family history. This, more than the circumstance of serial publication in the *Jewish Daily Forward,* is why the Book of Isaac is a series of narratives, a collection of personal stories, with a unity which is nominal. Such is the form of the effective life of Bashevis — modi bubbling in the turbulent cauldron which is the consciousness of Isaac Singer.

Samuel I. Mintz

14.

Spinoza and Spinozism in Singer's Shorter Fiction

The element of Spinoza in Isaac Bashevis Singer's work has only partly to do with Spinoza's system of ideas. What is also involved is Spinoza's personality and the paradoxical fact of his drawing upon the Jewish tradition at the same time that he is isolated from it. Figuratively, Spinoza is a way of focusing in Singer's work on the tension between rationalism and the spirit-world of demons, or between enlightenment and orthodoxy, or between Spinozist intellectualism and Chassidic emotion. In an even larger sense, Spinoza is a metaphor for the problem that has beset Yiddish literature from the time of its first great classical writer, Mendele Mocher Sforim, to Singer himself, namely, the problem of the writer who dwells simultaneously in the opposing cultures of Jewish enlightenment or the Haskalah and the Jewish tradition.

These issues are present in much of Singer's shorter fiction, but nowhere more so than in the remarkable story "The Spinoza of Market Street." The Yiddish title of this story, *"Der Spinozist,"* is less suggestive than is the English of the story's meaning, because the hero of the story, Dr. Fischelson, is more than a Spinozist philosopher, he is also

207

a type of Spinoza. Surrounded though he is by the teeming life of the Jewish community of Warsaw, Dr. Fischelson is nevertheless a figure of isolation. The exuberant, even violent, life of the people flows around him, but he is detached. He is a Jew but he is regarded by his neighbors with suspicion, because, although he is a man of evident and wide learning, the whole bent of his intellectual life appears to be guided by principles that lie outside the Jewish tradition. He does not pray; the object of his ceaseless study is not Scripture or Talmud; he entertains opinions so heterodox as to give currency to rumors that he is either a heretic or an apostate; he owns a telescope and peers through it at the stars — a curious interest, so it is thought, for a Jew — and although he is the son of a rabbi, he chooses to pursue a secular career in philosophy.

What Singer has done, without actually telling us that he has done so, is to create a portrait of Spinoza. It is an inexact portrait, to be sure, because two of the most attractive features of Spinoza's personality, his serenity and his tolerance, are missing. But in its broadest outlines the picture of Dr. Fischelson as Spinoza is accurate. Both the seventeenth-century philosopher and his twentieth-century disciple were born into orthodox Jewish families; both repudiated the tradition by calling into question various aspects of the orthodox creed. Spinoza was excommunicated; Dr. Fischelson is removed from his post as chief librarian of the Warsaw synagogue. Both depended for their daily bread on pensions from sympathetic friends, although Spinoza bore the loss of a pension with greater equanimity. Both had scientific interests. Both were plagued by ill health.

In these respects Dr. Fischelson resembles Spinoza unconsciously. But he also imitates his master. He tries to make reason the ruling principle of his life. "There is no rational life," Spinoza wrote, "without intelligence and things are good only insofar as they assist man to enjoy that life of the mind which is determined by intelligence. Those things alone, on the other hand, we call evil which hinder man from perfecting his reason and enjoying a rational life." Dr. Fischelson strives to perfect his reason. For thirty years he has been laboring over a massive commentary on Spinoza's *Ethics*. The precepts of the master are engraved in his mind, and his pleasures are wholly connected with the life of the mind. When he looks at the heavens through his telescope he feels the force of Spinoza's doctrine about the infinitude of God and the oneness of God and Nature.

> It comforted Dr. Fischelson to think that although he was only a weak, puny man, a changing mode of the absolutely infinite Substance, he was nevertheless a part of the cosmos, made of the same matter as the celestial bodies; to the extent that he was a part of the Godhead, he knew he could not be destroyed. In such moments, Dr. Fischelson experienced the *Amor Dei Intellectualis* which is, according to the philosopher of Amsterdam, the highest perfection of the mind.[1]

Similarly, although Dr. Fischelson is afflicted by a severe stomach disorder which might be an ulcer but could just possibly be cancer, he has no fear of death. He understands the meaning of the statement in the fourth part of the *Ethics* that "a free man thinks of nothing less than of death; and his wisdom is a meditation not of death, but of life." On Spinoza's showing, fear is one of the baser emotions; it does not partake of reason and it fails to apprehend the necessity of all things.

In the skillfully drawn portrait of Dr. Fischelson, Singer makes good literary use of Spinozist ideas. He has evidently read the philosopher with care and with an accurate understanding. Spinoza is not an easy philosopher to read; his geometrical method of demonstration and proof, essential though it is to his purpose, gives his style a crabbed appearance. Moreover, as Dr. Fischelson him-

self comes to agree, nuances of fresh meaning and ambiguities occasionally disturb the logical surface of Spinoza's
thought. But Singer has perceived very clearly the essential
shape of Spinoza's mind. He understands that Spinoza's
system embraces the whole universe and man's place in it
and that it is a powerful vision of moral order, an order
into which man can rise when he comprehends the universe under the aspect of eternity. Singer knows that
Spinoza's conception of freedom means the freeing of the
mind from the bondage of the particular and the temporal.
Singer has hold of the basic premises of Spinoza's thought
— the unity of God and nature and the determinism of all
things — and he understands the moral consequences that
flow from these premises. What is most important is that
Singer recognizes the fundamentally rationalist character
of Spinoza's system. Spinoza's ideas have been disfigured
both by their enemies as well as by some of their most
ardent admirers. Singer, however, reads these ideas coolly
and correctly. He rejects the notion sometimes advanced
that Spinoza is a mystic. It is true that a tincture of mysticism clings to Spinoza's teaching about the immersion of
the mind in the oneness of the universe, but, as Stuart
Hampshire has written, Spinoza "is not a mystic, but a
rationalist who makes greater claims for the powers of
pure reason than any other great philosopher has ever
made." [2] This observation about Spinoza is entirely ac-
ceptable to Singer, and its importance will be made clear
when we examine the second, climactic portion of Dr.
Fischelson's story.

The problem for Dr. Fischelson is that the life of the
mind is no proof against the demands of the flesh. He
cannot insulate his mind against the sounds, smells, triviali-
ties, vulgarities, cruelties, and travails of the world around
him, or against the pain of his own body, or against the
tribulations of poverty and of dependence on an uncertain
benevolence for his daily bread. He aspires to be Spinoza
but he is Spinoza-*manqué*. Only fitfully can he find repose

in the life of the mind; more often he feels himself afflicted by the world of particular things, and that world is full of surds and discomforts. The heat of the Warsaw summer is oppressive, Spinoza notwithstanding. And even the world of politics and of nations, in whose problems he takes no interest, appears to be entering a process of decay: an archduke assassinated, armies on the march, food and drink scarce, friends absent, money not forthcoming. The world is irrational, unSpinozan. In it lurk evil presences, such as were presumed to have been banished by Spinoza; tomcats scamper on the roofs like demons, raising unearthly sounds and taunting Dr. Fischelson. It is a "half-lit bedlam."

Insofar as Dr. Fischelson thinks of this world, that is to say, insofar as he takes a Spinozist view of it, he is able to detach himself from it. The difficulty is that his thoughts are not always under his control. The world presents itself to his senses with an immediacy, a hardness, which he cannot dispel, and some part of his reaction to it is unconscious, or only dimly perceived in a dream. He has a nightmare, a confused recollection of his childhood, in which a Catholic procession passes through the street of his *shtetl* Tishvitz. Long-robed figures walk by; in their hands they bear double-edged axes. The air is filled with the smell of incense and of corpses. Suddenly the sky turns red and the whole world begins to burn. The dream, suffused as it is in the emotion of fear and having no apparent rational structure, is a perfect antithesis to Spinoza. Dr. Fischelson "tried to meditate about his extraordinary dream, to find its rational connection with what was happening to him and to comprehend it *sub specie eternitatis,* but none of it made sense." "This earth," he thought, "belongs to the mad."

What is happening to Dr. Fischelson is that his health is giving way under the pressure of the conflict between his beloved Spinozism and the irrational world in which he lives. The turbulent life that had hitherto flowed around him now flows through him; it churns his emotions and makes him feel he is dying. When the tension inside of him becomes intolerable — when, that is to say, he is unable to live in either of the two opposing worlds — he lapses into unconsciousness; in this condition he is discovered by his neighbor Black Dobbe, a spinster, a singularly unattractive woman who bears masculine features and dresses like a man, who has been twice jilted, who is illiterate, and whose character is a curious mixture of patience and cunning. In sketching her portrait, which he does in bold, rapid strokes and with the utmost skill, Singer omits the irony which he has spent on Dr. Fischelson. He admires her, and he makes her the catalyst of Dr. Fischelson's salvation. She nurses the aging philosopher, feeds him, restores him; in the process she is able to overcome her awe of him and her superstitious fear of his black doctrines. For his part Dr. Fischelson is comforted by Dobbe's presence; but, curiously, when he returns to his study of the *Ethics,* its logical structure and meaning elude him. What could Spinoza have meant when he said that having an idea of the separate modes of the human body does not give adequate knowledge of the human body itself? Dr. Fischelson feels an obscure stirring in his blood; to tell the truth, he is becoming more interested in the modes of the human body than in the body regarded *sub specie eternitatis.*

And then a miracle takes place such as could not occur in a Spinozan universe. Dr. Fischelson and Black Dobbe are married. The bridegroom is the object of many good-natured jibes; he is even too feeble to break the glass at the wedding ceremony, and it has to be done by a younger guest. Nevertheless Dr. Fischelson takes his bride home with him, speaks to her not of Spinoza but of love, quotes Lessing and Goethe to her, embraces her, possesses her, and is restored to that passionate life from which he has been cut off — indeed cut himself off — for so many years past. The life of Spinoza and the life of Dr. Fischelson can no longer be said to intersect. We are told by Spinoza's earliest biographer that "although our philosopher was not one of those austere people who look upon marriage as a hinderance to the activities of the mind, he nevertheless did not enter into its bonds, either because he feared the ill temper of a woman, or because the love of philosophy took him up completely." [3] Earlier in the story, before Dobbe comes in to minister to Dr. Fischelson and while he is still in his anguish, he receives what might be considered a mild warning against marriage. It comes in the form of a vulgar music-hall song played on a gramophone record in some neighboring house:

> If a man takes a young wife
> He has bought himself grief;
> She isn't worth a penny
> And his joy is too brief.[4]

But Dr. Fischelson is not able to make better sense of this song than he is of the Hebrew prayer which mingles incongruously with it in the summer air. Nor are we given assurances as the story ends that Dr. Fischelson's marriage to Dobbe will succeed. We simply cannot tell. An element of contingency, thoroughly unSpinozan, clings to the experience and gives it zest. Singer's point is not that the marriage will succeeed or that it will fail, but that it has taken place; having taken place, it puts Dr. Fischelson on the side of experience — passionate, open-ended, full-bloodcd experience. Singer does not argue that the world opposed to Spinoza is an abode of happiness. Quite the contrary, it is a world in which pleasure and pain, joy and grief, good and evil are mixed together almost inseparably; they are, in Milton's phrase, "as two twins cleaving together."

Such a world cannot accommodate Spinozist rationalism. It is a mysterious, not a rational world. In the majority of Singer's short stories we are made to feel the presence of demons and supernatural beings. Some of them are no more than mischievous sprites but many of them are evil spirits. They are figures or types of evil or of death; so realistically are they treated in the stories that they give ground for thinking that Singer is persuaded of their real existence. Their appearances are sudden, uncaused and unexplained. In some of the stories their entrance is dramatic; at other times it is casual and hardly noticed. Their names are drawn from a variety of sources of which the most prominent is the mystical cabalist tradition well known to Chassidic lore. Spinoza knew the same tradition and rebelled against it, and it is interesting to note that the text of Spinoza's excommunication invokes the names of numerous benign angels and supernatural presences drawn from the cabalist tradition. What Spinoza thought of this tradition, of the existence of demons, specters, and evil presences, he made clear in a number of places: his *Short Treatise* has a chapter on devils, the burden of which is "that such a wretched thing could not exist, even for a moment." And in his correspondence with Hugo Boxel he equated ghosts and demons with centaurs and griffins, with the products, that is to say, of a febrile human imagination. Similarly, he argued that miracles are symptoms of human ignorance. And he associated the whole apparatus of supernature with periods of social stress and disorder, declaring that men tend to be rational when they are prosperous, and superstitious when they fall into misfortune. In short, Spinoza disbelieved utterly in a world inhabited by demons, in the kind of world brought vividly to life by Singer.

Singer's world is realized most fully in the *shtetl*, the village community of East European Jewry. At the peak of its development, this environment was comparatively immune to currents of European thought. Such ideas as came to it from the outside were brought by outsiders, as, for example, by the gentile Dr. Yaretzky in the story "The Shadow of a Crib." This is an imperfectly shaped but mysterious and very moving story. Dr. Yaretzky is a striking character, a troubled figure who belongs to the world of European thought but who is not happy in it and who is drawn, strangely, to the mystically ascetic rabbi of the town. Unable to enter the rabbi's world, he withdraws from the town, only to reappear in it many years later as an apparition. "Why would the soul of Dr. Yaretzky hover in the window of the rabbi's study? Why should a Christian heretic seek the house of a rabbi?" The answers to these questions is given implicitly; it is (to put the matter in a way that does only partial justice to the meaning of this story) that the life of the spirit, of the mind of the rabbi immersed in the *Zohar* and in touch with the spirit-world, is superior to the life of the mind trained only in the aridities of secular "enlightened" philosophy.

The same problem is broached in the story called "Caricature." Here the scene is Warsaw on the eve of World War II. Whereas Dr. Fischelson a generation before was only one remove from the *shtetl,* Dr. Boris Margolis, also a philosopher, is two removes away and the distance seems immense. Dr. Margolis is a child of the Jewish Enlightenment. He has in hand a large manuscript which is nothing less than the exposition of his own metaphysical system, but he is dissatisfied with it and cannot bring himself to publish it. What seemed to him penetrating when he first wrote it, now seems, after a lapse of years, to be jejune. He does not believe that it can withstand the criticism of the newer currents of philosophy. Moreover, Dr. Margolis is no longer enamored of the great metaphysical systems of the past. The scepticism of Hume put those systems finally to rest, and Kant's attempt at their resuscitation was a failure. Nineteenth-century metaphysics compounded the failure, succeeding only in providing footnotes to Kant. Dr. Margolis's disenchantment is complete. His intellectual life is now marked by hesitations and frustrations and his whole experience is a tissue of irritations. Even the scholarly life of enlightened Jews around him seems irrelevant. What is the point, for example, of producing a Hebrew encyclopedia when the shadow of Hitler draws closer?

Dr. Margolis is Dr. Fischelson writ large, and his wife Mathilda is Black Dobbe. She resembles Black Dobbe even in the masculinity of her features, a characteristic which Dr. Margolis interprets in the light of a remark by Schopenhauer to the effect that if a woman overcomes her natural immaturity of mind she takes on the features of a man. Mathilda is afflicted with financial anxieties and she is baffled by her husband's loss of intellectual vitality. She urges him to publish his manuscript. She is a more sophisticated, better educated version of Black Dobbe, but something of the *shtetl* still clings to her. At the end of the story Dr. Margolis discovers her asleep at his desk, his open manuscript spread before her. Her masculine features have deepened. He realizes that in almost every detail, not excluding the wisp of beard, her face resembles his own. This transformation, this mingling of appearances and of personalities, is a mystery, one that transcends rational and biological explanation, as Dr. Margolis now dimly begins to recognize, but only dimly, because he reverts very quickly to "rational" explanations. Thus the story ends as it began, on a note of despair.

What are we to make of Singer's repudiation of intellectualism? The issue between himself and Spinoza does not turn simply, as I have suggested earlier, on the differences in their outlook. It is a question of personality, of feelings and of feeling-tone. And it is a question, on Singer's part, of asserting the value of the emotional life. "We are the people of the idea," Lionel Trilling has written, "and we rightly fear that the intellect will dry up the blood in our veins and wholly check the emotional and creative part of the mind." [5] Singer's horror of this prospect is matched by the power of his contrary vision, by the spontaneity and creativity of the life he extols. His short

stories are written in a style of concentrated energy per-
fectly suited to the world of his imagination. That world is not a Spinozan world, but having said
this we must observe that Singer does not hold Spinoza
in contempt. It is in fact hard to see how any writer, committed to the creation of an imaginative world, could be
contemptuous of Spinoza, whose work, after all, was on
the order of a great imaginative achievement. Indeed there
is a sense in which Singer, opposed though he is to Spinoza's fundamental outlook, apprehends at least one of
Spinoza's positions. Spinozism is a philosophy of timeless-
ness, and the *shtetl*, that marvelous abode of Singer's imagination, existed, at the moment of its fullest development,
outside of history. Singer and Spinoza clasped hands in
their different achievement of that timeless order.

Notes

1. *The Spinoza of Market Street* (New York, 1963), p. 10.
2. Commentary upon Spinoza's *Ethics* in *The Age of Reason: The Seventeenth Century Philosophers* (New York, 1956), p. 132.
3. [J. M. Lucas], *The Life of the Late Mr. DeSpinosa* [1719], trans. and ed. Abraham Wolf (London, 1927), pp. 72–73. Spinoza may have had an unrequited love affair, but the evidence for this is con-flicting. See Abraham Wolfson, *Spinoza* (New York, 1932), p. 106.
4. These verses were omitted from the English version. They are translated freely here from the volume *Gimpl Tom un andere Derzaylungen* (New York, 1963), p. 67.
5. Lionel Trilling, "The Meaning of a Literary Idea," *The Liberal Imagination* (New York, 1957), p. 276.

Glossary

For fuller descriptions of the following terms see *The Jewish Encyclopedia;* Gershom G. Scholem, *Major Trends in Jewish Mysticism;* and Irving Howe and Eliezer Greenberg (eds.), *A Treasury of Yiddish Stories.*

Baal Shem Tov   The founder of the Hasidic movement who stressed the "divinity" of all men.

Cabala   A system or kind of occult theosophy or mystical interpretation of the Scriptures.

Chmielnicki   The Cossack leader responsible for the death of many Jews in the seventeenth century. (See *Satan in Goray.*)

Dybbuk   A spirit which dwells in a human being and controls his actions.

Hanukah   Feast of the Dedication.

Hasidism   A religious revival of the eighteenth century which stressed ecstacy and similar experience of the divine.

Haskalah   A religious movement of mideighteenth-century Germany which stressed rationalism and "assimilation" of currently modern ideas.

Jacob Frank   An eighteenth-century Sabbatian and cabalist who proclaimed himself the Messiah and later converted to Catholicism.

Sabbatai Zevi   An Oriental Jew who proclaimed himself the Messiah in the middle of the seventeenth century and later converted to Islam. (See *Satan in Goray.*)

Shtetl   A Jewish village (especially the "world" of East European Jews).

Simhath Torah   Feast of the Rejoicing of the Law.

Zadik   A "wise man" who set patterns of behavior for his Hasidic followers.

Jackson R. Bryer and Paul E. Rockwell

Isaac Bashevis Singer in English: A Bibliography

As of this writing — June 1, 1968 — it is fifteen years since Saul Bellow's translation of "Gimpel the Fool" introduced to readers of English the work of a writer long known to those familiar with Yiddish literature — Isaac Bashevis Singer. During this time, recognition has not come to Isaac Singer either quickly or spectacularly. Despite the fact that, to date, he is the author, in English, of five novels, three collections of short stories (a fourth volume appeared in September 1968), three children's books, a volume of autobiographical sketches, and a collection of his shorter prose in a Modern Library edition, he remains largely ignored by many serious critics of modern fiction and unread by a majority of the American and English reading public. Part of this can be attributed to the fact that, until very recently, Singer's prose appeared — before book collection — almost entirely in Jewish periodicals, many of them with very small circulations and all but one — *Commentary* — with no appreciable non-Jewish readership. But perhaps of equal importance in accounting for Singer's relative obscurity is his manner of writing. He is a story-teller in the folk tale tradition writing in an age which demands that its prose writers be interested in either psychological introspection or the problems of today. Singer continues to reach into his past for his settings and subjects at a time when critics and public alike cry for relevancy to today.

But within the last year or two there have been encouraging signs that such superficial and literal standards are not blinding intelligent editors and readers to the far more important excellences of Singer's work. His prose has begun to appear in such varied periodicals as *Cosmopolitan, Harper's,* the *New Yorker, Encounter, Playboy, Redbook,* and the *Saturday Evening Post.* He is not only the recipient of *Playboy's* Fiction Award for 1967 (in competition with a number of fine modern writers), but his last two books have been the subjects of front-page essays in the *New York Times Book Review.* In addition, the last two years have seen the first extended comment on Singer's work in critical journals, with recent and perceptive essays in *Critique, Encounter,* and the *Minnesota Review.* Thus, this bibliography appears at what may well be a turning point in Singer's critical reputation. With a book of short stories published last year and the sequel to *The Manor* surely soon to appear, there is no doubt that his work will continue to be reviewed and commented upon, and, undoubtedly, as it has almost always been in the past, in terms of great praise. But, more importantly, we can perhaps foresee the time when non-Jewish critics in non-Jewish, mass circulation, and critical journals will begin to focus serious attention on the range and richness of Singer's achievement. It is worth noting that, late in 1966, the most distinguished of all living American literary critics, Edmund Wilson, commended Singer's work to the attention of the Nobel Prize committee.

This bibliography is an attempt to list all of Singer's published work in English and a large sampling of the critical material about him. It is divided into two basic sections: works by Singer and works about him. Within the first, we have made no effort to list all editions of Singer's books but have included only the first American and British editions. The reviews listed in Section II, C refer almost exclusively to these editions. In Sections I, B and I, C, reprintings of shorter fiction and nonfiction are listed but this type of listing is a very difficult one to compile with any certainty of completeness and must therefore be regarded as partial.

In Sections II, A and II, B, we have exercised very little selectivity in listing book and periodical references about Singer, primarily because of the dearth of such material. Again, however, because Singer has been much commented upon in quite obscure journals, we have undoubtedly missed a few of these. Brief annotations in both these sections often indicate the scope and/or nature of the items.

Quite obviously, most of the important critical comment on Singer and his work has appeared in reviews of his books. Because of this fact, we have made a particular effort to locate and list as many reviews as we could. We have received invaluable assistance in this effort from the publicity departments of Singer's publishers, most especially Farrar, Straus & Giroux, Secker & Warburg, Harper & Row, and Scribner's. Without their help, and that of numerous editors and librarians throughout the country, we would have been unable to find and verify all but a very few of the reviews. Reviews of more than ordinary scope and interest are marked with an asterisk. Where only a few pages of a review (or an essay) refer specifically to Singer, the page numbers of the entire piece are listed first, followed by the pages on Singer, in brackets.

Finally, we wish to express our appreciation to Ellen Bungay, Mrs. Loretta T. D'Eustachio, and Mrs. Jacki Rockwell for their help with the bibliography.

I. Works by Singer

A. BOOKS

The Family Moskat, trans. A. H. Gross *et al.* New York: Alfred A. Knopf, 1950; New York: Farrar, Straus and Giroux, 1965; London: Secker and Warburg, 1966.

Satan in Goray, trans. Jacob Sloan. New York: Noonday Press, 1955; London: Peter Owen, 1958.

Gimpel the Fool and Other Stories, trans. Saul Bellow, Isaac Rosenfeld, Norbert Guterman, Elaine Gottlieb, *et al.* New York: Noonday Press, 1957; London: Peter Owen, 1958. Contents: "Gimpel the Fool," "The Gentleman From Cracow," "The Wife Killer," "By the Light of Memorial," "Candles," "The Mirror," "The Little Shoemakers," "Joy," "From the Diary of One Not Born," "The Old Man," "Fire," "The Unseen."

The Magician of Lublin, trans. Elaine Gottlieb and Joseph Singer. New York: Noonday Press, 1960; London: Secker and Warburg, 1961.

The Spinoza of Market Street, trans. Martha Glicklich, Cecil Hemley, *et al.* New York: Farrar, Straus and Cudahy, 1961; London: Secker and Warburg, 1962. Contents: "The Spinoza of Market Street," "The Black Wedding," "A Tale of Two Liars," "The Shadow of a Crib," "Shiddah and Kuziba," "Caricature," "The Beggar Said So," "The Man Who Came Back," "A Piece of Advice," "In the Poorhouse," "The Destruction of Kreshev."

The Slave, trans. Cecil Hemley and the author. New York: Farrar, Straus and Cudahy, 1962; London: Secker and Warburg, 1963.

Short Friday and Other Stories, trans. Mirra Ginsburg, Elizabeth Pollet, *et al.* New York: Farrar, Straus and Giroux, 1964; London: Secker and Warburg, 1967. Contents: "Taibele and Her Demon," "Big and Little," "Blood," "Alone," "Esther Kreindel the Second," "Jachid and Jechidah," "Under the Knife," "The Fast,"

"The Last Demon," "Yentl the Yeshiva Boy," "Three Tales," "Zeidlus the Pope," "A Wedding in Brownsville," "I Place My Reliance on No Man," "Cunegunde," "Short Friday."

Selected Short Stories of Isaac Bashevis Singer, edited and introduced by Irving Howe. New York: The Modern Library, 1966. Contents: "Gimpel the Fool," "The Gentleman from Cracow," "The Wife Killer," "The Mirror," "The Little Shoemakers," "The Old Man," "The Unseen," "The Spinoza of Market Street," "The Black Wedding," "A Tale of Two Liars," "The Beggar Said So," "The Man Who Came Back," "In the Poorhouse," "Taibele and Her Demon," "Blood," "Esther Kreindel the Second," "The Fast," "The Last Demon," "Alone," "Three Tales," "Zeidlus the Pope," "I Place My Reliance on No Man," "Short Friday."

In My Father's Court, trans. Channah Kleinerman-Goldstein, Elaine Gottlieb, and Joseph Singer. New York: Farrar, Straus and Giroux, 1966; London: Secker and Warburg, 1967.

Zlateh the Goat and Other Stories, trans. Elizabeth Shub and the author. Illustrated by Maurice Sendak. New York: Harper and Row, 1966. Contents: "Fool's Paradise," "Grandmother's Tale," "The Snow in Chelm," "The Mixed-up Feet and the Silly Bridegroom," "The First Shlemiel," "The Devil's Trick," "Zlateh the Goat."

The Fearsome Inn, trans. Elizabeth Shub and the author. New York: Charles Scribner's, 1967.

The Manor. New York: Farrar, Straus and Giroux, 1967.

Mazel and Shlimazel or The Milk of a Lioness, trans. Elizabeth Shub and the author. New York: Farrar, Straus and Giroux, 1967.

B. FICTION

"Gimpel the Fool," trans. Saul Bellow, *Partisan Review,* XX (May 1953), 300–13. Collected in *Gimpel the Fool* and *Selected Short Stories.*

Reprinted: *A Treasury of Yiddish Stories,* ed. Irving Howe and Eliezer Greenberg. New York: Viking Press, 1954. Pp. 401–14.

Reprinted: *Short Fiction: A Critical Collection,* ed. James R. Frakes and Isadore Traschen. Englewood Cliffs, N. J.: Prentice-Hall, 1959. Pp. 122–33.

Reprinted: *The World of Modern Fiction — American,* ed. Steven Marcus. New York: Simon and Schuster, 1960. Pp. 45–57.

Reprinted: *Modern Jewish Stories,* ed. Gerda Charles. Englewood Cliffs, N. J.: Prentice-Hall, 1965. Pp. 81–97.

Reprinted: *Great Modern European Short Stories,* ed. Douglas and Sylvia Angus. Greenwich, Conn.: Fawcett, 1967. Pp. 240–53.

Reprinted: *Short Stories: Classic, Modern, Contemporary,* ed. Marcus Klein and Robert Pack. Boston: Little, Brown, 1967. Pp. 437–50.

"The Little Shoemakers," trans. Isaac Rosenfeld. In *A Treasury of Yiddish Stories,* ed. Irving Howe and Eliezer Greenberg. New York: Viking Press, 1954. Pp. 523–33. Collected in *Gimpel the Fool* and *Selected Short Stories.*

"From the Diary of One Not Born," trans. Nancy E. Gross, *Partisan Review,* XXI (March 1954), 139–46. Collected in *Gimpel the Fool.*

"The Wife Killer," trans. Shlomo Katz, *Midstream,* I (Autumn 1955), 60–71. Collected in *Gimpel the Fool* and *Selected Short Stories.*

Reprinted: *The "Midstream" Reader,* ed. Shlomo Katz. New York and London: Thomas Yoseloff, 1960. Pp. 317–30.

"The Mirror," trans. Norbert Guterman. *New World Writing, No. 12.* New York: New American Library, 1957. Pp. 164–74. Collected in *Gimpel the Fool* and *Selected Short Stories.*

"Fire," trans. Norbert Guterman, *Commentary,* XXIII (February 1957), 135–38. Collected in *Gimpel the Fool.*

"The Gentleman from Cracow" [trans. Martha Glicklich and Elaine Gottlieb], *Commentary,* XXIV (September 1957), 231–39. Collected in *Gimpel the Fool* and *Selected Short Stories.*

"A Tale of Two Liars," trans. Joseph Singer and Cecil Hemley. In *Noonday 1,* ed. Cecil Hemley. New York:

Noonday Press, 1958. Pp. 30–52. Collected in *The Spinoza of Market Street* and *Selected Short Stories.*

"Hail, the Messiah," trans. Morris Kreitman. In *Jewish Short Stories of To-day,* ed. Morris Kreitman. London: Faber and Faber, 1958. Pp. 35–51.

"The Black Wedding," trans. Martha Glicklich. In *Noonday 3,* ed. Cecil Hemley and Dwight W. Webb. New York: Noonday Press, 1960. Pp. 3–12. Collected in *The Spinoza of Market Street* and *Selected Short Stories.* Reprinted (abridged): *Psychopathology and Literature,* ed. Leslie Y. Rabkin. San Francisco: Chandler, 1966. Pp. 181–82.

"At the Poorhouse," trans. Mirra Ginsburg, *Midstream,* VI (Winter 1960), 38–45. Collected in *The Spinoza of Market Street* and *Selected Short Stories* (as "In the Poorhouse").

"One Whom Came Back," trans. Mirra Ginsburg, *Commentary,* XXIX (February 1960), 122–27. Collected in *The Spinoza of Market Street* and *Selected Short Stories* (as "The Man Who Came Back").

"A Piece of Advice," trans. Martha Glicklich, *Hadassah Newsletter,* XLI (September 1960), 8–9. Collected in *The Spinoza of Market Street.*

    Reprinted: *The Bas Mitzvah Treasury,* ed. Azriel Eisenberg and Leah Ain Globe. New York: Twayne, 1965. Pp. 255–64.

"The Shadow of a Crib" [trans. Elaine Gottlieb and June Ruth Flaum], *Mademoiselle,* LII (March 1961), 148–49. 191. Collected in *The Spinoza of Market Street.*

"Shiddah and Kuziba," trans. Elizabeth Pollet, *Commentary,* XXXI (March 1961), 213–16. Collected in *The Spinoza of Market Street.*

"The Beggar Said So," trans. Gertrude Hirschler, *Esquire,* LV (May 1961), 79–81. Collected in *The Spinoza of Market Street* and *Selected Short Stories.*

    Reprinted: *Literature for Composition,* ed. James R. Kreuzer and Lee Cogan. New York: Holt, Rinehart and Winston, 1965. Pp. 349–57.

"Big and Little: An Old Wives Tale," trans. Mirra Ginsburg, *Midstream*, VII (Summer 1961), 57–63. Collected in *Short Friday* (as "Big and Little").

"The Spinoza of Market Street [trans. Martha Glicklich and Cecil Hemley], *Esquire*, LVI (October 1961), 144–48, 150–54. Collected in *The Spinoza of Market Street* and *Selected Short Stories*.
Reprinted: *The Short Story: An Inductive Approach*, ed. Gerald Levin. New York: Harcourt, Brace & World, 1967. Pp. 121–34.

"Caricature," trans. Shulamith Charney and Cecil Hemley, *Gentlemen's Quarterly*, XXXI (November 1961), 106, 134–39. Collected in *The Spinoza of Market Street*.

"The Last Demon," trans. Martha Glicklich and Cecil Hemley, *Prism 1* (1962), 7–17. Collected in *Short Friday* and *Selected Short Stories*.

"The Faster," trans. Mirra Ginsburg, *The Second Coming*, I (June 1962), 39–42. Collected in *Short Friday* and *Selected Short Stories* (as "The Fast").

"Yentl the Yeshiva Boy," trans. Marion Magid and Elizabeth Pollet, *Commentary*, XXXIV (September 1962), 213–24. Collected in *Short Friday*.
Reprinted: *The "Commentary" Reader*, ed. Norman Podhoretz. New York: Atheneum, 1966. Pp. 295–314.

"Alone," trans. Joel Blocker, *Mademoiselle*, LV (October 1962), 118–19, 172–75. Collected in *Short Friday* and *Selected Short Stories*.

"The Son," trans. Elizabeth Pollet, *Menorah Journal*, XLIX (Autumn-Winter 1962), 71–76.   )
Reprinted: *The Menorah Treasury*, ed. Leo W. Schwarz. Philadelphia: Jewish Publication Society of America, 1964. Pp. 447–53.
Reprinted (abridged): *Jewish Digest*, IX (March 1964), 41–45.
Reprinted: *The Jewish Caravan* (rev. ed.), ed. Leo W. Schwarz. New York: Holt, Rinehart and Winston, 1965. Pp. 626–30.

"Taibele and Hurmizah," trans. Mirra Ginsburg, *Commentary*, XXV (February 1963), 132–38. Collected in *Short Friday* and *Selected Short Stories* (as "Taibele and Her Demon").

"A Wedding in Brownsville," trans. Chana Faerstein and
Elizabeth Pollet, *Commentary*, XXXVII (March 1964),
43–49.
> Reprinted: *How We Live — Contemporary Life in Con-
> temporary Fiction,* ed. Penney Chapin Hills and L.
> Rust Hills. New York: Macmillan, 1968.

"Blood," trans. Elizabeth Pollet, *Harper's*, CCXXIX (August 1964), 87–94. Collected in *Short Friday* and *Selected
Short Stories.*

"Getzel the Monkey," *American Judaism*, XIV (Fall 1964),
12–13, 53–54, 56. Collected in *The Séance.*
> Reprinted: *The "American Judaism" Reader,* ed. Paul
> Kresh. London, New York, Toronto: Abelard-Schu-
> man, 1967. Pp. 119–27.

"Three Tales," trans. Ruth Whitman and Cecil Hemley,
Commentary, XXXVIII (October 1964), 40–45. Collected in *Short Friday* and *Selected Short Stories.*

"Esther Kreindel the Second" [trans. Elizabeth Pollet and
the author], *Saturday Evening Post*, CCXXXVII (October 17, 1964), 50–52, 54, 57, 59. Collected in *Short
Friday* and *Selected Short Stories.*
> Reprinted: *Best Modern Short Stories.* New York: Curtis
> Publishing Company, 1965. Pp. 157–71.

"Cockadoodledoo," trans. Ruth Whitman, *Hadassah Magazine*, XLVI (November 1964), 9, 27–30.

"Converts," trans. Joseph Singer, *Commentary*, XXXVIII
(December 1964), 46–48.

"Cunegunde" [trans. Elaine Gottlieb and the author],
Esquire, LXII (December 1964), 135, 282–84. Collected
in *Short Friday.*

"The Séance," *Encounter*, XXV (July 1965), 14–19. Collected in *The Séance.*
> Reprinted: *The Story Today — 1966/1967.* New York:
> Simon and Schuster, 1967. Pp. 109–23.
> Reprinted: *The International Short Story Anthology.*
> London: Jonathan Cape, 1967. Pp. 93–107.

"Two Corpses Go Dancing," trans. Joseph Singer and
Elizabeth Pollet, *Commentary*, XL (August 1965),
45–49.

"The Prodigal Fool," trans. Elizabeth Shub and the author, *Saturday Evening Post*, CCXXXIX (February 26, 1966), 64–66, 68–69.

"Boudoir," trans. Elizabeth Shub and the author, *Vogue*, CXLII (April 1, 1966), 148–49, 214.

"The Parrot," trans. Ruth Whitman, *Harper's*, CCXXXII (June 1966), 59–66. Collected in *The Séance*.

"Three Stories for Children" ["The Snow in Chelm," "The Mixed-up Feet and the Silly Bridegroom," "The First Shlemiel"], trans. Elizabeth Shub and the author, *Commentary*, XLII (July 1966), 39–48. Collected in *Zlateh the Goat*.

"Dreamers," *The Reporter*, XXXV July 14, 1966), 45–46.

"The Needle," *Cosmopolitan*, CLXI (August 1966), 113–15. Collected in *The Séance*.

"The Brooch," trans. Alma Singer and Elizabeth Pollet, *Chicago Review*, XVIII (Nos. 3 & 4, 1966), 7–17. Collected in *The Séance*.
Reprinted: *The American Literary Anthology*, Vol. I. New York: Farrar, Straus and Giroux, 1968.

"Zlateh the Goat," trans. Elizabeth Shub and the author, *Young Judaean*, LV (December 1966), 11–14. Collected in *Zlateh the Goat*.

"The Riddle," trans. Chana Faerstein and Elizabeth Pollet, *Playboy*, XIV (January 1967), 164–66, 253–54. Incorporated into *The Manor*.

"A Match for a Princess," trans. Elizabeth Shub and the author, *Redbook*, CXXIX (August 1967), 68–69, 149–51, 154–55. Incorporated into *Mazel and Shlimazel*.

"Pigeons," trans. Elizabeth Shub and the author, *Esquire*, LXVIII (August 1967), 76–79.

"A Wedding," *Dimensions in American Judaism*, II (Fall 1967), 14–16.

"The Courtship," *Playboy*, XIV (September 1967), 145, 200–202, 204, 206–207. Incorporated into *The Manor*.

"Powers," trans. Dorothea Strauss and the author, *Harper's* CCXXXV (October 1967), 76–78, 83–87.

" 'My Adventures as an Idealist,' " trans. Aliza Shevrin and Elizabeth Shub, *Saturday Evening Post*, CCXL (November 18, 1967), 68–73.

"The Slaughterer," trans. Mirra Ginsburg, *New Yorker,*
XLIII (November 25, 1967), 60–65. Collected in *The
Séance.*

"The Lecture" [trans. Mirra Ginsburg], *Playboy,* XIV
(December 1967), 184, 294–96, 298, 300. Collected in
The Séance.

"The Letter Writer," trans. Aliza Shevrin and Elizabeth
Shub, *New Yorker,* XLIII (January 13, 1968), 26–36, 38,
41–42, 44, 47–49, 52, 54. Collected in *The Séance.*

"Henne Fire," *Playboy,* XV (May 1968), 92–94, 204–205.
Collected in *The Séance.*

"Yanda," trans. Dorothea Straus and the author, *Harper's,*
CCXXXVI (May 1968), 43–47. Collected in *The Séance.*

"Yash the Chimney Sweep," trans. Mirra Ginsburg, *Saturday Evening Post,* CCXLI (May 4, 1968), 66–69.

"The Dead Fiddler," *New Yorker,* XLIV (May 25, 1968),
42–46, 48, 51–52, 54, 57–58, 60, 63, 66–68, 71–72. Collected in *The Séance* (as "The Dead Musician").

C. MEMOIRS, ESSAYS, BOOK REVIEWS

"The Everlasting Joke" [Review of *Der Judische Wits,
Soziologie und Sammlung (The Jewish Joke, Its Sociol-
ogy and a Collection)* by Salacia Landmann], *Commentary,* XXXI (May 1961), 458–60.

"Two Memoirs" ["A Gruesome Question," "Strange Merchandise"], trans. Channah Kleinerman, *Commentary,*
XXXIII (January 1962), 45–50. Collected in *In My
Father's Court* ("Strange Merchandise" as "The Salesman").

"A New Use for Yiddish" [Review of *Sovietish Heimland,*
No. 1 (July–August 1961)], *Commentary,* XXXIII
(March 1962), 267–69.

"From *My Father's Courtroom,*" trans. Channah Kleinerman, *Commentary,* XXXIII (April 1962), 299–305. Col.
lected in *In My Father's Court* (as "The Will" and "Reb
Moishe Ba-ba-ba").

"Why the Geese Shrieked," *This Month,* I (May 1962),
40–44. Collected in *In My Father's Court.*

"Realism and Truth," trans. Adah Auerbach Lappin, *The
Reconstructionist,* XXVIII (June 15, 1962), 5–9.

"Why I Write in Yiddish," *Pioneer Woman,* XXXVIII (January 1963), 13.

"My Father's Courthouse" ["The Purim Gift," "Reb Chayim Gorshkover," "A Day of Pleasures," "The Washwoman"], *Saturday Evening Post,* CCXXVI (May 4, 1963), 38–41, 43–45, 48–50, 52–54. Collected in *In My Father's Court.*

"Had He Been a Kohen," *Jewish Heritage,* VI (Summer 1963), 57–62. Collected in *In My Father's Court* (as "The Secret").

"What It Takes to Be a Jewish Writer," trans. Mirra Ginsburg, *National Jewish Monthly,* LXXVIII (November 1963), 54–56.

"The Dispensation: A Memoir," trans. Channah Kleinerman, *Mosiac* (Cambridge, Mass.), IV (Winter 1963), 39–44. Collected in *In My Father's Court* (as "The Dispensation").
Reprinted (abridged): *Jewish Digest,* X (October 1964), 75–80.

"Traitl," *American Judaism,* XIII (Winter 1963–1964), 10–11, 59. Collected in *In My Father's Court.*

"A Sacrifice," *Harper's,* CCXXXVIII (February 1964), 61–64. Collected, slightly revised, in *In My Father's Court* (as "The Sacrifice").
Reprinted: *The Best American Short Stories — 1965,* ed. Martha Foley. New York: Houghton Mifflin, 1965. Pp. 283–89.

"The Betrothal," *Jewish Heritage,* VI (Spring 1964), 57–62. Collected in *In My Father's Court* (as "A Broken Engagement").

"Sholem Aleichem: Spokesman for a People," *New York Times,* September 20, 1964, Sec. 2, pp. 1, 4.
Reprinted (abridged): *Jewish Digest,* X (January 1965), 17–19.

"Introduction," *Yoshe Kalb.* New York: Harper and Row, 1965. Pp. v–x.

"Rootless Mysticism" [Review of *Daniel: Dialogues on Realization* by Martin Buber], *Commentary,* XXIX (January 1965), 78–79.

"Indecent Language and Sex in Literature," trans. Mirra
Ginsburg, *Jewish Heritage,* VIII (Summer 1965), 51–54.
Reprinted (abridged): *Jewish Digest,* XI (December
1965), 21–24 (as "Four Letter Words — In Jewish
Literature").
"A Phantom of Delight," *Book Week* (July 4, 1965),
pp. 2, 7.
"To the Wild Cows," *The Critic,* XXIV (August–September 1965), 6–13. Collected in *In My Father's Court.*
"A Major Din Torah," trans. Channah Kleinerman, *Commentary,* XL (September 1965), 77–80. Collected in *In
My Father's Court.*
"The Secret," trans. Channah Kleinerman, *Commentary,*
XL (October 1965), 72, 74. Collected in *In My Father's
Court.*
"What's In It for Me," *Harper's,* CCXXXI (October
1965), 172–73.
[Review of *Pan* by Knut Hamsun], *Holiday,* XXXVIII
(December 1965), 166–67.
"The Strong," *American Judaism,* XV (Winter 1965–66),
20–21. Collected in *In My Father's Court* (as "The
Strong Ones").
"Once on Second Avenue There Lived a Yiddish Theatre
— (Did It Really Die?)," *New York Times,* April 17,
1966, Sec. 2, p. 3.
"Kafka's Trials" [*Review of The Diaries of Franz Kafka:
Vol. I, 1910–1913; Vol. II, 1914–1923,* ed. Max Brod],
Book Week, May 1, 1966, pp. 16–17.
"A Warsaw Hasid," *Hadassah Magazine,* XLVII (June
1966), 12. Collected in *In My Father's Court.*
"Hagigah," *American Judaism,* XVI (Winter 1966–67),
18–19, 48–49.
"The Future of Yiddish and Yiddish Literature," *The
Jewish Book Annual — Vol. XXV.* New York: Jewish
Book Council of America, 1967. Pp. 70–74.
"The Extreme Jews," *Harper's,* CCXXXIV (April 1967),
55–62.
"Civilising the Shtetl," *Jewish Chronicle,* December 8,
1967, pp. i–ii [On Mendele Mocher Sforim].

"The Writer of Inborn Goodness" [Review of *My Father, Sholem Aleichem* by Marie Waife-Goldberg], *Book World,* March 17, 1968, p. 4B.

"Editors' Prize," *Playboy,* XV (May 1968), 18 [Letter to the Editor acknowledging with gratitude the *Playboy* fiction award for 1967 — for "The Lecture"].

II. Works About Singer

A. BOOKS

Burgess, Anthony. *The Novel Now: A Guide to Contemporary Fiction.* New York: W. W. Norton, 1967. Pp. 193–94.

Frakes, James R., and Isadore Traschen. "Comment" and Questions [on "Gimpel the Fool"]. In their ed. *Short Fiction: A Critical Collection.* Englewood Cliffs, N. J.: Prentice-Hall, 1959. Pp. 133–35.

Hemley, Cecil. "Isaac Bashevis Singer," In his *Dimensions of Midnight — Poetry and Prose,* ed. Elaine Gottlieb. Athens: Ohio University Press, 1968. Pp. 217–33.

Howe, Irving. "Introduction." In his ed. *Selected Short Stories of Isaac Bashevis Singer.* New York: Modern Library, 1966. Pp. v–xxiv.

———. "Demonic Fiction of a Yiddish 'Modernist.' " In *On Contemporary Literature,* ed. Richard Kostelanetz. New York: Avon Books, 1964. Pp. 579–85 [Reprinted review of *The Magician of Lublin*].

———. "A Yiddish 'Modernist.' " In *The "Commentary" Reader,* ed. Norman Podhoretz. New York: Atheneum, 1966. Pp. 589–94 [Reprinted review of *The Magician of Lublin*].

Hyman, Stanley Edgar. "The Yiddish Hawthorne." In *On Contemporary Literature,* ed. Richard Kostelanetz. New York: Avon Books, 1964. Pp. 586–90 [Reprinted review of *The Slave*].

———. "The Yiddish Hawthorne." In his *Standards: A Chronicle of Books for Our Time.* New York: Horizon Press, 1966. Pp. 83–87 [Reprinted review of *The Slave*].

Kazin, Alfred. "The Saint as Schlemiel." In his *Contemporaries.* Boston: Little, Brown, 1962. Pp. 283–88 [Reprinted review of *Gimpel the Fool*].

Peden, William. *The American Short Story.* Boston: Houghton Mifflin, 1964. Pp. 151–53, 190.

B. PERIODICALS

Adler, Dick. "The Magician of 86th Street," *Book World,* October 29, 1967, p. 8 [Interview].

"Always the Devil Pops Up," *New York Times,* October 30, 1966, Sec. 2, pp. 23–24 [Interview].

Aptekar, Richard. "Yiddish Novelist I. Singer Relates Spiritual Conviction in Authorship," Detroit *Jewish News,* April 19, 1963, p. 16 [Interview].

"Arts Group Picks 18 Grant Winners; National Institute's Awards Total 3 More Than Usual; Others to Get Help," *New York Times,* April 28, 1959, p. 70 [IBS among recipients].

Ash, Lee. "Isaac Bashevis Singer," *Wilson Library Bulletin,* XXXVII (December 1962), 356.

"The Author's Advice to Authors," Providence *Sunday Journal,* June 10, 1962, p. W-24 [IBS's five "rules for fiction writers" quoted].

"Authors & Editors," *Publishers' Weekly,* CXCII (October 16, 1967), 17–18 [Interview].

Boroff, David. "The College Intellectual, 1965 Model," *New York Times Magazine,* December 6, 1964, pp. 36–37, 134–137 [135].

Breger, Marshall, and Bob Barnhart. "A Conversation With Isaac Bashevis Singer," *The Handle* (University of Pennsylvania), II (Fall 1964–Winter 1965), 9–21.

Buchen, Irving H. "The Art and Gifts of Isaac Bashevis Singer," *Chicago Jewish Forum,* XXIV (Summer 1966), 308–12.

———. "Isaac Bashevis Singer and the Eternal Past," *Critique* (Minneapolis, Minn.), VIII (Spring–Summer 1966), 5–17.

Cahnman, Werner J. "The Magician of Lublin," *The Reconstructionist,* XXVII (May 19, 1961), 30 [Letter to the Editor].

Cantor, Frank. "I. Bashevis Singer Revisited," *Jewish Currents*, XIX (November 1965), 10–13.

Cromie, Robert. "The Bystander," *Chicago Sunday Tribune Magazine of Books*, December 31, 1961, p. 6.

Cross, Leslie. "Reading and Writing — Keeping a Literary Heritage Alive," *Milwaukee Journal*, December 17, 1967, Part 5, p. 6 [Interview].

Dolbier, Maurice. "About Books and Authors," *New York Herald Tribune Books*, October 29, 1961, p. 2.

Duker, Abraham G. "Two Views of Isaac Bashevis Singer — The Shtetl in Transition," *The Reconstructionist*, XXIV (October 31, 1958), 25–27 [Review of *Beth Din*, Yiddish version of *In My Father's Court*].

Eisenberg, J. A. "Isaac Bashevis Singer — Passionate Primitive or Pious Puritan?" *Judaism*, XI (Fall 1962), 345–56.

Elman, Richard M. "The Spinoza of Canal Street," *Holiday*, XXXVIII (August 1965), 83–87.

————, and Joel Blocker. "An Interview With Isaac Bashevis Singer," *Commentary*, XXXVI (November 1963), 364–72.

Fields, Sidney. "Only Human — Writer of His People," New York *Daily News*, April 26, 1967, p. 48 [Interview].

Fixler, Michael. "The Redeemers: Themes in the Fiction of Isaac Bashevis Singer," *Kenyon Review*, XXVI (Spring 1964), 371–86.

Flender, Harold. "An Interview With Isaac Bashevis Singer," *National Jewish Monthly*, LXXXII (March 1968), 18–19, 78–79; LXXXII (April 1968), 14–16.

Frank, M. Z. "The Demon and the Earlock," *Conservative Judaism*, XX (Fall 1965), 1–9.

Girson, Rochelle. "The Author," *Saturday Review*, XLV (June 16, 1962), 19 [Interview].

Glanville, Brian. "Furrowed Brows on the New York Scene," London *Sunday Times*, September 2, 1966, p. 25.

————. "Speaking of Books: Anglo-Jewish Writers," *New York Times Book Review*, April 17, 1966, pp. 2, 40 [2]. Reprinted (abridged): in *Jewish Digest* (November 1966), pp. 63–66.

Glatstein, Jacob. "The Fame of Bashevis Singer," *Congress Bi-Weekly,* XXXII (December 27, 1965), 17–19.

Goodheart, Eugene. "The Demonic Charm of Bashevis Singer," *Midstream,* VI (Summer 1960), 88–93.

Gottlieb, Elaine. "A Talk With Isaac Bashevis Singer," *The Reconstructionist,* XXV (March 6, 1959), 7–11.

Hammel, Lisa. "The Novelist's Working Wife," *New York Times,* November 23, 1967, p. 56 [Interview with Mrs. IBS].

Harris, Russell. "Author Singer Speaks, Discounts Critics' Praise," Detroit *News,* April 13, 1963, p. 4-B [Interview].

Hindus, Milton. "Isaac Bashevis Singer," *Jewish Heritage,* V (Fall 1962), 44–52.

Hochman, Baruch. "I. B. Singer's Vision of Good and Evil," *Midstream,* XIII (March 1967), 66–73.

Howe, Irving. "I. B. Singer," *Encounter,* XXVI (March 1966), 60–70.

———. "The Other Singer," *Commentary,* XLI (March 1966), 78, 80–82 [On IBS and his brother, I. J. Singer].

Hyman, Freida Clark. "Jewish Themes in Recent Fiction," *Jewish Spectator,* XXVII (October 1962), 24–25.

"I. B. Singer, Researcher in Humanity," *Village Voice* (New York, N. Y.), April 2, 1958, p. 19.

"Isaac Bashevis Singer Speaks on His Philosophy as a Jewish Writer," *JWB Circle,* June 1966, p. 13 [Interview].

Jacobs, Arthur L. "Yiddish Dailies," *Commentary,* XXXVII (March 1964), 18, 20 [Letter to the Editor re. IBS's November 1963 *Commentary* interview; includes IBS's very brief reply].

Jacobson, Dan. "The Problem of Isaac Bashevis Singer," *Commentary,* XXXIX (February 1965), 48–52.

Kahn, Lothar. "The Art of Isaac Bashevis Singer," *Jewish Exponent,* CXXXIII (January 4, 1963), 21.

———. "Focus on the Spiritual Novel," *Congress Bi-Weekly,* XXX (December 30, 1963), 21–23.

———. "A World of Spirits and Imps — Isaac Bashevis Singer," *Commonweal,* LXXXI (January 22, 1965), 538–40.

Kemeny, Joan. "Isaac Singer, Yiddish on Campus," *Chicago Jewish Forum*, XXIII (Spring 1965), 218–19 [Account of and excerpts from lecture given by IBS at Syracuse University].

Lappin, Adah Auerbach. "Reply to I. B. Singer," *The Reconstructionist*, XXVIII (June 15, 1962), 9–13 [Answers IBS's "Realism and Truth" (see I, C, above)].

Lawrence, Wes. "Last Stand for Yiddish," Cleveland *Plain Dealer*, March 1, 1966, p. 11.

Leviant, Curt. "The Phenomenon of Isaac Bashevis Singer," *Congress Bi-Weekly*, XXXIV (December 18, 1967), 9–12.

Levin, Beatrice. "Isaac Bashevis Singer," *Jewish Spectator*, XXX (May 1965), 20–22 [Interview].

Liben, Meyer. "Jewish," *Commentary*, XXXVIII (September 1964), 74–78.

MacGregor, Martha. "The Week in Books," New York *Post*, November 4, 1967, p. 51 [Interview].

Maddocks, Melvin. "He Builds Bridges to the Past," *Christian Science Monitor*, October 28, 1967, p. 9 [Interview].

Mucke, Edith. "Isaac B. Singer and Hassidic Philosophy," *Minnesota Review*, VII (No. 3, 1967), 214–21.

"People Are Talking About . . . Isaac Bashevis Singer," *Vogue*, CXLVII (April 1, 1966), 147.

Ribalow, Reena Sara. "A Visit to Isaac Bashevis Singer," *The Reconstructionist*, XXX (May 29, 1964), 19–26.

Robinson, Barry. "Show Notes — Not Yet a Millionaire," Asbury Park (N. J.) *Evening Press*, November 15, 1966, Sec. 2, p. 22 [Account of talk by IBS in Rumson, N. J.].

Rosenfeld, Arnold. "The Storyteller," Houston *Post*, June 6, 1965, "Spotlight" Section, p. 26 [Interview].

Siegel, Ben. "Sacred and Profane: Isaac Bashevis Singer's Embattled Spirits," *Critique* (Minneapolis, Minn.), VI (Spring 1963), 24–47.

Sloan, Jacob. "I. B. Singer and His Yiddish Critics," *Congress Bi-Weekly*, XXXIII (March 7, 1966), 4–5.

Sloman, Judith. "Existentialism in Pär Lagerkvist and Isaac Bashevis Singer," *Minnesota Review*, V (August–October 1965), 206–12.

"To the Manor Born: Isaac Bashevis Singer," *Books,* IV (October 1967), 5 [Interview].

Wells, Leon W. "TV Mailbag — What Makes a Jewish Writer," *New York Times,* November 13, 1966, Sec. 2, p. 16 [Letter to the Editor re. IBS's "Always the Devil Pops Up" interview].

Wilson, Edmund. "The Invisible World of S. Y. Agnon," *Commentary,* XLII (December 1966), 31–32 [32].

Wolkenfeld, J. S. "Isaac Bashevis Singer: The Faith of His Devils and Magicians," *Criticism,* V (Fall 1963), 349–59.

"Yiddish," *New York Times Book Review,* July 10, 1966, p. 51 [Letter to the Editor from Mordecai Kosover about Richard Elman's review of *In My Father's Court* (see II, C, below) and Elman's reply].

C.   REVIEWS OF BOOKS BY SINGER

THE FAMILY MOSKAT

Beichman, Arnold. "Poet of Two Zions," *Christian Science Monitor,* April 15, 1965, p. 11.

The Booklist, XLVII (December 1, 1950), 138.

Buchen, Irving H. " 'Death Is the Messiah,' " Baltimore *Sunday Sun,* March 21, 1965, p. D7.

Burgess, Anthony. "New Novels," *The Listener,* LXXV (June 16, 1966), 883.

Butler, Martha. "Vanished World in Poland," Bridgeport *Sunday Post,* March 28, 1965, Sec. C, p. 4.

Chametzky, Jules. "The Old Jew in New Times," *The Nation,* CCV (October 30, 1967), 436–38 [437].

Daniel, John. "Who's Your Agent?" *The Spectator,* No. 7198 (June 10, 1966), 733–34 [734].

"Descent Into Abaddon," *Time,* LXXXV (March 26, 1965), 100, 102.

Duguay, Robert F. "Jewish Life in Warsaw in Between-Wars Novel," Hartford *Times,* March 13, 1965, p. 18.

Dumbell, James M. "This Tale of Polish Jews Could Become a 'Classic,' " Charlotte (N. C.) *Observer,* May 9, 1965, p. 18-A.

Elman, Richard M. *Cavalier,* XV (August 1965), 10–12.

" 'Family Moskat' — Novel By Singer," *Intermountain Jewish News* (Denver), March 5, 1965, Sec. X, p. 6.

Frisch, D. R. "A Realistic Singer," *American Jewish World*, LIII (July 30, 1965), 3.

Gregory, Charles. " 'Family Moskat' By Singer Tells of Warsaw Jews," Fort Wayne *News-Sentinel*, April 3, 1965, p. 4A.

Gross, John. "Crack of Doom," *New Statesman*, LXXI (June 17, 1966), 887–88.

Havens, Lori. "Disintegration of a Patriarch's Dynasty," Columbia *Missourian*, May 30, 1965, "Showtime" Section, p. 3.

Hindus, Milton. "A Monument With a Difference," *New York Times Book Review*, March 14, 1965, pp. 4, 44–45.

Hogan, William. "A Bookman's Notebook — The Little World of Isaac Singer," San Francisco *Chronicle*, March 30, 1965, p. 41.

*Hughes, Ted. "The Genius of Isaac Bashevis Singer," *New York Review of Books*, April 22, 1965, pp. 8–10 [9–10].

"Isaac B. Singer's 'The Family Moskat' Reissued by Farrar, Straus and Co.," Detroit *Jewish News*, March 19, 1965, p. 17.

Journal of the Screen Producers Guild, VII (June 1965), 46.

Kipnis, Tina. *American Zionist*, LV (March–April 1965), 32.

Kirkus, XVIII (September 1, 1950), 530.

Kunitz, Joshua. "Passion Without Nobility," *New York Herald Tribune Book Review*, November 19, 1950, p. 24.

Mandel, Siegfried. "Dramatic Study of Family Life," Denver *Sunday Post*, April 25, 1965, *Roundup* Magazine, p. 11.

Martin, Jean. "The Heir to Talents of Classical Russians," Chicago *Sun-Times*, August 1, 1965, Sec. 3, p. 2.

Melnick, Norman. "Warsaw Recalls Pre-Nazi Pogroms," San Francisco *News Call Bulletin*, July 10, 1965, Sec. 1, p. 7.

Miller, Alicia Metcalf. "Dying Culture — Symbolic View of Jewish Life," Cleveland *Plain Dealer,* March 14, 1965, p. 7-BB.

Mitchison, Lois. "Seventeen Year Stint," London *Sunday Telegraph,* June 5, 1966, p. 11.

Moore, Harry T. "New Fiction in Brief," St. Louis *Sunday Post-Dispatch,* March 28, 1965, p. 4C.

New Yorker, XXVI (November 18, 1950), 185.

Plant, Richard. "Frustrated, Undying," *New York Times Book Review,* October 22, 1950, p. 34.

Popkin, Henry. "A Waste of Dreams," *Saturday Review,* XLVIII (May 15, 1965), 31, 53.

Raphael, Frederic. "A Novel of Splendid Stature," London *Sunday Times,* June 5, 1966, p. 29.

Richler, Mordecai. "Waiting for the Messiah," London *Observer,* June 5, 1966, p. 27.

Rothman, Nathan L. "Jews Before 'The Wall,'" *Saturday Review,* XXXIII (November 25, 1950), 18.

S., G. Columbus (Ohio) *Dispatch,* August 15, 1965, "Tab" Section, p. 17.

Shuttleworth, Martin. "New Novels," *Punch,* CCL (June 15, 1966), 892.

Stone, Leonard W. "Life That Has Vanished," Hartford *Courant,* April 25, 1965, Magazine Section, p. 15.

"Waiting for Hitler," (London) *Times Literary Supplement,* June 9, 1966, p. 520.

Winegarten, Renee. "The Modern Jew: Two Interpretations," *Jewish Observer and Middle East Review,* XV (June 10, 1966), 18–19.

Wilkie, Brian. *Commonweal,* LXXXII (August 6, 1965), 568–69.

Worcester (Mass.) *Sunday Telegram,* March 21, 1965, Sec. E., p. 12.

Ziff, Howard M. "A Modern Classic," Chicago *Daily News,* March 20, 1965, "Panorama" Section, p. 7.

SATAN IN GORAY

A., R. "Isaac Singer, Master of Symbol, Allegory," *Northwest Arkansas Times* (Fayetteville), September 26, 1958, p. 12.

Apt, Jay. "Visited By the Devil," Philadelphia *Daily News,* November 23, 1955, p. 21.

Burstein. "Remarkable Novel of Time of False Messiah, Zabbatai Zevi, Now in Inexpensive Paperback," *National Jewish Post and Opinion,* May 8, 1959, p. 9.

Davie, Donald. "Jewish Idylls," *New Statesman,* LXXIII (May 19, 1967), 690–91.

Gay, Laverne. *Books on Trial,* XIV (February 1956), 234.

Greene, James. *Commonweal,* LXIII (December 2, 1955), 236.

*Hindus, Milton. "The False Messiah," *New Leader,* XXXVIII (November 28, 1955), 24–26.

*Howe, Irving. "In the Day of a False Messiah," *New Republic,* CXXXIII (October 31, 1955), 20–22.

*Hughes, Ted. "The Genius of Isaac Bashevis Singer," *New York Review of Books,* April 22, 1965, pp. 8–10 [8–9].

Kenyon, Theo Jean. "Nightmarish Horror As Satan Comes to Goray," Peoria *Journal Star,* November 16, 1955, Sec. A, p. 8.

*Kibel, Alvin Charles. "The Political Novel," *The Reconstructionist,* XXIV (October 31, 1958), 27–32 [28–31].

Kirkus, XXIII (October 15, 1955), 791.

Levin, Meyer. "A False Messiah," *New York Times Book Review,* November 13, 1955, p. 4.

Longstreet, Stephen. Los Angeles *Free Press,* October 11, 1956, p. 2A.

Rainer, Dachine. "Goray and the Devil," *Saturday Review,* XXXVIII (December 17, 1955), 36.

Sacramento *Bee,* February 2, 1956, Sec. F., p. 10.

Schenk, Faye. "False Messiah," *Hadassah Newsletter,* XXXVI (February 1956), 10.

Square Journal (New York, N. Y.), November 2, 1959, p. 4.

*Teller, Judd L. "Unhistorical Novels," *Commentary,* XXI (April 1956), 393–96.

GIMPEL THE FOOL AND OTHER STORIES

*Hughes, Ted. "The Genius of Isaac Bashevis Singer," *New York Review of Books,* April 22, 1965, pp. 8–10 [10].

*Kazin, Alfred. "The Saint as Schlemiel," *New Leader,* XLI (August 4, 1958), 21–23.

*Kibel, Alvin Charles. "The Political Novel," *The Reconstructionist,* XXIV (October 31, 1958), 27–32 [31–32].

Kirkus, XXV (October 15, 1957), 784.

Lauter, Paul. "The Jewish Hero: Two Views," *New Republic,* CXXXIX (November 24, 1958), 18–19.

*Ludwig, Jack. "The Two-Fold Nature of Truth," *Midstream,* IV (Spring 1958), 90–93.

Miller, Karl. *The Spectator,* No. 6799 (October 17, 1958), 526.

Phelps, Donald. "The Moral Tales of I. B. Singer," *The Second Coming,* I (January–February 1961), 47–48.

Ribalow, Harold U. "A Personal Devil," *Saturday Review,* XLI (January 25, 1958), 19.

———. "Tales of Evil and Magic," *Congress Bi-Weekly,* XXV (January 6, 1958), 16. See also *Jewish Affairs,* February 1958, pp. 52–53.

"Rooted in Unreality," (London) *Times Literary Supplement,* January 2, 1959, p. 5.

Shaw, Fred. "A Man of Words — English or Not," Miami (Fla.) *News,* July 17, 1960, Sec. B, p. 6.

Time, LXX (November 25, 1957), 134, 136.

Weinman, Jack W. "Yiddish Stories," *Jewish Currents,* XII (November 1958), 27–29.

Yezierska, Anzia. "With the Sap of Folklore," *New York Times Book Review,* December 29, 1957, p. 4.

THE MAGICIAN OF LUBLIN

Carew, Jan. "In the Shadows," *Time and Tide,* XLII (September 21, 1961), 1573.

Chametzky, Jules. "Stereotypes and Jews: Fagin and the Magician of Lublin," *Massachusetts Review,* II (Winter 1961), 372–75 [373–75].

Elman, Richard M. "No Easy Faith," *The Nation,* CXCII (March 11, 1961), 219–20.

Halpern, Ben. "A Modern Morality Tale," *Hadassah Newsletter,* XLI (December 1960), 17, 20.

Hindus, Milton. "Yasha Escaped Into a Prison," *New York Times Book Review*, June 26, 1960, pp. 26–27.

*Howe, Irving. "Demonic Fiction of a Yiddish 'Modernist,'" *Commentary*, XXX (October 1960), 350–53.

*Hughes, Ted. "The Genius of Isaac Bashevis Singer," *New York Review of Books*, April 22, 1965, pp. 8–10 [10].

Kibel, Alvin Charles. "Where Symbol Equals Reality," *New Republic*, CXLIV (January 2, 1961), 22.

King, Francis. "Egypt's Exodus," *New Statesman*, LXII (September 15, 1961), 355–56.

Kirkus, XXVIII (April 15, 1960), 335.

(London) *Times Literary Supplement*, October 13, 1961, p. 679.

Manning, Olivia. *The Spectator*, No. 6951 (September 15, 1961), 361.

Mercier, Vivian. "Sex, Success and Salvation," *Hudson Review*, XIII (Autumn 1960), 449–56 [455–56].

Newman, Louis I. "Sinner and Saint," *The Reconstructionist*, XXVII (March 24, 1961), 27–29.

Nyren, Dorothy. *Library Journal*, LXXXV (May 1, 1960), 1825–26.

Ribalow, Harold U. "One of the Greats," *Jewish Exponent*, CXXX (May 27, 1960), 55.

Rubinstein, Annette T. "An Obscurantist Yiddish Novel," *Jewish Currents*, XV (May 1961), 36–38.

Rugoff, Milton. "The Odd Saga of Yasha Mazur, Magician," *New York Herald Tribune Book Review*, August 28, 1960, p. 7.

Stilwell, Robert L. "Imaginative Yiddish Novel," Louisville *Courier-Journal*, July 31, 1960, Sec. 4, p. 7.

Time, LXXVI (July 11, 1960), 104.

THE SPINOZA OF MARKET STREET

Angoff, Charles. "A Universal Story Teller," *Congress Bi-Weekly*, XXIX (February 5, 1962), 13–14.

Berkman, Dave. *Library Journal*, LXXXVI (October 1, 1961), 3303.

The Booklist, LVIII (January 1, 1962), 278.

Culligan, Glendy. "A Boyhood in Poland," *Washington Post*, March 11, 1962, p. E7.

Dobbin, Muriel. "Miracles and Spells," Baltimore *Sunday Sun,* October 29, 1961, Sec. A, p. 5.

Dolbier, Maurice. "Books in Review — Wise Men, Fools and the Devil Appear in New Short Stories," Baltimore *News-Post,* October 31, 1961, p. 5C.

"Dybbuks and Demons," *Newsweek,* LVIII (October 30, 1961), 78–79.

Easley, John. "Three Visions of Unique Worlds," Raleigh (N. C.) *News and Observer,* December 31, 1961, Sec. III, p. 5.

"Fact and Fantasy," (London) *Times Literary Supplement,* May 4, 1962, p. 298.

Fass, Martin. " 'Welcome' to a Storyteller," Denver *Sunday Post,* November 26, 1961, *Roundup* Magazine, p. 17.

*Feldman, Irving. "The Shtetl World," *Kenyon Review,* XXIV (Winter 1962), 173–77.

Fink, Michael. "Man Is Weak, Life Is Holy," Providence *Sunday Journal,* December 10, 1961, p. W-20.

Fulford, Robert. "Ghosts Love Yiddish," Toronto *Daily Star,* November 22, 1961, p. 43.

Globe, Leah Ain. " 'The Spinoza of Market Street,' " *Mizrachi Woman,* April 1962, p. 7.

Goodheart, Eugene. "The Secrets of Satan," *Saturday Review,* XLIV (November 25, 1961), 28.

Gorn, Lester. "The Book Corner — Yiddish Legends," San Francisco *Examiner,* October 19, 1961, p. 33.

Hindus, Milton. "The Surface Isn't All," *New York Times Book Review,* October 22, 1961, pp. 4, 36.

Howe, Irving. "Stories: New, Old, and Sometimes Good," *New Republic,* CXLV (November 13, 1961), 18–19, 22–23 [19, 22].

*Hughes, Ted. "The Genius of Isaac Bashevis Singer," *New York Review of Books,* April 22, 1965, pp. 8–10 [10].

"Isaac Bashevis Singer's Stories — 'Spinoza of Market Street,' " Detroit *Jewish News,* October 20, 1961, p. 4.

Kahn, Lothar. *Books Abroad,* XXXVI (Summer 1962), 323.

Kirkus, XXIX (August 1, 1961), 699.

Kreigel, Leonard B. "Two Books of Modern Jewish Short Stories," Louisville *Courier-Journal,* December 17, 1961, Sec. 4, p. 7.

Kupferberg, Herbert. "Where Evil and Good Walk Side by Side," *New York Herald Tribune Books,* November 19, 1961, p. 7.

Levine, Rose. "Changes of Pace for Isaac Singer," Boston *Sunday Herald,* December 31, 1961, p. 46.

Lodge, David. "Instant Novel," *The Spectator,* No. 6985 (May 11, 1962), 628.

Ribalow, Harold U. "Eleven Short Stories," *Jewish Exponent,* CXXXII (November 3, 1961), 23.

Rodman, Maia. *Jubilee,* IX (March 1962), 48–49.

Rosenwasser, Rose K. *Jewish Spectator,* XXVII (April 1962), 29–30.

Smith, William James. "Irony, Earthiness and Wild Humor," *Commonweal,* LXXV (November 3, 1961), 158–59.

Steele, Harry. "Gratifying Wit, Wisdom," *Chicago Sunday Tribune Magazine of Books,* November 12, 1961, p. 7.

*Sundel, Alfred. "The Last of the Yiddish Mohicans," *New Leader,* XLIV (December 11, 1961), 20–22.

Time, LXXVIII (November 10, 1961), 106.

Wershba, Joseph. "Singer: New 'Classics,' " New York *Post,* November 5, 1961, Magazine Section, p. 11.

THE SLAVE

Adelman, George. *Library Journal,* LXXXVII (June 1, 1962), 2160.

Allen, Walter. "Faith and Fiction," *New Statesman,* LXV (February 22, 1963), 280–81 [280].

Appel, John J. "The Love of a Survivor of the Chmielnicki Massacres for a Peasant Woman," *Circle in Jewish Bookland,* October 1962, p. 1.

Barrett, William. "Exotic But Not Remote," *Atlantic* CCX (August 1962), 143.

The Booklist, LVIII (June 15, 1962), 719.

The Bookmark (Albany, N. Y.), XXI (May 1962), 224.

Boroff, David. "The Sins of a Good and Pious Man," *Saturday Review,* XLV (June 16, 1962), 18–19.

B[rady], C[harles] A. "Tale of Feudal Poland Created by Yiddish Art," Buffalo *Evening News,* June 16, 1962, p. B-10.

Brizzolara, Robert. *Ave Maria,* XCVI (September 8, 1962), 28–29.

*Buchen, Irving H. "The Present Revealed Through the Past," Baltimore *Sunday Sun,* June 24, 1962, Sec. A, p. 5.

Cruttwell, Patrick. "Fiction Chronicle," *Hudson Review,* XV (Winter 1962–1963), 589–98 [593].

Doblier, Maurice. "Daily Book Review — 'The Slave,'" New York *Herald Tribune,* June 12, 1962, p. 23. See also Baltimore *News-Post,* June 15, 1962, p. 8C.

Elman, Richard M. "The Realism of Isaac Singer," *Commonweal,* LXXVI (July 6, 1962), 381–82.

"Faith Survives All in Bitter Challenge," Miami (Fla.) *News,* July 8, 1962, Sec. B, p. 6.

Fink, Michael. "A Wild and Superstition-Haunted World," Providence *Sunday Journal,* June 10, 1962, p. W-24.

Fogarty, Robert S. "Birth and Death Solve a Riddle," Denver *Sunday Post,* July 8, 1962, *Roundup* Magazine, p. 13.

Garison, Eudora. "'The Slave' Is Cruel Old Tale With Familiar Parallels," Charlotte (N. C.) *Observer,* July 22, 1962, p. 17-F.

Glassheim, Eliot. "Conflict Over God's Demands," Washington *Post,* June 10, 1962, p. E9.

*Goodheart, Eugene. "Singer's Moral Novel," *Midstream,* VIII (September 1962), 99–102.

H., B. H. "'The Slave' by Isaac Singer," Springfield (Mass.) *Republican,* July 22, 1962, p. 2D.

Highet, Gilbert, *Book-of-the-Month-Club News,* July 12, 1962, pp. 12–13.

Hindus, Milton. "An Upright Man on an Eternal Landscape," *New York Times Book Review,* June 17, 1962, p. 4.

*Hughes, Ted. "The Genius of Isaac Bashevis Singer," *New York Review of Books,* April 22, 1965, pp. 8–10 [10].

*Hyman, Stanley Edgar. "The Yiddish Hawthorne," *New Leader,* XLV (July 23, 1962), 20–21.

Kirkus, XXX (August 15, 1962), 398.

Kirsch, Robert R. "Jewish Theme Handled With Power, Poetry," Los Angeles *Times,* July 15, 1962, "Calendar" Section, p. 14.

Laird, James H. "The Yiddish Master — Jewish Tragedy Knows No Age," Detroit *Free Press,* July 1, 1962, Sec. B, p. 5.

Lavine, Sigmund. "Imaginative Conception," Worcester (Mass.) *Sunday Telegram,* June 10, 1962, Sec. E, p. 10.

Le Clair, Edward E. "Singer's 'Slave' Warm Story," Albany (N. Y.) *Time Union,* July 22, 1962, Sec. G, p. 6.

Mindlin, Hilary. "Vision Wilder Than the Self," *Jewish Floridian,* June 15, 1962, p. 14A.

Monson, Frances. Brooklyn Heights (N. Y.) *Press,* July 12, 1962, p. 4.

Moore, Harry T. "A Great Novel For Readers of All Faiths," Boston *Sunday Herald,* June 24, 1962, Sec. III, p. 8.

Morton, Robert. *Show,* II (July 1962), 94.

Newcomb, Richard F. "Unusual Novel Possesses the Qualities of Fable," Victoria (Texas) *Advocate,* June 9, 1962, *Fun* Magazine, p. 12.

Nott, Kathleen. "New (Translated) Novels," *Encounter,* XX (May 1963), 88–90 [90].

P[erlman], M[ilton] B. "Booknotes," *Bulletin of the East Midwood Jewish Center* (Brooklyn, N. Y.), XXX (September 14, 1962), 6.

"Piety and Peasant in Ancient Poland," Detroit *News,* August 12, 1962, p. 15-E.

Prescott, Orville. "Books of The Times," *New York Times,* July 6, 1962, p. 23.

Raphael, Frederic. "Questionings of Upbringing," London *Sunday Times,* February 17, 1963, p. 31.

Ribalow, Harold U. "In Which the Ghosts Play Second Fiddle," *Pioneer Woman,* XXXVIII (January 1963), 13–14.

——. "A Romantic Bit of Folklore," *Jewish Exponent,* CXXXIII (June 29, 1962), 21.

Rodman, Maia. *Jubilee,* X (December 1962), 49.

Ross, Fred. "There's Nothing Neutral in Life," Raleigh (N. C.) *News and Observer,* August 12, 1962, Sec. III, p. 5.

Rugoff, Milton. *New York Herald Tribune Books,* June 17, 1962, p. 5.

"The Same Jacob," *Time,* LXXIX (June 29, 1962), 78.

Scheer, Serena. " 'The Slave' Tells a Vivid Story of 17th Century Poland," Oakland (Cal.) *Sunday Tribune,* June 24, 1962, p. EL-4.

Schott, Webster. "The Will Sustains When Logic Fails," Kansas City *Star,* July 1, 1962, p. 8D.

Shalett, Jo Fields. Chicago Heights *Star,* September 13, 1962, p. 23.

Shapiro, Charles. "Alive With Passion and Wisdom," Louisville *Courier-Journal,* July 8, 1962, Sec. 4, p. 7.

*Sontag, Susan. "Demons and Dreams," *Partisan Review,* XXIX (Summer 1962), 460–63.

Stafford, Jean. "The Works of God, the Ways of Man," *New Republic,* CXLVI (June 18, 1962), 21–22.

Sullivan, Richard. "A Noble Novel Treats of Passionate Man," *Chicago Sunday Tribune Magazine of Books,* June 17, 1962, pp. 1–2.

"The Torah and the Whale," (London) *Times Literary Supplement,* February 22, 1963, p. 121.

Towery, Elizabeth. "One Man Learns the Way to Obtain Peace of Mind," Columbia *Missourian,* December 9, 1962, p. 8.

Uhlig, Inna. "Those Good Old Days Were Sad," Washington (D. C.) *Sunday Star,* July 15, 1962, p. C-5.

"Wandering Jew," *Newsweek,* LIX (June 25, 1962), 90–91.

Weddeck, Dr. Harry E. "17th Century Polish-Jewish Life," *National Jewish Monthly,* LXXVII (May 1963), 52.

Weintroub, Benjamin. *Chicago Jewish Forum,* XXI (Winter 1962–1963), 169–70.

White, Ellington. "Throw Out the Paddle and Get a Reactor," *Kenyon Review,* XXIV (Autumn 1962) 749–55 [754–55].

Whittington, Harold. "Yiddish Storyteller," Houston *Post,* June 24, 1962, *Houston Now* Magazine, p. 9.

Ziff, Howard M. " 'The Slave' — Jews In Another Time," Chicago *Daily News,* June 27, 1962, p. 35.

SHORT FRIDAY AND OTHER STORIES

Alter, Robert. "Of Sex and Demons," *Hadassah Magazine,* XLVI (December 1964), 12.

Barrett, William. "Visionary Tales," *Atlantic*, CCXV (January 1965), 129–30.

Baumbach, Jonathan. "A Wish for the Impossible," *Saturday Review*, XLVII (November 21, 1964), 49.

Beichman, Arnold. "Poet of Two Zions," *Christian Science Monitor*, April 15, 1965, p. 11.

Brady, Charles A. "Singer Tops as Teller of Stories," Buffalo *Evening News*, November 21, 1964, p. B-12.

Buchen, Irving H. "Masterful Stories By Singer," Baltimore *Sunday Sun*, November 29, 1964, Sec. D, p. 5.

Burgess, Anthony. "Singer at the Feast," *Manchester Guardian Weekly*, March 9, 1967, p. 11.

Burke, Hatton. "Marked Departure — 'Short Friday' Has Genuine Humanity," Pensacola *News-Journal*, February 7, 1965, p. 6B.

Butler, Martha. "Yarns Labeled as Ambiguous," Bridgeport *Sunday Post*, January 3, 1965, Sec. C, p. 4.

*Cantarow, Ellen. "Isaac Singer," Providence *Sunday Journal*, December 27, 1964, p. H-6.

Chayefsky, Paddy. "Of Dybbuks and Devilkins," *The Reporter*, XXXII (April 22, 1965), 40, 42–43.

Choice, I (February 1965), 558.

Clarkson, Paul R. *Best Sellers*, XXIV (December 1, 1964), 365.

*"A Dance on the Grave," *Newsweek*, LXIV (November 23, 1964) 120, 120A, 120B.

Davie, Donald. "Jewish Idylls," *New Statesman*, LXXIII (May 19, 1967), 690–91.

Dolbier, Maurice. "16 By Singer: Weird Stories About Demons," New York *Herald Tribune*, November 20, 1964, p. 23.

Elliott, George P. *Harper's*, CCXXX (April 1965), 111–12.

Fagereng, Per. "Impish Stories of Poland's Past," San Francisco *News Call Bulletin*, December 5, 1964, Sec. 1, p. 6.

Feinstein, George W. Pasadena (Cal.) *Independent Star-News*, January 10, 1965, "Scene" Section, p. 4.

Fey, Isabella. "Yiddish Is for Ghosts," Norfolk *Virginian-Pilot*, November 22, 1964, p. B-6.

Flynn, Judith A. "Absorbing Collection," Hartford *Courant*, March 14, 1965, Magazine Section, p. 13.

Gold, Arthur R. "The Last of the Old-Time Demons," *Book Week*, December 6, 1964, p. 5.

Gregory, Charles T. "Singer Tales Modern But Medieval Too," Fort Wayne *News-Sentinel*, December 19, 1964, Sec. A, p. 4.

G[rusd], E[dward] E. "The Magic of I. B. Singer," *National Jewish Monthly*, LXXIX (April 1965), 42–43.

Hamilton, Iain. "Inside View of Modernism," *Illustrated London News*, CCL (March 4, 1967), 32–33 [33].

Hindus, Milton. "Singer's Latest Book Entertaining Series," Boston *Globe*, December 2, 1964, p. 24.

*Hughes, Ted. "The Genius of Isaac Bashevis Singer," *New York Review of Books*, April 22, 1965, pp. 8–10 [10].

Hutchinson, James D. "Human Ordeal, God's Mysteries Pitted in Singer's Series of Short Stories," Denver *Sunday Post*, January 3, 1965, *Roundup* Magazine, p. 8.

*Hyman, Stanley Edgar. "Isaac Singer's Marvels," *New Leader*, XLVII (December 21, 1964), 17–18.

Journal of the Screen Producers Guild, VII (June 1965), 46.

Kirsch, Robert R. "Isaac Singer in Fine Fettle," Los Angeles *Times*, December 17, 1964, Part V, p. 12.

Kleinstein, David M. "They Found Their Greatest Happiness on Fridays," *JWB Circle*, XXII (May 1965), Sec. 2, p. 1.

*Kolatch, Mollie. "With Singer in the Shtetl," *Jewish Life*, XXXIII (November–December 1965), 51–54.

Lavine, Sigmund A. "The Problems Are Everyman," Worcester (Mass.) *Sunday Telegram*, November 22, 1964, Sec. E, p. 10.

Malin, Irving. *Studies in Short Fiction*, III (Spring 1966), 383–85.

Margoshes, Miriam K. *Library Journal*, LXXXIX (November 1, 1964), 4389.

Martin, Jean. "Picks a Potential Classic," Chicago *Sun-Times*, March 21, 1965, Section Four, p. 2.

Mathewson, Joseph. *Harper's Bazaar*, XCVIII (February 1965), 98.

Merril, Judith. *The Magazine of Fantasy and Science Fiction,* XXVIII (April 1965), 68.

Miller, Alicia Metcalf. "Time Is Not of Essence to Yiddish Author," Cleveland *Plain Dealer,* December 6, 1964, p. 8-I.

*Miller, Henry. "Magic World of Imps and Villagers," *Life,* LVII (December 11, 1964), 14, 20.

Miller, Warren. "Last of the Line," *The Nation,* CC (January 4, 1965), 15–16.

Moore, Harry T. Boston *Sunday Herald,* December 27, 1964, Sec. 4, p. 8.

———. St. Louis *Sunday Post-Dispatch,* March 28, 1965, p. 4C.

Mudrick, Marvin. "All That Prose," *Hudson Review,* XVIII (Spring 1965), 110–23 [122–123].

Powers, Dennis. " 'Yiddish Hawthorne' Spins Tales of Timeless People," Oakland (Cal.) *Sunday Tribune,* November 15, 1964, p. 11-EN.

Prescott, Orville. "Books of The Times — Demons, Devils and Others," *New York Times,* December 14, 1964, p. 33.

Ribalow, Harold U. "A Master Story-Teller," *Congress Bi-Weekly,* XXXII (March 15, 1965), 14–15.

Richler, Mordecai. "Boy at the Keyhole," London *Observer,* February 26, 1967, p. 26.

Rogers, W. G. "Eerie Evocations — A Delightful Ghost Story Book Written With Wand, Not Pen," Toledo *Sunday Blade,* November 22, 1964, Sec. B, p. 5. See also Grand Rapids *Press,* November 22, 1964; Philadelphia *Sunday Bulletin,* November 22, 1964.

Rosenfeld, Arnold. "An Ancient Teller of Tales," Houston *Post,* November 22, 1964, '64 Magazine, p. 8.

Schott, Webster. "Yiddish Yoknapatawpha," *New York Times Book Review,* November 15, 1964, pp. 5, 64.

Scott, Paul. "Jewish Childhood," London *Times,* March 23, 1967, p. 7.

Seymour-Smith, Martin. "Terror and Fable," *The Spectator,* No. 7237 (March 10, 1967), 281–82.

Share, Bernard. "Book of the Day," *Irish Times* (Dublin), March 4, 1967, pp. 9, 14.

"Singer Does It Again," *American Jewish World,* LIII (January 1, 1965), 8.

Spiegel, Moshe. *Chicago Jewish Forum,* XXIII (Summer 1965), 323–24.

Sullivan, Richard. "Triumph and Absurdity," *Chicago Sunday Tribune Books Today,* December 27, 1964, p. 5.

Symons, Julian. "Singer," *Punch,* CCLII (April 5, 1967), 503.

Time, LXXXIV (November 20, 1964), 119.

Yoggerst, Jim. "Singer Captures Times and Feeling of People," Waukegan (Ill.) *News-Sun,* November 14, 1964, p. 13.

Ziff, Howard M. "Strange World of the Ghetto — Powerful Short Stories," Chicago *Daily News,* November 21, 1964, "Panorama" Section, p. 10.

IN MY FATHER'S COURT

Allschwang, John. "In a World That Is No More, a Rabbi Held Court for the Poor," *Milwaukee Journal,* May 8, 1966, Part 5, p. 4.

[Alter, Harry]. "Recollections of Jewish Poland," Youngstown *Jewish Times,* May 6, 1966, p. 4.

Ashford, Gerald. "Short Stories Tell About Warsaw Rabbinical Court," San Antonio *Express,* May 1, 1966, p. 6-H.

Atkin, Helen. *Pioneer Woman,* XLI (November 1966), 14–15.

B., J. "The 'Red Rabbi' to Isaac Singer," *People's World* (San Francisco), June 25, 1966, p. 6.

Ben-Joseph, Marc. "A Unique 'Gallery of Types' — These Sketches Are Departure From Singer's Preoccupation," Charlotte (N. C.) *Observer,* May 1, 1966, p. 7F.

Berkow, Ira. "His Father's Court Was Rich With Life and Love," Minneapolis *Tribune,* June 12, 1966, Entertainment Section, p. 6.

Black, H. Gilbert. " 'In My Father's Court,' " Springfield (Mass.) *Republican,* August 28, 1966, p. 16C.

Bleck, Tim. Dayton *Journal Herald,* May 14, 1966, p. 26.

B'nai B'rith Women's World (Washington, D. C.), LVI (June 1966), 6.

The Booklist, LXII (June 15, 1966), 988–89.

Bray, Barbara. "Jewish Fables," *The Scotsman* (Edinburgh), March 11, 1967, Week-End Magazine, p. 4.

Buchen, Irving H. "A World That Roars, Snarls and Moans," Baltimore *Sunday Sun,* May 8, 1966, Sec. D, p. 5.

Bunke, Joan. Des Moines *Sunday Register,* July 17, 1966, p. 19-G.

Burgess, Anthony. "Singer at the Feast," *Manchester Guardian Weekly,* March 9, 1967, p. 11.

Cevasco, George. *The Sign,* XLV (July 1966), 55–56.

Chametzky, Jules. "In the Shtetl of Bilgoray," *The Nation,* CCIII (October 17, 1966), 392–93.

Coulter, Prevost. "Autobiography Reads Like Novel," Pensacola *News-Journal,* June 26, 1966, Sec. C, p. 10.

Crane, B. Kendall. "Mantle of Reminiscence — Silken Thread of Memory," Pittsburgh *Press,* May 8, 1966, Sec. 6, p. 5.

The Critic, XXIV (June–July 1966), 74.

Davie, Donald, "Jewish Idylls," *New Statesman,* LXXIII (May 19, 1967), 690–91.

Derleth, August. "A Warsaw Childhood," *Capital Times* (Madison, Wis.), May 26, 1966, Sec. 1, p. 10.

*Elman, Richard M. "Singer of Warsaw," *New York Times Book Review,* May 8, 1966, pp. 1, 34–36.

"Faith and Fable," (London) *Times Literary Supplement,* March 16, 1967, p. 213.

Fanning, Garth. "Yiddish Writer Opens Up Well of Memory," Sacramento *Bee,* June 19, 1966, Sec. L, p. 5.

Feinstein, George. "Isaac Singer's Fiction Is a Blend of Simple, Grotesque, Humorous," Pasadena (Cal.) *Independent Star-News,* May 29, 1966, "Scene" Section, p. 13.

*Fiedler, Leslie. "The Circumcized Philistine and the Unsynagogued Jew," *American Judaism,* XVI (Fall 1966), 20, 33–36 [20, 33].

Fink, Michael. "Isaac Singer's Art: Ancient, Just, True," Providence *Sunday Journal,* May 22, 1966, p. N-47.

Fixler, Michael. "The Memoirs of Isaac Singer," *Commonweal,* LXXXIV (September 23, 1966), 615–16.

Friedlander, Albert H. "Rabbis, Angels, and Demons," *Saturday Review,* XLIX (May 7, 1966), 90–91.

G., E. "Innocence, Integrity Flowered," Roanoke (Va.) *Times,* August 14, 1966, p. C-8.

G., P. Charleston (S. C.) *News and Courier,* June 19, 1966, p. 5-B.

Glazer, Dr. Joseph. "Isaac Bashevis Singer's Memoirs," *Southern Israelite* (Atlanta, Ga.), XLI (May 13, 1966), 2.

"God in the Ghetto," *Newsweek,* LXVII (May 2, 1966), 106–107.

Goldman, Albert. *"In My Father's Court,* 'a magic door,' " *Vogue,* CXLVIII (July 1966), 29.

Goldsmith, Judith R. *Temple Sinai News* (New York, N. Y.), XVI (November 1966), 3.

Govan, Gilbert E. "Of Books and Writers," Chattanooga *Times,* July 3, 1966, p. 18.

Greene, A. C. "The Strictures of a Devout Life," Dallas *Times Herald,* May 1, 1966, Sec. D, p. 18.

Greenspan, Lou. *Journal of the Screen Producers Guild,* June 1966, pp. 42–43.

Grusd, Edward E. "A Splendid Memoir," *National Jewish Monthly,* LXXXI (November 1966), 56–57.

H., J. "Pre-World War I Life in Warsaw," Charleston (S. C.) *Evening Post,* July 29, 1966, p. 10-C.

Hadas, David. "A Fragmentary Autobiography," *Judaism,* XV (Fall 1966), 508–10.

Halio, Jay. "Second Skins," *Southern Review,* n.s. IV (January 1968), 236–47 [243–44].

Hamilton, Iain. "Inside View of Modernism," *Illustrated London News,* CCL (March 4, 1967), 32–33 [33].

Heiney, Donald. "Memoir of a 'born storyteller,' " *Christian Science Monitor,* May 12, 1966, p. 11.

Highet, Gilbert. *Book-of-the-Month-Club News,* June 1966, p. 9.

Hogan, William. "World of Books — The Little World of Isaac Singer," San Francisco *Chronicle,* May 11, 1966, p. 47.

Honig, Nat. "Today's Book," Long Beach (Cal.) *Independent Press Telegram,* May 11, 1966, Sec. B, p. 2.

Jacobson, Dan. "Family Troubles," *New York Review of Books,* July 7, 1966, pp. 24–25.

"Jewish Scholar Recalls Boyhood," Tulsa *Sunday World,* August 28, 1966, *Your World* Magazine, p. 12.

Kahn, Lothar. *Books Abroad,* XLI (Winter 1967), 96–97.

*———. *Jewish Horizon,* XXX (November–December 1966), 16, 18.

Kay, Jane. "The Shop on Krochmalna Street" Quincy (Mass.) *Patriot-Ledger,* June 14, 1966, p. 26.

*Kazin, Alfred. "His Son, the Storyteller," *Book Week,* April 24, 1966, pp. 1, 10.

Keith, Robert Q. "Memoirs of Youth in Poland Told," Beaumont (Texas) *Journal,* August 19, 1966, p. 25.

Kipnis, Tina. *American Zionist,* LVII (October 1966), 28.

Kirkus, XXXIV (March 1, 1966), 289.

Kirsch, Robert R. "Memoirs Reveal Life in a Beth Din," Los Angeles *Times,* May 5, 1966, Part V, p. 6.

Kitching, Jessie. *Publishers' Weekly,* V (April 18, 1966), 110–11.

Klein, Esther. "The Publisher Speaks," Philadelphia *Jewish Times,* June 3, 1966, pp. 1, 9.

Kornstein, Marcus. "A Vineyard of Vignettes," Charleston (W. Va.) *Sunday Gazette Mail,* April 24, 1966, p. 22m.

La Fleche, Duane. "Books and Authors — A Very Human Court — at Home," Albany (N. Y.) *Knickerbocker News,* May 28, 1966, p. B-2.

Lask, Thomas. "Books of The Times — Gone With Ninevah and Tyre," *New York Times,* May 9, 1966, p. 41. See also Hartford *Times,* June 4, 1966; El Paso *Times,* July 10, 1966.

Leibowitz, Herbert. "A Lost World Redeemed," *Hudson Review,* XIX (Winter 1966–1967), 669–73.

Levin, Abraham. "Book Review—'In My Father's Court,'" Baltimore *Labor Herald,* October 21, 1966, p. 4.

Library Journal, XCI (September 15, 1966), 4374.

Logan, Floyd. "Tied to His Father's Court Tales," Indianapolis *News,* July 30, 1966, p. 32.

Mahoney, W. J., Jr. Montgomery (Ala.) *Advertiser-Journal,* July 3, 1966, Sunday Magazine, p. 6.

Malin, Irving. "A Look Back," *The Progressive,* XXX (August 1966), 34–35.

Marbrook, Del. "Tales of Warsaw — Ghetto Arbiter," Winston-Salem (N. C.) *Journal and Sentinel,* May 22, 1966, Sec. C, p. 4.

Margoshes, Miriam K. *Library Journal,* XCI (May 1, 1966), 2326.

Mathewson, Joseph. *Harper's Bazaar,* XCIX (November 1966), 116, 118.

"Memories of a Polish Boyhood," *Time,* LXXXVII (May 27, 1966), 102.

Michaels, Herb. Springfield (Mass.) *Jewish Weekly News,* May 12, 1966, p. 4.

Mintz, Donald. " 'Father's Mouth Spoke the Torah,' " Washington (D. C.) *Evening Star,* May 4, 1966, p. A-18.

New Yorker, XLII (May 14, 1966), 204.

Newquist, Roy. Chicago Heights *Star,* May 1, 1966, p. 10.

"Novelist Recalls Boyhood," Allentown (Pa.) *Call-Chronicle,* May 8, 1966, Sec. E, p. 7.

"Old-World Fantasies Revivified in Singer's 49 Tales Narrated in 'In My Father's Court,' " Detroit *Jewish News,* April 29, 1966, p. 11.

Pasley, Virginia. "Critic's Corner," *Newsday* (Garden City, N. Y.), April 30, 1966, p. 15W.

Perley, Maie E. "An Era That Is Past Recreated With Vitality," Louisville *Times,* July 26, 1966, p. A-7.

Perlman, Milton B. *Bulletin of the East Midwood Jewish Center* (Brooklyn, N. Y.), XXXIV (September 23, 1966), 6.

Petrakis, Harry Mark. "Making the Endless Waiting Bearable," *Chicago Sunday Tribune Books Today,* May 8, 1966, p. 1.

Powers, Robert L. "Tribute Paid to Hemley in New Volume," Athens (Ohio) *Messenger,* May 15, 1966, p. 18.

Poyurs, A. "A Book of Memoirs," *Jewish Affairs,* XXI (July 1966), 42.

Prescott, Peter S. *Women's Wear Daily,* April 29, 1966, p. 28.

Publishers' Weekly, CXCI (February 20, 1967), 151.

Raiz, Seymour. "Isaac Singer Wrote From His Own Life," Cleveland *Press,* May 27, 1966, *Showtime* Magazine, p. 19.

Raskin, Anita. "Superb Chronicle of Slice of History," Savannah (Ga.) *Morning News,* May 8, 1966, Magazine Section, p. 9.

Read, David W. "Poignant, Delightful," St. Louis *Sunday Post-Dispatch,* August 7, 1966, p. 4-B.

Richler, Mordecai. "Boy at the Keyhole," London *Observer,* February 26, 1967, p. 26.

Rogers, W. G. "Isaac Singer Recalls Boyhood in Warsaw," Youngstown *Vindicator,* May 1, 1966, p. B-12. See also Grand Rapids *Press,* May 1, 1966, p. 76; Toledo *Sunday Blade,* May 8, 1966; Eugene (Ore.) *Register-Guard,* May 8, 1966; Lewiston (Idaho) *Tribune,* May 8, 1966; St. Petersburg *Times,* May 8, 1966; Norfolk (Va.) *Virginian-Pilot,* May 8, 1966; Gary (Ind.) *Sunday Post-Tribune,* May 1, 1966; Knoxville *News-Sentinel,* May 1, 1966.

*Rosenthal, Raymond. "The Darkness of the Glass," *New Leader,* XLIX (May 9, 1966), 13–14.

S., J. L. *Best Sellers,* XXVI (June 15, 1966), 112–13. See also *Catholic Witness* (Harrisburg, Pa.), June 23, 1966.

Sandrof, Martha. "I Remember Childhood," Worcester (Mass.) *Sunday Telegram,* May 15, 1966, Sec. E, p. 12.

Schaer, Sidney C. "Jewish Childhood," Wilmington (Del.) *Morning News,* June 22, 1966, p. 21.

Scott, Paul. "Jewish Childhood," London *Times,* March 23, 1967, p. 7.

Seymour-Smith, Martin. "Terror and Fable," *The Spectator,* No. 7237 (March 10, 1967), 281–82 [282].

Sharp, H. Jay. Kansas City *Jewish Chronicle,* July 22, 1966, p. 11.

Silver, Adele Z. "Mysterious Forces in Singer's World," Cleveland *Plain Dealer,* May 8, 1966, p. 7-I.

Simon, Marian. "Isaac Singer Returns to His Boyhood for Fable-like Tales of a Rabbi's Court," *National Observer,* May 9, 1966, p. 25.

Steinbach, A. Alan. "Human Experiences Woven Into Fabric," *JWB Circle,* XXI (October 1966), Sec. 2, p. 1.

Stone, Gerald C. *"In My Father's Court* — Book Will Have Limited Appeal," Baton Rouge (La.) *Sunday Advocate,* August 7, 1966, Sec. E, p. 2.

Stone, Leonard W. "Rabbi-Father," Hartford *Courant,* May 15, 1966, Magazine Section, p. 13.

Stuart, Mark A. "Colorful Blend," Hackensack (N. J.) *Record,* June 4, 1966, Weekend Magazine, p. 14.

Symons, Julian. "Singer," *Punch,* CCLII (April 5, 1967), 503.

Taylor, Ted. Albuquerque *Tribune,* April 28, 1966, Sec. A, p. 4.

Trevor, William. "Remembering Well," *The Listener,* LXXVII (March 2, 1967), 298.

Turner, Julian. *The Queen,* CCCCXXVIII (March 1, 1967), 10.

W., M. L. [Maxwell L. Wiesenthal]. "Memories of Warsaw Ghetto," Portland (Me.) *Evening Express,* May 16, 1966, p. 13.

Wall, Mary R. *Woods County Enterprise* (Waynoka, Okla.), July 21, 1966, p. 2.

Warnes, Danielle A. Columbus (Ohio) *Dispatch,* May 15, 1966, "Tab" Section, p. 49.

Weintraub, Benjamin. *Chicago Jewish Forum,* XXV (Winter 1966–1967), 156.

Ziprin, Nathan. "Off the Record," *Wisconsin Jewish Chronicle,* XCVII (May 27, 1966), 6.

ZLATEH THE GOAT AND OTHER STORIES

American Zionist, LVII (December 1966), 30.

Best Sellers, XXVI (December 1, 1966), 342.

The Booklist, LXIII (November 15, 1966), 378.

Bulletin of the Center for Children's Books, XX (January 1967), 79.

C[rawshaw], H[elen] B. *Horn Book,* XLII (December 1966), 712.

*Feldman, Irving. "Fools' Paradise," *Book Week,* October 30, 1966, p. 4.

Gillespie, John T. *Grade Teacher,* LXXXIV (May–June 1967), 32.

Graves, Elizabeth Minot. *Commonweal,* LXXXV (November 11, 1966), 174.

Hodges, Margaret. *Library Journal,* XCI (December 15, 1966), 6197.

Jackson, Charlotte. *Atlantic,* CCXVIII (December 1966), 150, 152.

Jacobs, William Jay. "Folk Literature: The Unconscious Memory of Mankind," *Teachers College Record,* LXVIII (December 1966), 275–76 [275].

Kirkus, XXXIV (October 1, 1966), 1045–46.

Lurie, Alison. *New York Review of Books,* December 15, 1966, p. 29.

Nissenson, Hugh. *New York Times Book Review,* October 9, 1966, p. 34.

Ostermann, Robert. *National Observer,* December 19, 1966, p. 19.

P., E. "Seven By Singer," *Christian Science Monitor,* November 3, 1966, p. B10.

Rothchild, Sylvia. *Hadassah Magazine,* XLVIII (November 1966), 19.

Russ, Lavinia. *Publishers' Weekly,* CXC (October 10, 1966), 74.

Shaw, Spencer G. *Top of the News,* XXIII (January 1967), 196.

Sheehan, Ethna. *America,* CXV (November 5, 1966), 554.

Sutherland, Zena. *Saturday Review,* XLIX (November 12, 1966), 49.

Whitman, Digby B. "Universal Tales," *Chicago Sunday Tribune Books Today,* November 6, 1966, p. 14A.

Woods, George A. *New York Times Book Review,* December 4, 1966, p. 66.

Young Reader's Review, III (December 1966), 1.

THE FEARSOME INN

Birmingham, Mary Louise. *Commonweal,* LXXXVII (November 10, 1967), 178.

The Booklist, LXIV (November 1, 1967), 338.

Dorsey, Margaret A. *Library Journal,* XCII (September 15, 1967), 3190.

Goodwin, Polly. *Book World,* March 3, 1968, p. 21.

Harmon, Elva. Tulsa *World,* October 29, 1967, p. 19E.
Kellman, Amy. *Grade Teacher,* LXXXV (December 1967),
113.
Kirkus, XXXV (August 1, 1967), 880.
National Jewish Monthly, LXXXII (April 1968), 52.
Nelson, Robert Colby. "Russia From Serf to Sputnik,"
Christian Science Monitor, November 5, 1967, p. 66.
New York Times Book Review, November 5, 1967, p. 66.
Nissenson, Hugh. *New York Times Book Review,* October
8, 1967, p. 38.
Ostermann, Robert. "Books for Young Readers," *National
Observer,* March 18, 1968, p. 23.
Publishers' Weekly, CXCII (August 28, 1967), 277.
Sauter, Alayne. "An Awareness of the World," Boston
Sunday Globe, October 29, 1967, "Children's Books"
Section, p. 11.
Sutherland, Zena. *Saturday Review,* L (September 16,
1967), 49.
V[iguers], R[uth] H[ill]. *Horn Book,* XLIII (December
1967), 751–52.

THE MANOR

Allschwang, John. "In Holy Poland, Christian and Jew Fill
a Rich Novel," *Milwaukee Journal,* October 29, 1967,
Part 5, p. 4.
[Alter, Harry]. Youngstown *Jewish Times,* March 22, 1968,
p. 3.
Alter, Robert. "Down to Lilith's Domain," *Saturday Review,* L (November 4, 1967), 33.
Anderson, H. T. *Best Sellers,* XXVII (November 1, 1967),
306–307.
Billings, Jim. "Jew in Poland Fights to Top," Springfield
(Mo.) *Sunday News & Leader,* November 19, 1967, p. B5.
Bischoff, Barbara. *Oregon Journal* (Portland), October 21,
1967, p. 6J.
Boardman, Anne Cawley. "Singer Hero Tormented By 2
Worlds," Minneapolis *Tribune,* October 29, 1967, Sec.
E, p. 5.
Bonomo, Josephine. "Novel of Jewish Family Absorbing,"
Newark (N. J.) *News,* December 31, 1967, Sec. 1, p. 26.

Brady, Charles A. "19th Century Poland Is Brought to Life With Charm, Power," Buffalo *Evening News,* October 21, 1967, p. B-12.

Buchen, Irving H. "Singer Conquers Defects," Baltimore *Sunday Sun,* November 5, 1967, Sec. D, p. 5.

Caldwell, Stephen F. "Novel By a Master," Hackensack (N. J.) *Record,* October 21, 1967, Weekend Magazine, p. 14.

Chametzky, Jules. "The Old Jew in New Times," *The Nation,* CCV (October 30, 1967), 436–38.

Curtin, Anne. "Moral Dilemmas," *The Progressive,* XXXII (February 1968), 50–51 [50].

Daughtrey, Anita. "An Era of Change," Fresno *Bee,* November 12, 1967, Sec. F, p. 17.

Donow, Herbert S. "Composite Forces in the Jewish Experience," *Daily Egyptian* (Southern Illinois University, Carbondale, Ill.), January 13, 1968, p. 5.

Duhamel, P. Albert. "I've Been Reading — The Odyssey [*sic*] of Jews From Poland to U. S.," Boston *Sunday Herald Traveler,* October 22, 1967, *Show Guide* Magazine, p. 17.

Edelstein, Arthur. "A Jew's Travail Unfolds Against the Frightening Sweep of History," *National Observer,* October 30, 1967, p. 20.

Epstein, Joseph. "I. B. Singer: to the manor born," *Book World,* October 29, 1967, pp. 4–5.

Fagin, Bryllion. "A Lively Novel in the Old Fashioned Style," Baltimore *Evening Sun,* November 22, 1967, p. A-16.

Falleder, Arnold. "The Enlightened," *Dimensions in American Judaism,* II (Winter 1967–1968), 52.

Feldman, Garrick. "Manorisms," Chicago *Skyline,* October 25, 1967, p. 24.

French, Warren. "The Old Fashioned Novel — Very Good If By Singer," Kansas City *Star,* December 17, 1967, p. 3D.

Friend, James. "Isaac Singer Pens a Novel in the Grand Tradition," Chicago *Daily News,* October 28, 1967, "Panorama" Section, p. 8.

Goldberg, Joseph E. "To All Men, To One God," Seattle *Post-Intelligencer,* October 8, 1967, *Northwest Today* Section, p. 5.

Goolrick, Esten. "A True Vision of Their Woes," Roanoke (Va.) *Times,* December 17, 1967, Sec. C, p. 18.

Harris, Isabelle W. " 'The Manor' Is Study of Enlightenment," *Mizrachi Woman,* XL (January 1968), 5.

Hindus, Milton. "Isaac Singer's 'The Manor' — Yarn Spinner's Realism," Boston *Sunday Globe,* November 12, 1967, p. 24-A.

Howe, Marjorie. " 'The Manor' Paints Broad Picture of Warsaw and Poland in 1860 Era," Burlington (Vt.) *Free Press,* November 7, 1967, p. 9.

Hubler, Richard G. "Scope of Jewish Life in Poland a Century Ago," Los Angeles *Times,* November 6, 1967, Part IV, p. 18.

*Hughes, Catharine R. "The Two Worlds of Isaac Singer," *America,* CXVII (November 18, 1967), 611–13.

"Isaac Bashevis Singer, Great Tale Weaver — His Immense 'Manor' and 'Mazel' Stories," Detroit *Jewish News,* December 22, 1967, p. 43.

*Jonas, Gerald. "People With a Choice," *New York Times Book Review,* November 5, 1967, pp. 1, 52.

Journal of the Screen Producers Guild, IX (December 1967), 42.

Kirkus, XXXV (August 15, 1967), 990.

Kresh, Paul. "An Early Masterpiece By I. B. Singer," *Hadassah Magazine,* XLIX (December 1967), 18–19.

Lask, Thomas. "The Search for the Way," *New York Times,* October 31, 1967, p. 43.

Levinson, Milton A. "Author Depicts Terror of Jews," Pensacola *News-Journal,* November 19, 1967, Sec. B, p. 5.

Levow, Mordecai. Kansas City *Jewish Chronicle,* December 8, 1967, p. 4B.

McCullough, David. *Book-of-the-Month-Club News,* November 1967, pp. 9–10.

M[aloff], S[aul]. "Portrait of a World Gone," *Newsweek,* LXX (October 30, 1967), 102.

Margoshes, Miriam K. *Library Journal,* XCII (October 1, 1967), 3447–48.

Monette, Paul L. "A Vast, Ambitious, Successful Novel," Lawrence (Mass.) *Eagle-Tribune,* December 23, 1967, Sec. 1, p. 12.

Murray, Michele. "Bringing the Past to Life," *National Catholic Reporter* (Kansas City, Mo.), November 15, 1967, p. 11.

Nordell, Roderick. "From the book reviewer's shelf: Isaac Singer: Architect of an Old World Firmament," *Christian Science Monitor,* October 28, 1967, p. 9.

Norris, Hoke. "A Little Madhouse in Each Brain," Chicago *Sun-Times,* October 29, 1967, *Book Week,* pp. 7, 9.

Parill, William. Nashville *Tennessean,* November 5, 1967, p. 6-B.

Pasley, Virginia. "A Panoramic Novel," *Newsday* (Garden City, N. Y.), October 7, 1967, p. 31W.

Patterson, Ann. "Singer's Epic Novel One of Life," *Arizona Republic* (Phoenix), November 5, 1967, p. N-9.

Perley, Marie E. "The Book Scene — Isaac Singer's 'The Manor' Proves His Literary Artistry," Louisville *Times,* October 5, 1967, p. A-13.

Playboy, XIV (December 1967), 54, 56.

Raiz, Seymour. " 'Manor' Is Marred By Over-Quantity," Cleveland *Press,* December 29, 1967, *Show Time* Magazine, p. 17.

Ribalow, Harold U. "I. B. Singer's Latest Novel," *Jewish Exponent,* CXLII (December 22, 1967), 21.

Rogers, W. G. "Isaac Bashevis Singer — Lives End, Living Goes On in a Chagall-Like Story," Toledo *Blade,* October 29, 1967, Sec. J, p. 5. See also Grand Rapids *Press,* October 29, 1967; Norfolk (Va.) *Virginian-Pilot,* November 19, 1967; Lakeland (Fla.) *Ledger,* October 29, 1967; Ft. Lauderdale *News,* November 26, 1967; Wichita Falls *Times,* October 29, 1967.

Rosenfeld, Arnold. "Old Tradition," Houston *Post,* December 3, 1967, *Spotlight* Magazine, p. 10.

Sale, Roger. "Good Servants and Bad Masters," *Hudson Review,* XX (Winter, 1967–1968), 666–74 [673–74].

Shaw, Mildred Hart. Grand Junction (Colo.) *Daily Sentinel,* November 19, 1967, Sec. 1, p. 4.

Silver, Adele Z. "Plums From Daily Forward," Cleveland *Plain Dealer,* October 29, 1967, p. 9-G.

Smith, Miles A. "Novel By Isaac Singer Has 19th Century Line," Washington (D. C.) *Sunday Star,* October 29, 1967, p. E-2.

Spearman, Walter. Greensboro (N. C.) *Record,* November 13, 1967, p. A15.

"Special From No Man's Land," *Time,* XC (October 20, 1967), 105.

Stanley, Donald. "A Novel From Yiddish," San Francisco *Examiner,* November 1, 1967, p. 37.

Thomas, W. H. J. "Singer Novel Called Story of an Epoch," Charleston (S. C.) *News and Courier,* November 5, 1967, p. 3-D.

Thompson, John. *Commentary,* XLIV (December 1967), 79–80.

Toynbee, Philip. "Inside the Pale," *New Republic,* CLVII (November 11, 1967), 39–40.

Traynor, John, Jr. "One Man's Family," *Extension,* LXII (January 1968), 55.

Wain, John. "Trouble in the Family," *New York Review of Books,* October 26, 1967, pp. 32–55 [32–33].

Waters, Craig. "The Conflicts," Camden (N. J.) *Courier Post,* December 14, 1967, p. 20.

Weigel, John. "Novel Is Nicely Balanced Between Fiction and History," Cincinnati *Enquirer,* December 23, 1967, p. 18.

Wellejus, Ed. "Poland in 1863," Erie (Pa.) *Daily Times,* December 5, 1967, Sec. 1, p. 5.

*Wincelberg, Shimon. "Probing a Vanished Past," *New Leader,* LI (February 26, 1968), 26–29.

Woods, Harriett. "A Tapestry of Poland," St. Louis *Sunday Post-Dispatch,* November 12, 1967, p. 4B.

Young, Sonia Winer. "Choice and Conflict," Chattanooga *Times,* January 14, 1968, p. 22.

Zaiman, Mildred. "Bows to Change," Hartford *Courant,* November 5, 1967, Magazine Section, p. 14.

MAZEL AND SHLIMAZEL OR
THE MILK OF A LIONESS

The Booklist, LXIV (January 15, 1968), 595.

Daltry, Patience M. "Newbery and Caldecott Medal Winners," *Christian Science Monitor,* February 29, 1968, p. 5.

Fremont-Smith, Eliot. "For Young Readers," *New York Times Book Review,* January 7, 1968, p. 30.

Goodwin, Polly. *Book World,* March 3, 1968, p. 21.

"Isaac Bashevis Singer, Great Tale Weaver — His Immense 'Manor' and 'Mazel' Stories," Detroit *Jewish News,* December 22, 1967, p. 43.

Jackson, Charlotte. "Adventure and Fun in Fact and Fiction," Chicago *Sun-Times,* March 3, 1968, *Book Week,* p. 11.

New York Times Book Review, December 3, 1967, p. 70.

Ostermann, Robert. "Books for Young Readers," *National Observer,* March 18, 1968, p. 23.

Publishers' Weekly, CXCII (November 20, 1967), 55.

Roth, Susan A. *School Library Journal,* XIV (December 1967), 64.

Sutherland, Zena. "A Stocking Full of Wealth," *Saturday Review,* L (December 16, 1967), 35.

V[iguers], R[uth] H[ill]. *Horn Books,* XLIV (February 1968), 62.

Notes on Contributors

Ruth Whitman is the author of *Blood and Milk* and the translator of several stories by Singer.

J. A. Eisenberg, a Canadian critic, holds degrees in English and philosophy from the University of Toronto and the University of Pennsylvania.

Michael Fixler teaches at Tufts University. He is the author of *Milton and the Kingdoms of God*.

J. S. Wolkenfeld teaches at Kingsborough Community College. He is the author of *Joyce Cary: The Developing Style*.

Irving Howe teaches at Hunter College. He is the author of books on Sherwood Anderson, Faulkner, and Hardy and the co-editor of *A Treasury of Yiddish Stories*.

Baruch Hochman teaches at Bard College. He is the author of several essays on Jewish writers published in *Commentary, Judaism,* and *Midstream*.

Max F. Schulz teaches at the University of Southern California. He is the author of *The Poetic Voices of Coleridge* and the forthcoming *Radical Sophistication*.

Karl Malkoff teaches at The City College of New York. He is the author of a book on Theodore Roethke and a pamphlet on Muriel Spark.

Jules Chametzky, who teaches at the University of Massachusetts, is the editor of *The Massachusetts Review*. His essays on minority writers have appeared in many important periodicals.

Melvin J. Friedman teaches at the University of Wisconsin-Milwaukee. He is the author of a book on the stream of consciousness, and the editor of critical collections on Flannery O'Connor, Beckett, and Styron.

Edwin Gittleman teaches at Dartmouth College. He is the author of *Jones Very: The Effective Years, 1833–1840.*

Samuel I. Mintz teaches at The City College of New York. He is the author of *The Hunting of Leviathan,* a study of Hobbes.

Jackson R. Bryer teaches at the University of Maryland. He has compiled the definitive bibliography on F. Scott Fitzgerald's critical reputation. His co-author, Paul E. Rockwell, is a graduate student at the University of Maryland.

Irving Malin teaches a
He is the author of *Willia*
New American Gothic, j
Bellow's Fiction; he is th
American Fiction, Saul B
Capote's In Cold Blood: A
Irwin Stark, *Breakthrough*
American-Jewish Literatur

About the Author

Irving Malin teaches at the City College of New York. He is the author of *William Faulkner: An Interpretation, New American Gothic, Jews and Americans,* and *Saul Bellow's Fiction;* he is the editor of *Psychoanalysis and American Fiction, Saul Bellow and the Critics, Truman Capote's In Cold Blood: A Critical Handbook,* and, with Irwin Stark, *Breakthrough: A Treasury of Contemporary American-Jewish Literature.*